Cooking
with the
Wolfman

Cooking
with the
Wolfman
INDIGENOUS FUSION

**David Wolfman
and Marlene Finn**

 Douglas & McIntyre

Douglas and McIntyre (2013) Ltd.
P.O. Box 219, Madeira Park, BC, V0N 2H0
www.douglas-mcintyre.com

Edited by Cheryl Cohen
Indexed by Nicola Goshulak
Cover design by Anna Comfort O'Keeffe and Mauve Pagé
Text design by Mauve Pagé
Printed and bound in Canada

Douglas and McIntyre (2013) Ltd. acknowledges the support of the Canada Council for the Arts, which last year invested $153 million to bring the arts to Canadians throughout the country. We also gratefully acknowledge financial support from the Government of Canada and from the Province of British Columbia through the BC Arts Council and the Book Publishing Tax Credit.

Library and Archives Canada Cataloguing in Publication
Wolfman, David, author
　　Cooking with the Wolfman : Indigenous fusion / David Wolfman and Marlene Finn.
Includes index.
Issued in print and electronic formats.
ISBN 978-1-77162-163-2 (softcover).
ISBN 978-1-77162-164-9 (HTML)
　　1. Indian cooking. 2. Cookbooks. I. Finn, Marlene (Marlene Esther), author II. Title.
TX715.6.W599 2017　　641.59'297　　C2017-904452-4
　　C2017-904453-2

To Delores Wolfman, my late mother, to Laura Marjorie Finn, Marlene's mother, and to everyone out there in TV land who watches my show!

Contents

Foreword

I am a huge fan of preparing dishes with a rich history that's rooted in our past. Through food, we have the ability to strengthen community bonds and celebrate our differences. I am encouraged by Chef David and Marlene's goal of inspiring people to discover ways to prepare dishes that highlight the exciting richness of flavours that are unique to Canada's history and Indigenous cuisine.

As I flip through the amazing array of easy-to-follow recipes, there are several incredible must-try dishes that have caught my eye. I am excited to make not only traditional Indigenous recipes like bannock but also some of the creative chef-inspired modern dishes like the Urban Indian Ice Cream. How delicious does that sound? I am also very excited by the idea that some of the dishes are recipes handed down from generation to generation.

Chef David is enthusiastic in his desire to bring people together through our shared love of food. He is inspiring home cooks to make dishes from the heart, and inspiring people from all walks of life to appreciate and connect with Indigenous culture.

More than ever, people are looking for ways to prepare nutrient-rich food from local sustainable sources. We want to know where our food is coming from. Through this book, you will not only get some truly inspiring dishes, it will teach you how to connect with and celebrate our local farmers.

Cooking with the Wolfman includes an incredible range of dishes and recipes that blend tradition with modern flavours and ingredients.

Enjoy cooking every recipe, you will discover how delicious Indigenous Fusion can be!

—**Chef Lynn Crawford**

Preface

One day when I was nine years old, I went into the kitchen, hungry, and offered to help my mom make supper, but really I was hoping just to get my hands on something to eat. She dressed me in an apron, handed me a spoon and told me to stir a pot of stew. That special time together (and a little slice of hot bread fresh from the oven, with margarine smothered all over it) was all I needed to return, time and time again, to "help" her. Each time we cooked together, she'd tell me stories about her childhood adventures on the Xaxli'p First Nation in the southern interior of British Columbia. Mom would make my two older sisters clean up the kitchen after we cooked, and from that point on, she called me her "Little Cheft"—just one of many words she used to say in her own way.

My sisters and I grew up in the disadvantaged downtown Toronto neighbourhood of Regent Park, Mom and Dad having moved to the city from western Canada in the 1950s. Dad is Russian Jewish and my late mother was First Nations. We never visited our parents' relatives in Manitoba or BC and just blended as best we could into our downtown neighbourhood. I didn't get to visit my mom's First Nation until 2007. With me then was Marlene Finn, who has played a major role in the writing of this book and is both my business partner and my wife.

Long before I met Marlene—by the age of 15 in fact—my first exposure to fast-paced cooking was at the take-out counter doing both day and night shifts in Fran's Restaurant in Toronto and then doing busboy service in the formal dining rooms of the National Club in the city's financial district. George Chen, the former night chef at the club, saw my budding interest in cooking and arranged for me to get chef training at George Brown College of Applied Arts and Technology and journeyman training at the National Club. I've tried to pay it forward since then. It's been over 30 years now and I haven't looked back.

I was already a certified chef when I volunteered at a reception honouring a First Nations playwright and Aboriginal theatre group he was working with in the early 1990s. A lot of cooked food had been donated potluck style in plastic containers and the like, so when I showed up in chef whites, I was given the job of putting it all together. I assembled the food on attractive platters, garnishing and arranging food service the way I was trained to in hotels. I threw a dessert together that was a memorable hit. There weren't any Indigenous caterers around at that time, so my phone started ringing the very next day with requests for my professional services. I ended up leaving my full-time cooking job to run my own catering company and start culinary consulting on the side.

My catering specialized in what I called Aboriginal Fusion back then—Indigenous Fusion these days—and the business grew pretty quickly. Of course, with lots of business came lots of excess food supplies, so I decided to start a soup kitchen at the local friendship centre that would feed elders and the homeless every day. I kept the soup kitchen and catering going for six years. Catering turned out to be a smart business move, and the First Nations, Métis and Inuit people I met were from all over the country, so catering really increased my interest in their local foods and traditions. Suddenly I had the freedom to be creative with food, hire and train my own catering staff, travel to First Nations to do cooking demonstrations, design restaurants, and train community cooks. I don't have time to devote to catering anymore, but my consulting business has expanded a lot since those days.

The demand for my cooking motivated me to learn more about the diet of First Nations peoples in what is now Canada (long before French explorer Jacques Cartier made

| Mom (Delores Wolfman) and Dad (Rubin Wolfman) in 2006.

his way over here in the sixteenth century). The deeper I got into learning about food and Indigenous culture, the more I wanted to share my knowledge.

In 1994, I became a professor of culinary arts at George Brown College of Applied Arts and Technology, my alma mater, where I discovered pretty quickly that teaching groups of young people how to cook can be quite challenging—but very rewarding. More than two decades later I still love my job and have tried to make good use of my teaching experience in writing the recipes in this cookbook. This is why I also included a lot of specific cooking tips. One example is my advice to always read a recipe through to the very end before starting to prepare it so that you don't discover halfway through making it that it needs specific ingredients or equipment, and so on.

I met Marlene in the 1990s. She was a high school teacher on leave from the Toronto District School Board and seriously thinking about quitting the profession. She was hired at my college to do research on the postsecondary education needs of Indigenous people in the Greater Toronto Area. I helped her out by making some introductions to people at local organizations whom she could interview for the project, and we became friends. It just so happened that Marlene's parents had also moved to Toronto from the west in the 1950s and had very little contact with family for several years, until they were able to start making annual car and camping trips west. She is a member of the Métis Nation of Ontario, although her family is originally from Saskatchewan. Her mom is Métis and her late father was Irish and Scottish.

Once we got to know each other, Marlene and I were surprised to learn that we had so much else in common. Her family lived in the east end, and both of our families regularly went to the same petting zoo at Riverdale Park. She and her sisters used to take part in all the drumming and dancing and craft activities and the L'il Beavers youth program at the same local friendship centre where I had set up the soup kitchen and catering. In the late eighties, we used to work in buildings that were literally next door to each other in Don Mills. And it turns out that when we met, we were living about a block apart and even walked our dogs in the same park. Marlene moved on when the research project was done and finally resigned from teaching to work in the Indigenous community doing television production, marketing and event planning, but we'd bump into each other every now and then at fundraisers and other local events.

Cooking with the Wolfman was my next big adventure. The show first aired in 1999 on APTN (the Aboriginal Peoples Television Network) in Canada. Tapings were done in the summer months when I wasn't busy teaching, but I ran myself ragged doing a lot of advance planning and coordination for production. I was the host, but most people don't realize that I was also responsible for the budget, recruitment of the production crew and talent, the shooting schedule, recipe development, food shopping, wardrobe, crew meals, ground transportation and more. My wife at the time was a big help on all of this.

Fan mail started pouring in from people wanting recipes, wanting to be on the show, wanting to know where to get the ingredients and wanting me to take the show on the road so that they could participate. The budget did not allow for travel, so I invited artists, novelists, musicians, dancers, actors, educators, political leaders, elders and herbalists living in Toronto to come to the studio kitchen instead. Many Indigenous people of all walks of life live here. We taped three to five different shows a day, requiring me to produce about twelve to fifteen recipes each day just for the show, and buffet style meals for the crew between tapings. It was a mad house! The show aired until 2017 in Canada and is airing in the United States on FNX and NativeFlix now, so the fan mail comes from farther away. But one thing hasn't changed: the energy I have for sharing good food with friends.

It wasn't until I had several seasons of the show under my belt and was separated, that Marlene and I met again and she joined the production team. By then she had set up her own consulting business in Muskoka, Ontario, co-authored a teacher's resource on the Indigenous peoples of Canada, had a long list of Indigenous business and social service agency clients, and had television production experience to boot.

Marlene returned to Toronto and joined forces with me to build my business. These days I design special events menus that feature Indigenous Fusion, speak at conferences, deliver my Recipe for Success goal setting workshop, deliver a healthy eating and healthy weights workshop geared to low-income families, and customize hospitality training on reserves. Together we coordinate live cooking competitions, conduct restaurant makeovers, deliver a cultural and culinary tourism training workshop for First Nations communities, and sell Cooking with the Wolfman knives. Marlene is my culinary assistant and videographer at live events and handles all my marketing and event bookings. She continues to operate her own business on the side as an Indigenous education consultant, curriculum developer and program evaluator. In 2009, we got married.

Introduction

The words of an elder inspired me to write this book. I was demonstrating how to cook large game to an audience of Gwich'in youth in Inuvik, a community in the Northwest Territories located two degrees above the Arctic Circle. They were surprised to learn that the frozen game they ate so regularly could be jazzed up and made as appealing as lasagna, just by adding some new ingredients and changing the cooking process from frying to other methods. But it was what one elder said to me afterwards that really hit me. He told me that it was great that I was bringing the food back home. He watched the whole cooking demonstration but was impressed the most by the fact that the youth were really paying attention and showing interest in learning more about food.

So many Indigenous food customs are fading away along with the languages and cultural traditions that have become extinct. Some of us, though, are lucky enough to have access to elders who can still source indigenous plants and who still know how to traditionally hunt or fish and prepare food. I try to take every opportunity to learn from grannies and elders; this is how I first began developing recipes to feature foods indigenous to the Americas—recipes that include long-forgotten food sources and cooking methods.

People ask me what Indigenous people ate before contact with Europeans, and I tell them what I know: each nation had its own resources and its own way of hunting, fishing, gathering and harvesting foods, planting foods, and cooking, for that matter; they didn't all eat the same thing—how could they, when they lived in different climates, different regions and different environments, and had different lifestyles? It would be like asking, "What do Europeans eat?" Food staples that were plentiful in one region were rare or non-existent in others. Also, diets changed over time as a result of colonization.

It's interesting to me that the food movement to "eat local" is gaining ground worldwide. More and more health- and environment-conscious people are encouraging people to eat foods that are produced in their own region rather than those that are transported or imported from other regions or countries. Eating local is what every culture did before food

trade networks were ever created! The "slow food" movement is also a sign that people are wising up to the ways of the past.

Modern society is making a full circle: recognizing the value of cutting out processed foods, artificial foods, genetically modified foods and so on, and validating ancient ways of living in harmony with our environment, rather than against it. Among the Indigenous peoples of the Americas, the growing interest now is not to eat local as much as it is to return to a "traditional" diet of foods that originated from these lands—including foods traded between nations on these continents. Corn is one example of a staple food of the Iroquois nations in northeastern North America. This plant is not indigenous to Canada or the United States but came from much farther south and took thousands of years to make its way north to Iroquois territory. Now corn is most definitely considered an Iroquois food.

To be clear, my recipes are not about making a meal out of whatever you can gather on a walk in the bush or about eating only those foods that were available in North America before the lost Spaniards reached the so-called New World in the fifteenth century—new to whom? My recipes are about taking the essence of indigenous ingredients and putting it under the spotlight. I blend the traditional with modern tastes and ingredients that are generally available in stores these days. This is the style of cooking that I call Indigenous Fusion.

Because of the great variety of foods indigenous to Turtle Island, there is no shortage of culinary inspiration for me. (Turtle Island is what some Indigenous peoples, including the Ojibway and Haudenosaunee, call North America; the term is based on their creation stories.) I love combining root vegetables of the plains with fish from the Arctic and wild edibles from the woodlands, with a touch of hot pepper from our brothers to the south, as long as these ingredients complement one another from a culinary perspective. Remember, we didn't cross the border—the border crossed us! Some of the Métis recipes I included in this cookbook come from my mother-in-law, Marge Finn, and reflect the distinct heritage of the historic mixed-blood people born of the European explorers and Indigenous women.

There are some unusual ingredients in my recipes, but most ingredients can be found in supermarkets in Canada and the United States, and substitutions are provided for items that might be hard to find. I expect that anyone who doesn't have access to wild game would use farmed game from a local butcher shop instead, and anyone who can't get wild-caught fish would use farm-raised fish; this sort of substitution won't affect the recipe outcome much. Beef can usually be used instead of game; the dish will taste great, but it won't be the same. (Read more about cooking large game in Chapter 5 on page 118). However, using a lean fish when a fatty fish is called for (or vice versa) will affect the taste, texture and overall appearance of the dish—and could ruin it—so stick to the recipe or use the recommended substitution only. Recipes that require seasonal fresh ingredients may be a challenge due to lack of availability, so I have suggested alternatives that should ensure recipe success.

This book also includes some information about salt and sugar alternatives, but readers are advised to turn to medical professionals for nutritional and dietary advice.

So here it is, after all these years—my first cookbook, written with my wife, Marlene. She had the joy of replaying all the *Cooking with the Wolfman* TV show tapes to find the gems to update and include in this cookbook. She managed to force me to sit down long enough to review the many recipes I've developed over the years to complement those from the show. Together we filled in the blanks to provide the background information and instructional details that a 22-minute TV show doesn't allow for. We hope that this book will increase readers' awareness of the cultural diversity of Indigenous peoples of North, Central and South America while demystifying contemporary cooking methods. We also hope that it will satisfy the writers of the many emails and Facebook messages I get each week from viewers who have run out of ideas on how to cook wild goose and bush rabbit.

Enjoy!

Indigenous Fusion

After all these years, the traditional diet of Indigenous peoples is making a comeback. The idea of looking to food for holistic healing is catching on. Many people across the continent have succeeded in completely changing their lives by following a pre-Columbian diet. I have read about Indigenous people on both sides of the borders between Canada, the United States and Mexico who, by adopting this diet, not only lost weight and lowered their blood pressure and blood sugar levels, but also developed a whole new way of living their culture at every meal by planning their diet based on the seasons and working as a community to harvest and prepare everything from scratch. Health researchers are investigating whether a traditional diet holds the key to reversing chronic disease among Indigenous people—especially type two diabetes. Some First Nations and Native American communities are piloting projects to find out.

The University of Northern Michigan calls their project the "Decolonizing Diet," to make clear that it's all about returning to the diet Indigenous peoples had before they were colonized, before some of our most valuable food sources were virtually exterminated through settlement, railways and sport hunting (e.g., for bison), and before food was industrialized. The return to ancient foods is happening in Latin America for similar reasons, and it provides an opportunity for Indigenous people there to stimulate economic growth through the manufacture of foods that used to be food staples before the Spaniards deliberately destroyed them—quinoa, for example.

The traditional diets of Indigenous people across the North American continent relied heavily on large game, small game, waterfowl, eggs, fish, seafood, tubers, berries, leaves, roots, trees, grasses and seeds. Although this diet was high in protein and nutrients and low in fat, it varied greatly from region to region and from season to season. In the Far North, the Inuit thrived on seaweeds, fish, caribou, seal meat and tundra greens, a diet that was high in animal fat but nutritious

Arctic willow is an example of a food source that is suited to a harsh environment.

and perfectly suited to life in a harsh, cold environment. The Arctic willow that grows in the eastern Arctic, for example, has more vitamin C than oranges.

Not all Indigenous people led a hunter-gatherer lifestyle, however, as Hollywood would have us believe. In the US Midwest, the Wichita, Chippewa and Winnebago regularly harvested wild rice. On the Pacific coast, the Tlingit and Qualicum cultivated shellfish. In 2016, archaeologists uncovered clam gardens on the BC coastline dating back 3,000 years. Plant cultivation and trading with Indigenous peoples in South America increased the numbers of North American nations that developed an agricultural lifestyle. In the Great Lakes region, the Haudenosaunee became highly skilled farmers of corn, beans and squash.

Indigenous elders value the old ways that have kept our people strong and healthy since time immemorial, but elders have also become dependent on both imported and convenience foods just like the rest of us. Long ago it was understood that food is medicine—physically, spiritually, mentally and emotionally—but some people are just waking up to that concept now. Those who have returned to a

traditional diet say that instead of becoming simply a way of eating, it becomes a very physical, spiritual, mental and social way of life. If you eliminated all the things that pass for food these days and focused on eating only those foods that existed before the arrival of Europeans, you would realize how difficult it is to even find indigenous foods let alone know what to do with them. Then, if you considered the changing seasons and eliminated anything that was not truly indigenous to the region in which you live, and factored in what you would have to do in advance to keep yourself going through the winter months, you'd realize how much you'd rely on others, how hard it would be on your body to obtain the food, and how much mental energy would go into planning everything. How connected we'd be to our food, one another and our world if we had to do that every day!

It's no coincidence that the Paleo (or Paleolithic) Diet, Caveman Diet and Primal Diet have been trending worldwide, too, and more and more alternative health care practitioners are recommending that people try them out, which just goes to show that Indigenous people are not the only ones who are trying to control their health and prevent or reverse disease through food. The dedication of all these converts is amazing, but I prefer a less extreme approach to food. Indigenous Fusion is my way of enjoying natural foods from North, Central and South America while adding select ingredients from the Old World.

The reality is, the bulk of our diet is made up of either imported foods or foods that are not indigenous to North America but became naturalized over time after European settlers brought them here and cultivated them. Just as the settlers got used to foods like potatoes, collard greens, corn and tomatoes, and techniques such as pit-roasting beans, barbecuing meats and smoking fish, Indigenous people became accustomed to wheat, citrus fruits, beef, dairy, pork, and metal cooking pots and utensils. Indigenous Fusion brings them all together.

CHAPTER 1

Are You Ready?
Kitchen Essentials and
Food-Handling Techniques

L ove of food, love of friends and love of family—they all come together when we eat. Mom used to say that you shouldn't cook if you are not feeling good, since it will affect the meal, one way or another. I say, make cooking an enjoyable experience; prepare for it with the proper tools and equipment and get in there with your hands to feel the spirit of food.

Animal bones, antlers, shells and wood historically played a large role in the making of tools to dig roots, scrape trees, pull up seaweed, harvest berries, grind corn, clean hides, cook, and smoke fish. For about 10,000 years, the ulu has been the all-purpose tool of Inuit women and their Thule and Sivullirmuit ancestors. The semicircular blade of this knife was suitable for cutting red meat, large marine animals and bones, and for removing fat and hair from animal skins. Oddly enough, many modern-day chefs use a curved blade reminiscent of the ulu for mincing herbs (*un hachoir* in French) or cutting pizza (*una mezzaluna* in Italian) as part of their kitchen tool kit.

Kitchen tool kits have expanded since the days when a cook had just one or two tools to work with. That wasn't all that long ago. My Métis mother-in-law, Marge Finn, remembers watching her mother mix bannock dough right in a sack of flour because she didn't have a bowl—something hard to imagine today. It's almost ridiculous how many gadgets and appliances cooks have nowadays; but the right tools make the job easier, safer and quicker if you cook a lot or on a regular basis, so they are worth it. If you live in a shoebox-sized condo in Toronto or Vancouver, oh well, no storage room for you. That's why I live in a house with a shed in the suburbs!

Culinary Terms

The type of kitchen equipment you need depends on the type of cooking you want to do. There are basic skills and tools you need just to get started, and more specialized ones for barbecuing, baking or making soup, for instance. When new to cooking, you tend to notice that recipe instructions refer to specific actions that you have to perform, as well as objects that you need to use. If you are just learning to cook and don't have everything you need for the kitchen, go to garage sales and thrift stores to find great used equipment. Marge and I go out garage-saling on Saturdays and find all sorts of neat stuff.

Here are some basic terms that all cooks, whether inexperienced or highly experienced, need to know:

- **Blanching** means cooking food—such as vegetables or stone fruit—briefly in boiling water before transferring it to ice water to stop the cooking process.
- **Chopping** means coarsely cutting food into more or less evenly sized pieces, usually about 1 inch (2.5 cm) or so.
- **Dicing** means cutting food into evenly sized cubes. Does it matter how big or small the pieces are or if they are all uniform? Yes. Use smaller cuts for quick-cook dishes and larger cut for slow-cook dishes. Regardless of size, uniformity promotes even cooking. Unless indicated otherwise, dicing usually refers to medium-sized cubes.

  Large dice are ¾ inch (2 cm) square.
  Medium dice are ½ inch (1.5 cm) square.
  Small dice are ¼ inch (1 cm) square.

- **Folding** is a very gentle method for mixing ingredients (like whipped cream) into dry ingredients, using a spatula.
- **Grating** or shredding of hard and soft foods like cheese, carrots, apples, boiled eggs and chocolate is done on a box grater. A microplane will do the same job but make finer cuts more suitable for fresh garlic, ginger or Parmesan.
- **Hulling** a strawberry means cutting around the base of the stem and pulling it out.
- **Mincing** means finely chopping—herbs or garlic cloves, for example.
- **Peeling** means removing the outer skin or rind of fruit or vegetables.
- **Reducing** means cooking a liquid long enough to reduce its volume and thicken its texture through evaporation (to create a stronger flavour). This is done when making sauces.
- **Scoring** means making shallow cuts through the skin of a food. Recipes sometimes require scoring a tomato, which means cutting an X about 2 inches by 2 inches (5 × 5 cm) through the skin at the base of the tomato before blanching it. This technique makes it easier to remove the thin skin.
- **Seeding** (or deseeding) means removing all seeds from a vanilla bean or a pumpkin, for instance.
- **Slicing** means cutting evenly sized pieces of pie, cucumber or carrots, for example. The size of the slice depends

on the purpose and what is reasonable. The thickness of sliced onions, for instance, would be determined by how long they will be cooking.

Kitchen Equipment Essentials

I dream of having a kitchen that is large enough to hold all of my kitchen equipment, appliances, gadgets, smallwares, dishes, glassware, food storage containers, baking pans and, and, and . . . you get the idea. The kitchen would have to be huge, even though I've downsized since I shut down my catering business; but for the average home cook, the primary tools required are knives, cutting boards, pots and pans, a couple of appliances and a few smallwares.

Knives

I can cook in big kitchens, small kitchens, dark longhouses and smoky tipis, and on rocky boats, windy docks, leaning decks and shaky stages. I can work in hot kitchens, freezing cold flapping tents, noisy arenas, silent churches and chaotic community centres. But I cannot work without my knives! They are literally the tools of my trade and worth grabbing if the house was on fire.

These are the most important knives any home cook needs to have:

01 **Chef knife** (French knife, cook's knife). This is an all-purpose knife for mincing, chopping, slicing, dicing and disjointing meat. A home cook might prefer a 6 inch (15 cm) or 7 inch (18 cm) chef knife (especially if he/she has small hands) or a Santoku, or Japanese-style, all-purpose knife. An 8 inch (20 cm) blade is the most common size, but a person with large hands might prefer a 10 inch (25 cm) blade. Long blades are preferable for cooking large quantities.

02 **Paring knife** (vegetable knife). This knife is usually 3 to 4 inches (7.5 to 10 cm) long and is used for peeling vegetables, as well as deveining shrimp, seeding chilis or removing the skin from fruits—delicate jobs, in other words.

03 **Boning** knife. This knife is used for separating meat from the bone. Since I do a lot of that, I prefer a semi-flexible blade that easily cuts through ligaments and connective tissue, and removes bones.

When my students ask me which kinds of knives to get, I tell them it's essential to invest in these three knives first, even if they end up with different types, makes, models and colours. Then when they can afford it, they can build up tool kits later on.

Other knives of note include these:

· **Bread knife.** This knife has a long, serrated edge and is good for slicing hard foods (like melon or pineapple rinds) and soft foods (like tomatoes, bread and cake) without crushing them. Bread knives don't need sharpening.

· **Cleaver.** I don't often use one at home since my chef's knife is strong enough for cutting through most bone, but if you do your own hunting and butchering where you cut through very thick bones, a cleaver would make the job easier.

· **Fillet knife.** This is specifically designed for removing the fillets from fish. I do a lot of work with fish so have several of these knives that are flexible enough to allow me to slice the flesh away from the skin in seconds. A filleting knife not only makes for a quicker job, but also helps to avoid wasting food.

· **Slicing knife** (carving knife, salad knife). This knife is good for cutting fruits and vegetables (like heads of lettuce) and carving poultry. The blade is very long and thin so the knife can also be used for carving even, thin slices of meat off a turkey or roast when using with a roasting fork.

Good-quality knives are safer to use and more efficient than poor-quality knives, and, with proper care, will last longer. The quality of a knife is based on the type of steel used to make the blade, followed by the proper tempering and grinding. Stainless steel is less expensive than carbon steel, but you have to sharpen stainless steel frequently. High-carbon stainless steel is a new surgical steel technology and the best culinary knife steel that gives you the best of both stainless and carbon steels with additional resistance to rust and corrosion. That is the type that I sell.

Experienced chefs like me are pretty protective of their knives and don't like to share them, so don't even ask. It's pretty common to use a carrying case to take them to and from work each day, and some chefs go to a lot of trouble to get their names engraved on their knives so that none of the knives mysteriously ends up in somebody else's bag. I had my knives disappear so many times when I was working at different restaurants, hotels and catering functions that now, whenever we are out doing a cooking demonstration somewhere, I have Marlene stand guard to keep an eye on them if I leave the room.

Two other items I use regularly are kitchen shears (with blades that come apart for easy cleaning) and a sharpening steel, which is a long, rounded metal rod with a handle at one end.

The shears are for cutting through twine, herbs, poultry and tough food packages. The steel is for honing your knives.

A dull knife needs sharpening on a whetstone but once it's sharp, you straighten it by honing it with the steel. If you can't remember when you last sharpened your knives, it's time! An electric knife sharpener will do the job but it will also take a few years off your knife, and you will still need to hone it. You could get a diamond steel to do both jobs, but it's not necessary unless you are going into business involving high-volume cooking. The best way to learn how to sharpen a knife is to watch and learn. Go online and check out the many videos on the subject.

> ## Tip
> Hand wash your knives to keep them sharper longer.

Chef Masaharu Morimoto said Japanese chefs believe their souls go into their knives once they start using them, so "You wouldn't put your soul in a dishwasher!" Good advice.

The safest way to store knives and accessories is in a knife block—not loose in a drawer. A knife block also protects your knives from chips and dents. It's also wise never to leave knives in a sink, wet or dry, since they are apt to get banged around and damaged, or cut someone who doesn't know they are there.

Cutting Boards

Wood: good. Teakwood: really good. Plastic mat: poor. Plastic cutting board: great. Glass: don't even go there. Wooden cutting boards will get damaged in a dishwasher so really need to be washed by hand. I sanitize mine with a mild bleach solution since they are vulnerable to bacteria buildup over time. They sometimes split and crack if dropped or when left soaking in water (no, no, no!), but most people still prefer wooden cutting boards to glass or plastic because of the feel of the wood and the pleasant sound of cutting on it. Teak is supposed to be better over time than maple or bamboo, but it's harder to find. My buddy Stevo just gave me a hand-made cross-grain tamarack cutting board (made by Trevor's Boards on Manitoulin Island) that is quite unique, so I am trying it out to see if it stands up to teak.

Now I don't like to name names, but I have a certain sister-in-law whose name begins with N who used a tiny, wobbly glass cutting board and an even smaller beat-up paring knife for cutting just about everything—that is, until I went rummaging through my storage unit of kitchen equipment and found her a large wooden cutting board and an old chef knife. Even though she has to wash the board by hand and was shocked at the size of the knife, she was happy to learn how to cut up food more efficiently. And I am happy not to hear that awful clicking noise of metal on glass anymore when she hosts family dinners at her place. There's nothing really wrong with using glass as a cutting board. In fact, it's easy to sanitize, which is a plus, but it will dull your knives.

Thick plastic is what we use in the food industry, with colour-coded boards to ensure we don't contaminate lettuce with pork, or fruit with fish, for example. Plastic cutting boards should be replaced if they have any deep cuts that could harbour bacteria. At home, I happen to prefer plastic since it is lighter to use than wood and easier to clean, but when entertaining, I often serve dishes on wooden boards. Consider using the very thin plastic cutting boards available at discount stores so you can change them more frequently.

Tip
Put a damp dish cloth under your cutting board to keep it from slipping when in use.

Pots and Pans

What separates a good set of pots and pans from a poor set is durability, heat conductivity and maintenance requirements. Pots and pans also have to be comfortable to use. These qualities are typically, but not always, reflected in the price.

There are several kinds of cookware to choose from:

· **Cast iron** is really affordable, adds a little iron to your diet (if you get an uncoated pan) and has been around forever it seems. It is high on my list for its durability, especially for cooking meat. My favourite way to do roasts is in a very heavy enameled cast iron Dutch oven.

Tip
Use minimal soap when cleaning cast iron pans and "season" them from time to time to avoid rust and corrosion; to season a cast iron pan, heat it in the oven for 30 minutes at 350F (175C) and then oil it with vegetable oil. Cool and wipe the pan before using.

· **Stainless steel** cookware is very practical and affordable and a good choice for the majority of cooks. Heavy gauge stainless steel also browns foods better than non-stick surfaces. One step up from stainless steel cookware is stainless steel with copper bottoms.
· **Aluminum** cookware is lightweight and affordable; it is the type of cookware used in industry and for teaching cooking because of its durability and ability to transfer heat so well, but when exposed to acid the metal can discolour and change the taste of food. Health concerns about aluminum prompted lots of home cooks and chefs to switch to other types of cookware.

- **Magnetic** cookware is required if you have an induction cooktop. Aluminum, glass and copper will not work on these stoves. Also known as induction cookware, magnetic pots and pans would include those that are cast iron, steel, magnetic stainless steel, ceramic clad or enameled. If you don't know what kind of cookware you have, hold a magnet to the bottom of your pot; if it sticks, then you are good to go.
- **Non-stick** cookware is the easiest type to clean and a good option for pan-frying. I prefer to use a non-stick frying pan at home for quick breakfasts. Minimal oil is needed, but you have to be careful to use rubber spatulas or wooden spoons on non-stick pans to avoid scratching them. That's the primary problem with non-stick cookware: once it gets scratched, metal is exposed and can be a health concern. When that happens, replace the pan.
- **Copper** cookware (lined with stainless steel) is an excellent heat conductor and for generations has been chefs' ultimate preference for searing, frying, simmering and sauce making. But copper tarnishes, unless you get the modern type that has a brushed finish. Still, copper is a luxury few can afford (including me, but I dream of buying a whole set and hanging them from the ceiling).

Tip

Look for cookware that can do double duty on stovetops and in the oven. These pots and pans normally have metal handles.

Equipment Must-Haves

I have cooking equipment preferences for home cooking, large-volume cooking, cooking on the road and cooking on television, but in addition to knives and cutting boards, at a minimum every home kitchen should have the following:

- A cast iron frying pan
- Small, medium and large saucepans (also known as pots), with lids
- A Dutch oven (a large, heavy pot with two handles and a tight-fitting lid)
- A stockpot with a lid (also known as a soup pot, or *marmite*, in French)
- Baking sheets of varying sizes
- Baking pans of varying sizes
- Baking dishes of varying sizes (round, square or rectangular, made of metal, ceramic or glass)
- Small, medium and large mixing bowls (made of non-reactive materials like your baking dishes)
- Blender (or hand blender)
- Hand mixer (or stand mixer)
- Vacuum sealer
- Thermometers (fridge thermometer, freezer thermometer, oven thermometer and digital thermometer to check meat or fish for doneness)
- Wet and dry measuring cups (cups for measuring liquids are usually made of ovenproof glass with a spout for pouring, whereas cups for measuring dry ingredients are made of metal or plastic and come in various increments)
- Measuring spoons
- Parchment paper

A vacuum sealer is a hunter's best friend. If you are going to all the time and trouble of hunting or fishing, why not get a sealer to preserve the catch properly? I swear you will be glad you did. When I cook meat or fish that has been frozen and not vacuum sealed, I can often tell how long it's been in the freezer just by the taste and texture. That is why I think this little appliance is so fabulous: it makes freezing quick and easy and produces a higher-quality food for cooking or reheating. No more freezer burn or freezer taste.

A note on parchment paper: it's simply indispensable for cooking and baking. This disposable paper is sold in rolls, or in stacks if you buy large quantities. Also known as baking paper, parchment paper looks like wax paper but it has so many more uses. I use it all the time for lining my baking sheets (so that I don't have to grease them), for keeping oily or sweet foods from sticking to my pans (so I can transfer a cake or meatloaf from the pan to the serving plate in seconds) and to speed up cleaning afterwards. Using parchment paper rather than foil is also recommended for wrapping chicken or fish for baking *en papillote*, due to the health risks associated with aluminum. Marlene uses it to roll out pastry so that the dough doesn't stick to the rolling pin.

Food-Handling Techniques

There are proper ways to handle and store every kind of food whether it's fresh, frozen, canned or dried. According to Health Canada, about four million, or one in eight, Canadians are affected by a food-borne illness each year, resulting in over 11,000 hospitalizations and 230 deaths. The risk of exposure to bacteria, bacterial toxins, parasites and viruses is minimized by following proper food safety practices. This is especially important for seniors, pregnant women, young children and babies, and people with chronic medical conditions or compromised immune systems.

Here are some food-handling tips:

Keeping Things Clean

- Wash your hands for 20 seconds with soap and water before and after handling food, using the bathroom, coughing, sneezing, smoking, changing diapers or touching animals.
- Dip a cloth in a sanitizing solution (1 tsp/5 mL chlorine bleach to 3 cups/710 mL water) to sanitize your sink, countertops and cutting boards *after* cleaning them.
- Sanitize dish cloths in the washing machine and scrubbers in a dishwasher.

Caring for Fresh Food

- Rinse greens, fruits and vegetables thoroughly before consuming, including organic foods, even if planning to peel them; scrub potatoes and carrots with a vegetable scrubber.
- Dedicate one cutting board to fruits and vegetables and others to meat, poultry and fish (consider using colour-coded cutting boards: blue for fish, yellow for poultry, green for vegetables, and red for meat).

Storing

- Keep your fridge set to 40F (4C) or lower.
- Refrigerate fresh produce apart from meats and fish.
- When storing food in bags, use food-safe plastic bags only.
- See specific storage tips for meat in "Preparing Large Game" (page 117) in Chapter 5, for fish in "Preparing Fish and Shellfish" (page 155) in Chapter 6 and for poultry in "Preparing Birds" (page 190) in Chapter 7.

- Refrigerate leftovers as soon as possible and discard after a maximum of three to four days.
- Store dry goods (rice, dried beans, dried corn, cornmeal, pasta, cereal, etc.) in airtight containers and keep in a cool location away from direct light.

Cooking

- Use a thermometer to make sure meats, fish and poultry reach the appropriate internal temperature when you cook (see "Safe Internal Temperatures" chart, page 14, for specifics).

Reheating

- Thoroughly reheat cooked foods to a minimum of 165F (75C) before consuming.

Freezing

- Keep your freezer set to 0F (-18C) or lower.
- Label and date all packages going into the freezer and discard anything more than six months old unless it was vacuum sealed.
- Use only airtight food-safe storage containers, butcher wrap, freezer bags, and so on.
- Thaw proteins in the refrigerator (in a container to prevent dripping) rather than at room temperature on the counter.

Canning

- Follow proper canning procedures for making preserves; you will find accurate instructions on packages of liquid or dry pectin, as well as on the websites of canning jar manufacturers.
- Make appropriate adjustments for canning if you live in a high-altitude location.
- Never eat canned food that appears to be bubbly on top or food from dented or bulging tin cans or glass jars that have been damaged.

Testing for Doneness

Standards for cooked food "doneness" are high in the Canadian food industry—even higher than in the United States. Businesses in the food industry are obligated to follow federal guidelines to prevent food poisoning, and home cooks should do the same. Taking accurate readings of internal temperatures requires the use of thermometers whether you are cooking poultry, fish, meat or stuffing, or heating up leftovers. Digital thermometers are reasonably cheap to buy and measure the temperature instantly and accurately. They have a spike at one end that you insert an inch or two (2.5 to 5 cm) deep into the food. Once you get the hang of using a thermometer, you will never want to be without one. The temperatures in the "Safe Internal Temperatures" illustration (below) are for general reference but if you are immune compromised, pregnant or elderly, it's a very good idea to follow these guidelines.

Tip

To test the internal temperature of meat, insert the thermometer at the thickest part: at the joint (for a roast), in the centre (for a burger) or in the side (for a steak), close to the bone without touching it.

You will find additional information about smoked meat doneness in the Smoked Deer Sausage recipe (page 142) and about readying raw meat in the Elk Carpaccio on Salad Greens recipe (page 55). Similarly, the recipes for Cold-Smoked Juniper Salmon (page 48) and Hot-Smoked Salmon (page 45) address doneness in more detail with regard to smoking fish; and the Cod Martinis with Strawberry Peach Salsa recipe (page 52) addresses doneness for marinating fish.

All that being said, if I were a chef running my own restaurant and I followed Health Canada's meat and fish doneness guidelines faithfully, I'd probably go out of business. When I was head chef on the Kraft General Foods account while employed by Marriott Management Services (1985–93), I was required to follow federal guidelines, even though several customers sent my food back to the kitchen because it was overdone. So although there are guidelines to follow, the customer is always right and when you are running your own food business you have to adjust your standards to stay competitive. My recipes advise when I would remove food from heat, but the decision is yours.

Part of making sure your food is cooked properly is to have an oven that works properly. You'd be surprised at how far off your oven could be without your knowledge. Test your oven's accuracy at different temperatures using an oven thermometer. Then read the instructions that came with your oven to learn how to calibrate it yourself or get it done under warranty. Sometimes it's just a matter of cleaning. I had an old beast of an oven that went wonky for a while after Marlene sprayed it with oven cleaner. We didn't notice it was off kilter for a week or two, and then I started to wonder what was going on. She had missed wiping the thermostat clean, but once I did that, we were back in shape—for a while. Accuracy is particularly important when baking, since temperatures need to be precise, so we ended up having to replace our 30-year-old stove with a new one.

Illustration adapted from Health Canada's Safe Internal Cooking Temperatures chart.

Safe Internal Temperatures

BEEF	CHICKEN/DUCK	CRAB	DEER	FISH	RABBIT
170F/77C Well done	180F/82C Whole	165F/74C	165F/74C Medium well	158F/70C	165F/74C
160F/71C Medium	165F/74C Parts				
145F/63C Medium rare					

CHAPTER 2

Tricks of the Trade:
Basic Cooking Methods and Recipes

Indigenous culinary creativity must have impressed the explorers who arrived in these lands centuries ago. When their own food supplies ran out, the hungry and sickly newcomers in what was to become Canada were fortunate that First Nations and Inuit people were willing and able to help them out not only with New World foods, but with the knowledge of how to harvest and prepare them. In time, Indigenous people taught settlers what to hunt, fish, cultivate and store, and how to cook foods and prepare medicines. Some of the foods, cooking techniques and recipes that have come to be known as "Canadian" or "American" classics actually came from Indigenous nations: roasted venison, stuffed turkey, smoked salmon, steamed lobster, dried buffalo, maple baked beans, mashed potatoes, cranberry sauce, barbecue sauce, chili, guacamole, corn on the cob, roasted peanuts, fruit pudding and chocolate. Indigenous foods were prepared in a number of ways, depending on the nation:

- **Air-drying.** Berries, mushrooms, seaweed, strips of meat, inner bark and greens were air dried on woven mats or wooden racks, and seaweed was spread on beach rocks to sun dry.
- **Baking.** Root vegetables were wrapped up and buried under hot coals to bake.
- **Boiling.** Soups and stews were made by boiling tubers, seaweed, meat and plant roots in an earthen bowl over a fire, in a dug-out tree stump, or in a wooden bowl heated by hot stones.
- **Broiling.** Meat and fish were broiled on a wooden canopy over a fire or on a stick frame leaning over a fire.
- **Curing.** Fish was cured by salting.
- **Preserving.** Fish and root vegetables were preserved underground in caches with water, oil, berries and herbs (sometimes inside a sealskin), as a form of pickling.
- **Roasting.** Meat and stuffed game birds were roasted on a spit over a fire, or on a stake surrounded by multiple fires, or under hot coals.
- **Smoking.** Meat and fish were smoked on a wooden canopy built over a fire.
- **Steaming.** Root vegetables and fish were steamed in a pit in the ground lined with hides and filled with water heated by hot stones, and shellfish was steamed wrapped in leaves or bark set over hot rocks.
- **Wind-drying.** Fish was wind dried on tree branches stripped of leaves and bark.

Dry Heat and Moist Heat Cooking Methods

One thing that hasn't changed since the origin of cooking is that it involves applying dry heat or moist heat, or a combination of the two. Dry heat cooking includes grilling, broiling, roasting, baking, sautéing and stir-frying, pan-frying and deep-frying. Moist heat cooking includes poaching, simmering, boiling, blanching and steaming.

In general terms, if the meat/fish/poultry is dry (lean), then you should cook it in a moist fashion, but if the food is oily or high in fat to begin with, then use a dry cooking method. In many respects, moist heat cooking methods are healthier than dry heat cooking due to the absence of oil or fat that is used for frying or grilling. Many of my recipes suggest how you can reduce fat consumption when cooking.

Dry versus Moist Heat Cooking Methods

	METHOD	DESCRIPTION
DRY HEAT COOKING	Grilling	Cooking food on an open grill over a heat source
	Broiling	Cooking food with radiant heat from above
	Roasting	Cooking food by surrounding it with hot, dry air in an oven or on a spit in front of an open fire
	Baking	Cooking food by surrounding it with hot, dry air. Similar to roasting but usually applies to breads, pastries, vegetables and fish
	Sautéing	Cooking food quickly in a small amount of fat, usually while mixing or tossing the food by occasionally flipping the pan
	Sweating	Cooking slowly in fat without browning, sometimes under a cover
	Stir-frying	Cooking cut-up food quickly in a small amount of fat by tossing the food in a wok or pan with a spatula or similar implement. Similar to sautéing, except that when stir-frying the pan is stationary
	Pan-frying	Cooking food in a moderate amount of fat in an uncovered pan
	Deep-frying	Cooking food submerged in hot fat
	Barbecuing	Roasting or grilling food using a wood fire or a barbecue
	Smoking	Cooking food in a closed container in which wood chips are burned to create heat and smoke
MOIST HEAT COOKING	Poaching	Cooking food gently in water or other liquid that is hot but not actually bubbling (160–180F/70–80C)
	Simmering	Cooking food in water or other liquid that is bubbling gently (180–200F/80–95C)
	Boiling	Cooking food in water or other liquid that is bubbling rapidly (212F/100C)
	Blanching	Cooking food partially and very briefly in boiling water or hot fat as a preparation technique
	Steaming	Cooking food by direct contact with steam
COMBINATION METHODS	Braising	Browning food using dry heat followed by cooking the food covered in a small amount of liquid
	Stewing	Simmering or braising food in a small amount of liquid, which is usually served with the food as sauce

Elements of a bouquet garni. See recipe on page 35.

There are also combination cooking methods, such as braising and stewing. Drying, salting, pickling and smoking are generally considered to be food preservation techniques rather than cooking methods. The secret to knowing which cooking method to use lies in the texture of the food you are working with, its moisture level, the amount of time you have to cook, and the flavour and texture you are after.

Cooking methods are explained further in Chapter 5 (see "Cooking Large Game," page 118, and the "Recommended Venison Cooking Methods" illustration, page 119), Chapter 6 (see "Cooking Fish," page 156), and Chapter 7 (see "Cooking Birds" and the "Differences between Wild and Domesticated Birds" illustration, both on page 192).

Fat, Salt and Health

The health status of Indigenous peoples in Canada today is bleak. There's a high infant mortality rate, an epidemic in type two diabetes and a life expectancy that is as much as 15 years shorter for Indigenous men and 10 years shorter for Indigenous women than the national average. A major factor contributing to mortality and disease among Indigenous people is poor nutrition. Once Europeans arrived, the diet and lifestyle of First Nations and Inuit people started to change and underwent further change when they were reduced to living on reserves and in settlements. Generations of

Indigenous people were forced to live in residential schools, which caused the disruption of their traditional knowledge, customs and practices relating to food, hunting, fishing and harvesting. Now it is a battle to restore the health status of Indigenous people.

The majority of the cooking demonstrations I do in Indigenous communities are at the request of community health workers, nurses, dieticians and diabetes educators. One of the greatest challenges they face is getting people to eat food that is not heavily dosed with salt, fat, sugar, and so on. Health care workers struggle to find ways to help their communities get access to affordable fresh foods, to teach them healthy ways to prepare "country" food, and to promote cooking education overall.

What I try to show in my cooking demonstrations is that foods can be flavoured many different ways while controlling the amount of salt, fat and sugar it contains. This is much easier when you cook from scratch and control what goes into your food from the beginning. Even though the recipes in this book are not designed for diabetics, I have included various techniques for flavouring food without using salt or by reducing salt content.

Marlene and I deliver a workshop to demonstrate cooking for families on a budget. Our idea was to support health educators and low-income families to approach food from a more holistic perspective, by connecting all of the dots between cooking and eating, as a daily cycle that engages the mind, the body, the spirit and the emotions. Two of the most common points I make in the workshop are that learning how to cook using herbs and spices and natural ingredients is beneficial not just to diabetics, but to everyone, and cooking from scratch actually saves money in the long run.

About Fat

Indigenous people traditionally used bear grease and fish oil for cooking, but they also found other practical uses for these fats—such as keeping bugs away, heating their igloos, lighting their lodges, preserving foods and making medicine. Times have changed a lot, but First Nations people still cook with animal fats and make use of them outside the kitchen. Every so often Marlene will get a little jar of bear grease or goose grease (enhanced with ground leaves, roots or barks) from her sister Pat Chum, of Moose Factory First Nation, or brother-in-law Kenn Pitawanakwat of Wikwemikong Unceded Indian Reserve in northern Ontario, to be used for skin problems or aches and pains. A friend recently sent me a jar of eulachon fish oil from BC to use for cooking. He uses it when pan-frying potatoes, for making salad dressings and as a dip for bread.

The Blackfoot and Cree used buffalo marrow as fat to bind dried chokecherries and dried buffalo meat together to make pemmican long ago; woodlands peoples used deer suet and cranberries in the same way. When made properly, pemmican lasts indefinitely. Survivalists have experimented with new ways of making it so that they are prepared in case of a nuclear disaster, and the fats trending for this purpose now are beef tallow or coconut oil, although I am not sure where you would find either of those after a nuclear catastrophe.

Fats do go bad at some point. Some oils go rancid just sitting in the kitchen, especially if exposed to sunlight or heat, whereas others (stable fats) can tolerate high degrees of heat before reaching their smoking point—this is the point when they quickly deteriorate, lose their nutritional value, produce harmful compounds and take on a burnt taste.

We all need fat in our diet, and we get it from solid fats, liquid fats and hidden fats (like those in nuts, milk and avocados). There are so many different types of fats to choose from for cooking now, and there doesn't seem to be much agreement on which ones are best to use. Cardiologists generally advise that saturated fats (the ones that solidify when chilled, like butter, lard and shortening) need to be avoided. These practitioners recommend canola, corn, safflower, sunflower, soybean and peanut oils, advising that they are better for you. Alternative health experts disagree because of how the fat is altered through the refining process; they believe saturated fats are healthier. From a chef's perspective, fat is important in cooking. Butter, lard and shortening all have their rightful place in the kitchen, as do clarified butter, chicken skin, pork back fat, olive oil and peanut oil. Fat adds flavour, softens texture and adds moisture to food.

Each type of oil has a unique taste and smoking point, so chefs choose fats depending on what they are making and how they plan to cook. I prefer regular (pure) olive oil as my go-to oil for day-to-day cooking and recommend it for all the recipes in this cookbook that do not state any other type. Extra-virgin olive oil is great too, but not for high-temperature cooking. We have a cupboard of various oils at home and keep some of the less stable ones (like walnut oil) in the fridge. If you don't cook much, get small quantities of oil and keep them refrigerated so that they don't spoil. Olive oil will get cloudy when chilled, but that doesn't affect the flavour when you cook with it; just leave it out so it warms up first.

About Salt

Chefs cringe when they present a meal only to see a diner immediately reach for the salt and pepper shakers before even tasting the food. I know what salt adds to food in terms of taste, texture and appearance, so of course I use it. But I also know that when we eat salt, we get a hit of dopamine, the chemical that makes us feel good in the pleasure centre of the brain. Unfortunately, the more salt you eat, the more you want.

There are many kinds of salt, and they don't all share the same qualities in taste, appearance, texture, dissolvability or purity, so it helps to know the natural properties and qualities of salts. Get a small quantity of different salt types and use them as needed. Here are a few popular types of salt:

· **Iodized table salt.** This is very economical and is what most people use as an all-purpose salt, although it is heavily refined and lacking in trace minerals. It's good for salting water for pasta or vegetables, or for baking, since it has a fine texture and is easy to measure, but it has a strong flavour and lacks texture for finishing a meat or fish dish, a salad, vegetables or desserts.

- Kosher salt. This coarse salt is mildly flavoured, dissolves easily and is less refined than table salt. Kosher salt comes from inland salt deposits from ancient seabeds, and its original purpose was for koshering meat—removing blood from meat by salting it, thereby making it fit to eat. Kosher salt is more expensive than regular table salt but is excellent for brining, pickling, smoking and finishing dishes (such as french fries), so it might just be the most versatile of all salts.

- Himalayan salt. This crunchy salt is hand mined from an ancient sea salt deposit in Pakistan and is full of trace minerals that are easily absorbed in the body, which is why it has so many health benefits; alternative health practitioners believe it reduces inflammation, boosts the immune system and detoxifies organs. Himalayan salt is more expensive than table salt and kosher salt and is also coarse. Himalayan salt can be briny, sweet or bitter and can be white, pink or red due to the iron oxide it contains.

- Sea salt. Many types of salt come from evaporated seawater from different corners of the world, including Hawaii, Japan and the north of France (hand harvested salt from there is called Celtic salt). Sea salt adds wonderful flavours and textures to popcorn, meat, fish and salads, is great for brining, pickling, sauce making and grilling, and is free of the toxins found in refined salt, but it could contain heavy metals from polluted seas. Sea salt is more expensive than the other salts mentioned above and can be too coarse for everyday use unless you grind it. Flaked sea salt (from England) is very quick to dissolve and adds a briny flavour to freshly cooked foods, but the rarest and most delicate of salts, fleur de sel, is the crust that forms on the surface of Atlantic Ocean seawater as it evaporates. Fleur del sel is very expensive but has a delicate, earthy flavour, perfect for finishing a dish.

- Pickling salt. To prevent the liquids in home canned foods from becoming cloudy, home cooks use fine grain pickling salt, a pure salt that has none of the additives found in table salt (or some brands of kosher salt).

- Rock salt. This salt is the very coarse type used to melt ice in winter but is also used to make ice cream and to display oysters on the half shell at oyster bars.

In my recipes, I specify which type of salt to use when there is an advantage to doing so. In the case of pickling and brining, it's more than a preference—it's essential to recipe success.

Flavoured Salt Mixes

When salt is combined with herbs, spices or other seasonings, the result is flavoured, or seasoned, salt. Flavoured salt mixes can be coarse or fine, depending on the type of salt chosen for seasoning. Typically, flavoured salt mixes have added herbs, spices and citrus peels, and can even be combined with vinegars, oils or other ingredients. The following two recipes have a lot of uses in a typical household.

Lemon Pepper Salt

MAKES ¼ CUP (60 ML)

This has got to be one of the easiest salt combos around for seasoning poultry, steaks, pasta, fish, side dishes, cocktails and eggs.

2 lemons
2 Tbsp (30 mL) whole black peppercorns
1 Tbsp (15 mL) kosher salt (or sea salt or Himalayan salt)

01 Wash lemons. Zest the peels using a zester or fine grater. Dry zest in a bowl at room temperature for a day (or on a baking sheet for 30 minutes in a 200F/95C oven).

02 Crush peppercorns in a mortar and pestle or spice mill. Add the zest and grind. Combine with the salt (do not grind) and store in an airtight spice jar. It will keep for about four weeks.

03 Rub the mixture into a steak for a quick hit of flavour before tossing the meat on a sizzling grill, or use on poultry (rubbed with oil) before roasting. Alternatively, use this salt mix to season omelettes, boiled rice and steamed green beans or other vegetables.

Vanilla Salt

MAKES ¼ CUP (60 ML)

You've heard of garlic salt, onion salt and lemon pepper salt. Well, imagine what you could do with vanilla salt—Vanilla Salted Maple Duck Breast comes to mind (see recipe, page 194). Examples of sweet and savoury dishes to use with Vanilla Salt are listed at the end of this recipe.

1 vanilla bean
¼ cup (60 mL) kosher salt (or sea salt or Himalayan salt)

01 Trim the ends of the vanilla bean. Make an incision down the bean, lengthwise, without cutting through to the other side. Spread the bean open and use the tip of a sharp knife to scrape out the tiny seeds into a mortar and pestle. Add 1 tablespoon (15 mL) of the salt to the seeds and combine well. Alternatively, use a spice mill. Grind until well combined.

02 Add the rest of the salt to the mixture and combine using a spoon (but do not grind).

03 Cut the seeded bean into small pieces (large enough not to fall out of a spice shaker) and add them to the mixture to build up more flavour in the salt over time.

04 Store mixture in an airtight spice jar for up to four months. Wait at least a week before using.

05 Sprinkle vanilla salt over chocolate brownies, chocolate cake, ice cream, crème brûlée or fresh fruit cup for an intriguing quick dessert. Or try it on your main dishes.

Tip
When making your own spice mixes, use good-quality herbs and spices that have been properly harvested and stored, making for a fresher tasting product.

Spice Mixes

Herbs and spices fill in the blanks to round out flavours in food. Most herbs come from the green parts of a plant (stem and leaves), while spices come from the seeds, flowers, bark, root or bulb of a tree or shrub. Herbs can be used fresh or dried, but spices are practically always dried. Black pepper is probably the best-known spice used in cooking worldwide and it comes from India. Few classic culinary herbs are indigenous to North America, and most originate from more temperate regions of the world. Before the arrival of Europeans, Indigenous peoples of Canada and the United States used many plant species either for cooking or medicine; wild leeks, nodding onion, Indian celery, meadow garlic, wild bergamot, wild rose hips and wild mint are just a few examples.

One of the easiest ways to flavour meat, fish and poultry—so that it tastes just the way you want and has the texture you like—is to use a spice mix containing the flavours you love. If you want to make your own, try the mixes below. You will find that they can save you a lot of time when you want to throw something together for supper in a hurry, and they will save you money too. Just remember to shake or stir the mix before using, since it will not contain any anticaking agents. (Shake it every time you use it. Otherwise you might get too much of one spice and not enough of another.) Whatever you do, don't contaminate the spice mix in the container: just measure out what you need and throw out excess rather than pouring it back into the jar.

Store the spice mixes in labelled spice bottles or shakers with lids; they should keep for 6 to 12 months.

SPICE BAGS A HIT

The spice mixes I use in my cooking demonstrations have always generated a lot of interest. So one hot July a few years ago, Marlene and I made some to sell. We were in Thunder Bay, Ontario, doing a demo at a powwow, and we sold tiny bags of our spice mixes at our booth. They sold like hotcakes and people kept coming back wanting more. We ran out in no time on the first day. That was great, but then we wondered what we would do on the second day. We talked it over and made the decision to make more. But where? How? We were away from home and from our production kitchen and supplies.

In between demos we took off to the nearest shopping mall and loaded up on jumbo containers of all the spices we needed for our three best-sellers, as well as small food storage bags, plastic gloves, plastic drop sheets, hairnets, surgical gloves and masks, and printer paper. We were all set. We stayed up making spice bags and printing labels in our hotel room till 4:00 a.m. that night. But we got it done. I am glad we were gone by the time the room cleaning staff showed up, since it smelled like we'd been cooking all night in there (which would be weird, considering there was no kitchen). We sold out again the next day.

After that, we revised the recipes a little and made spice bags to give away at Christmas. The family loved them.

WET RUB VARIATION: A wet rub is recommended for cuts with bones (especially ribs) and very lean dishes, like Big Buffalo Pot Roast (see recipe, page 129). Combine 1½ tablespoons (22 mL) of spice mix with 3 tablespoons (45 mL) of pure olive oil per pound (500 g) of meat.

Big Buffalo Spice Mix (Red Meat Rub)

MAKES 1 CUP (250 ML)

This dry rub will season deer, moose, buffalo, beef or lamb, particularly tender cuts. The recipe makes a small batch so that you can try it before committing to making a big batch. The next time you make it, add more of what you like and less of what you might not care for.

¼ cup (60 mL) kosher **salt** (or sea salt or Himalayan salt)
2 Tbsp (30 mL) **brown sugar**
2 Tbsp (30 mL) dried **rosemary**
2 Tbsp (30 mL) **paprika**
1½ Tbsp (22 mL) dried **thyme**
1 Tbsp (15 mL) **chili flakes**
1 Tbsp (15 mL) granulated **garlic**
1½ tsp (7.5 mL) **cayenne pepper**
1½ tsp (7.5 mL) ground **black pepper**
1½ tsp (7.5 mL) ground **cumin**
1½ tsp (7.5 mL) **mustard powder**

01 Mix all the ingredients well. Keep the rub in an airtight jar out of direct sunlight. It should keep for 6 to 12 months.

02 Use 1½ tablespoons (22 mL) of spice mix per pound (500 g) of meat. Rub the mix in with your fingers a minimum of five minutes before cooking the meat, unless the recipe directs otherwise.

Swimming with the Fishes Spice Mix (Fish Rub)

MAKES ½ CUP (120 ML)

This is a dry rub that will season and add some texture to any kind of fish, especially fatty fish like sablefish, salmon or whitefish. The recipe makes a small batch so that you can try it before committing to making a big batch. The next time you make it, add more of what you like and less of what you might not care for.

2 Tbsp (30 mL) kosher **salt** (or sea salt or Himalayan salt)
1 Tbsp (15 mL) ground **black pepper**
1 Tbsp (15 mL) granulated **garlic**
1 Tbsp (15 mL) **onion powder**
1 Tbsp (15 mL) **paprika**
1 tsp (5 mL) **chipotle powder**
1 tsp (5 mL) dried **marjoram**
1 tsp (5 mL) dried **parsley**
1 tsp (5 mL) dried **tarragon**
Pinch **cumin**

01 Mix all the ingredients and keep in an airtight jar out of direct sunlight. It should keep for 6 to 12 months.

02 Use 2 teaspoons (10 mL) of spice mix per pound (500 g) of fish. Rub the mix in with your fingers for a minimum of five minutes before cooking the fish, unless the recipe directs otherwise. Most people don't eat the skin of fish, so I usually only season the flesh side. If seasoning fish for longer than a few minutes (for deeper flavour), cover the fish in a nonreactive dish (glass, ceramic or stainless steel) with a lid or with food wrap, and chill. To prevent the wrap from removing the spice mix, make sure the wrap doesn't touch the fish.

WET RUB VARIATION: A wet rub is recommended for lean fish, like perch, pike or trout. Combine 2 teaspoons (10 mL) spice mix with 1½ tablespoons (22 mL) pure olive oil per pound (500 g) of fish. See the Swimming with the Whitefish recipe (page 173).

Sexy Chicken Spice Mix (Poultry Rub)

MAKES ¾ CUP (180 ML)

This dry rub is good for chicken and duck. See the Sexy Duck Legs recipe (page 198). The recipe makes a small batch so that you can try it before committing to making a big batch. The next time you make it, add more of what you like and less of what you might not care for.

3 Tbsp (45 mL) kosher salt (or sea salt or Himalayan salt)
2 tsp (10 mL) ground black pepper
2 Tbsp (30 mL) ground rosemary
2 Tbsp (30 mL) paprika
1 Tbsp (15 mL) chili flakes
1 Tbsp (15 mL) dehydrated onion
1 Tbsp (15 mL) granulated garlic
1 Tbsp (15 mL) ground thyme
1 tsp (5 mL) cayenne pepper
1 tsp (5 mL) ground cinnamon
1 tsp (5 mL) ground ginger
½ tsp (2.5 mL) celery seeds
½ tsp (2.5 mL) ground nutmeg

01 Mix all the ingredients and keep in an airtight jar out of direct sunlight. The rub should keep for 6 to 12 months.

02 Use 1½ tablespoons (22 mL) of spice mix per pound (500 g) of meat. Rub the mix in with your fingers for a minimum of five minutes before cooking the meat, unless the recipe directs otherwise. If seasoning birds for longer than a few minutes (for deeper flavour), cover the meat in a nonreactive dish (glass, ceramic or stainless steel) with a lid or with food wrap, and chill. To prevent the wrap from removing the spice mix, make sure the wrap doesn't touch the meat.

WET RUB VARIATION: A wet rub is recommended for lean birds such as turkey, goose, quail and pheasant. Combine 1½ tablespoons (22 mL) of spice mix with 3 tablespoons (45 mL) of pure olive oil per pound (500 g) of meat.

Pickling Spice

MAKES ⅔ CUP (160 ML)

Indigenous peoples invented various ways of storing food for future needs. Storing it underground and covered with heavy rocks was one method. In Canada, the Inuit fermented greens, berries and fish underground as a form of pickling. The foods softened and became sweeter over time.

The standard spices found in store-bought pickling spice are mustard seeds, peppercorns, coriander seeds and bay leaves. I happen to like a little extra kick with additional ingredients in this recipe, but you could do without if you want a very simple mixture.

This mixture is what I used for pickling herring (see Pickled Herring Salad with Blackberry Vinaigrette recipe, page 72) and melon (see Swimming with the Whitefish, Served with Pickled Melon recipe, page 173).

2 dried **bay leaves**
2 **cinnamon sticks**, broken into pieces
2 tsp (10 mL) **juniper berries**
2 tsp (10 mL) **red pepper flakes**
2 whole **cloves**
3 Tbsp (45 mL) whole **mustard seeds**
1 Tbsp (15 mL) whole **coriander seeds**
2 Tbsp (30 mL) whole **peppercorns** (black or mixed)
1 Tbsp (15 mL) whole **allspice**
1 tsp (5 mL) ground **ginger**

01 Use a mortar and pestle or spice mill to lightly crush the bay leaves, cinnamon, juniper berries, red pepper flakes, and cloves. Then combine with the remaining ingredients.

02 Store mix in an airtight spice bottle out of direct sunlight. This rub will keep for up to a year.

03 Follow the directions in the recipe to determine how much pickling spice to use for pickling beans or eggs, making pickles or making chutney. On average, you would use about 2 teaspoons (10 mL) per quart (1 L) jar for pickles, or you would double that amount if parboiling ribs (3–4 lb/1.5–2 kg).

Smoked Foods

Smoking is one way to simultaneously cure and flavour food. Whether you're working with meat, fish, vegetables, salt or nuts, smoke enhances the food with the flavour of the wood of your choosing. Each wood has its own unique scent and smoke quality from light, to medium or heavy. One way Indigenous people traditionally smoked meat and fish was to lay it on top of tree branches set up as a rack above a smoky fire. Smoking technology advanced to the use of tented enclosures and boxed containers for better smoke and heat control. If you are curious, you can go online and find all sorts of DIY smokers using pans clipped together, cardboard boxes or filing cabinets. My brother-in-law has plans to make a smoker out of an old fridge he's got, but something tells me he's going to have a lot of visitors snooping around in his backyard once they see a fridge out there and smell food!

There are two types of smoking methods—cold-smoking and hot-smoking—and both of them involve the use of brining or dry salting for curing to take place. After the curing has been set in motion, the food is thoroughly dried. Then it is exposed to the smoke of smoldering wood dust, chips or chunks in a smoker, barbecue, wood hut or other type of closed container. Because fish has a fragile texture, a lighter, sweeter smoke is generally used (alderwood or cherrywood) rather than a strong smoke aroma better suited for smoking meat (wood of mesquite, oak or hickory), but it all depends on your taste buds.

Charcoal or briquettes are normally used to get the fire going in a smoker. Pure hardwood charcoal lumps give the best woodsy smoke aroma for smoking, but they do not burn as evenly or as long as briquettes made from crushed hardwood charcoal. Standard coal briquettes burn even longer than hardwood briquettes but don't generate as much heat; but this is, in fact, a bonus for cold-smoking.

For cold-smoking, you need to use a smoker with temperature settings below 85F (30C), whereas for hot-smoking you need temperature settings above 85F (30C) to actually "cook" the food, whether you use an electric smoker, water smoker, charcoal barbecue or gas barbecue. Hot-smoking is

CONTINUED ...

a better technique for actually preserving food for the long term, whereas cold-smoked food has to be refrigerated and will keep for a few days only. The greatest challenge of smoking food, regardless of the technology you use, is keeping the temperature consistent. A smoker is not like a slow cooker that you can plug in and leave unattended for 8 to 10 hours at a time. You've got to keep an eye on it. Over-smoked food tastes like soot from the fireplace. (Don't ask how I know that.)

Tip

Don't rely on the thermostat of the smoker (especially if yours is second-hand). Get an oven thermometer and put it inside the smoker when using it. Or get a food thermometer and test your food every so often for even better accuracy.

Keep the smoker closed as much as possible and put up shelter around the smoker to protect it from sun (so that it doesn't overheat in the summer) or cold wind (so that it doesn't lose heat in the winter).

Tip

If you smoke oysters in the dead of winter like I do, when it's -5F (-20C), set the smoker up to 50F (10C) higher than what is called for, because as soon as you open the smoker door, the temperature inside the smoker will drop that much in seconds.

A couple of years ago I was lucky enough to find a gently used water smoker at a garage sale. I was even luckier to find it about five minutes before another man came along and eyed it. This guy offered to buy it from me and even followed me down the street to my truck, hoping I'd change my mind, and I felt bad later on, since a couple of years went by before I even tried to use it, but eventually I did. It took a while to experiment with it using different types of foods, wood smokes and vent positions before I was satisfied with the results and felt in control, but now there is no need to buy smoked fish, meat,

salt or nuts. As long as my eyes hold out long enough for me to remove bones from fish, I will continue to smoke it instead of buying it smoked.

Water Smoker

Naturally, using a smoker with a built-in thermometer and metal grates is not the traditional Indigenous way of smoking food, but it is legal and manageable for city dwellers so that you don't end up with firefighters at your place blasting your buffet table into wet smithereens. I have plans to build a man cave/shack for smoking meat and fish. Several of my neighbours have volunteered to help me with this project, since they are looking forward to having a place where they can escape to from their domestic duties from time to time and to sharing in the proceeds of the smoker. My friend Rob was nice enough to loan me his brand-new electric Bradley smoker and it was impressive. That's what I used for all the smoked food recipes in this cookbook. Here are some tips for those of you with the most popular types of smokers.

A water smoker works well with standard charcoal briquettes. Adding wood chips or chunks provides aromatic smoke so you get the best of both worlds. Use wood of your choice and decide whether to use wood dust, chips or chunks, depending on the length of time you intend to smoke the food. The longer it is, the better off you are using a larger grade of wood. It saves you time, because you don't have to refill the tray as often.

I always soak wood chips for at least 30 minutes before smoking. Then I drain the wood and wrap it in aluminum foil and poke some holes into it with a fork to let the smoke out. This flat little package sits neatly on top of the briquettes in the tray at the bottom of the smoker once you've got them burning (that could take anywhere from 15 minutes to 35 minutes, but you'll know it's ready when you see white ash on the edges of the briquettes). I made the mistake of using lighter fluid to start the briquettes when I first got my little red smoker, and OMG what a mistake! Take it from me: find some other way of heating the briquettes that won't make your food taste like it was soaked in gasoline. (Marlene didn't care for that so much.) A chimney starter might be a good investment. Fill the water bowl and open the vents to control the smoke intensity.

Charcoal Barbecue

As with the water smoker, smoking on a barbecue requires burning briquettes. Because these barbecues don't come with a tray to hold the wood chips, you would be wise to make a little foil package of soaked wood chips as mentioned above. For small, delicate foods that smoke quickly, you can smoke the food on a grill directly over the heat, but use a two-zone smoking method for whole birds, ribs or roasts; to do this, place briquettes on one side of the barbecue only. Once they get going, place the foil package directly on top of the briquettes. Place the food to be smoked on a grill on the other side of the barbecue, away from direct heat. Close the lid but experiment with the vents until you get the proper balance of smoke.

Propane Gas Grill

Propane gas gives you the key advantage of heat consistency and a wider range of smoking temperatures, including low heat, which is ideal for cold-smoking in particular. But as with the water smoker and the charcoal barbecue, smoking on a propane gas grill requires a foil package of soaked wood. Otherwise the only flavour you get will be from the smoke of pan drippings from previous barbecues. Use the two-zone smoking method: heat up all of the grill and, after it reaches temperature, turn half of the burners down (i.e., one burner on a two-burner grill or two burners on a four-burner grill). Place the foil package on the burner(s) that you just turned down to get it smoking. Place the food on the other half of the grill that is still turned on. If your grill is equipped with a smoker box, then you will have even more control over the intensity of the smoke and won't have to bother making a foil package, but don't forget to check your wood chips from time to time, since you may need to replenish them before the food is done.

Electric Smoker

Unlike the water smoker, charcoal barbecue or propane gas grill, electric smokers rely on the smoke generated by dry biscuits of wood that are fired up electrically in a metal box. This type of smoker was adapted from fridges, originally, and can be programmed for a specific temperature, amount of time and smoke level. Even more conveniently, electric smokers come in various sizes and have an auto-feed that pops in wood biscuits when required (usually every 20 minutes).

The "Smoke Flavour Intensities" chart below is simply a guide to get you started to figure out which kind of wood to use. There are no set rules when it comes to woods for smoking—just tradition and personal taste. The chart includes some of the more commonly smoked foods and flavours.

Smoke Flavour Intensities

SMOKE FLAVOUR INTENSITY		USES	WOOD TYPE
LIGHT	Musky		Alder
LIGHT	Sweet		Apple
LIGHT	Fruity		Cherry
MEDIUM	Smoky		Maple
MEDIUM	Somewhat acidic		Oak
MEDIUM	Rich		Pecan
HEAVY	Earthy		Mesquite
HEAVY	Bacon-like		Hickory

Health note: I'm not a doctor, but smoked foods really should be avoided by people on restricted salt diets, due to the high levels of salt used in the curing process. There is more on the subject in hot- and cold-smoked food recipes later in this cookbook.

Cold-Smoked Alderwood Salt

MAKES 2 CUPS (475 ML)

Vikings are said to have evaporated seawater over wood fires of juniper, cherry, elm, beech and oak to produce flavoured sea salt a millennium ago. That may be true, but Indigenous peoples along the Pacific coast in Canada are big on wood-smoked salt too, and they use it regularly when cooking salmon—alder is a favourite. Smoked salt can also be used for snacks, sweets, meat rubs and other purposes. Marlene's brother, Joe Finn, really loves it when I give him this salt.

Tip

Do not smoke multiple types of food simultaneously or their flavours will combine.

To make your own all-natural smoked salt, you need bark-free wood chips and coarse salt.

Kosher and sea salt are the best types of salt to use, since they are coarse; kosher salt is the cheaper of the two. In either case, smoke can easily penetrate through the salt crystals due to their irregular shape (whereas table salt is iodized and too fine for this to happen).

Using the right kind of wood is important too. If you intend to use your smoked salt on vegetable or fish dishes, then you would do well with a wood that has a light smoke intensity, whereas a medium or heavy wood flavour would better suit salt smoked for using on game, beef or pork. Refer to the "Smoke Flavour Intensities" chart (page 29) for suggestions. If you want to experiment, do it! I made this recipe in an electric smoker, but see pages 28–29 for more information on using a water smoker, charcoal barbecue or propane gas grill.

2 cups (475 mL) kosher salt (or sea salt)
Alderwood biscuits

01 Preheat the smoker to 85F (30C) to start the smoking process. Activate the smoke biscuits.

02 Once the smoker reaches temperature, spread the salt evenly in a disposable aluminum foil pan, place it in the smoker and close the door. Alternatively, place a 12 inch (30 cm) grease splatter guard (with plastic handle removed) directly on the grill, pour the salt on it and shake to spread out evenly. (My only complaint about using a grease splatter guard is that the fine grains of salt will slip through the screen, reducing your yield and making a bit of a wasteful mess.)

03 Timing will depend on outdoor temperatures, wind, sun and how hot your smoker can get. Keep an eye out for an even stream of smoke, and add more biscuits as necessary to keep the smoke going. Try to stir the salt every couple of hours, regardless of the type of container you use, without letting the heat escape.

04 Smoke for 12 to 24 hours (the longer, the better).

05 Let salt cool (while still in the smoker) before removing. Store smoked salt in an airtight jar to retain flavour. The salt can be kept for up to a year.

06 Use smoked salt as needed on foods such as popcorn or sliced avocado, melon, apple or tomato; on fudge, ice cream or roasted stone fruit; and as a meat rub for steak, burgers or ribs.

Above and Beyond Salt and Pepper

As a seasoning, salt was not traditionally used by many of the First Nations of the eastern part of the United States and Canada, even among those who had lots of access to it. The Iroquois, Delaware, Montagnais and Shawnee were just a few of the Indigenous peoples who preferred to use other ingredients like hickory ash, seaweed, berries or maple syrup for seasoning food. The adoption of salt into their diets was relatively recent, in historical terms, as there were enough alternatives to make food taste appealing.

When my mom was told she had diabetes and had to cut out salt, she was not a happy camper. In fact, she got really depressed. All she could think of was all the foods she couldn't eat anymore, and that made her mad. She felt like there was nothing good to eat and she was so frustrated she didn't know what to do. She hated the salt substitutes that were made out of potassium chloride but was encouraged when I was able to suggest alternatives. I remember one meal I made for her when she said, "This food is great, but don't tell my dietician." She thought I made it from things on her no-no list, but it actually contained herbs, spices and citrus peels that I combined to flavour the chicken before baking it. The chicken was so good she thought it had been fried.

Here are some recipes that you can make to build flavour in various types of dishes without using any salt.

Cold-Smoked Alderwood Salt (recipe on page 30).

Salt Alternative

MAKES ½ CUP (120 ML)

I like using this mix on fresh steamed green vegetables or mashed potatoes, although it's great on fish and seafood too. This recipe makes a small batch, so once you've used it for a while, you can figure out which spices you might want more of next time. You will probably have a few sneezing episodes during the course of this exercise, but in the long run making your own mixes is worthwhile.

2 tsp (10 mL) **lemon zest**
2 Tbsp (30 mL) **onion powder**
1 Tbsp (15 mL) **garlic powder**
1 Tbsp (15 mL) dried **marjoram**
2 tsp (10 mL) **paprika**
2 tsp (10 mL) dried **oregano**
2 tsp (10 mL) ground **sage**
1½ tsp (7.5 mL) ground **black pepper**
1½ tsp (7.5 mL) dry **mustard**

1½ tsp (7.5 mL) dried **thyme**
1 tsp (5 mL) **celery seeds**
1 tsp (5 mL) **chili powder**
1 tsp (5 mL) dried **rosemary**

01 Leave the lemon zest in the open air for several hours (or overnight) to dry completely, or bake it on a baking sheet at 200F (95C) for 30 minutes.

02 Combine all the ingredients and grind in a mortar and pestle or spice mill (or coffee grinder dedicated to this purpose).

03 Store the mix in a large-holed salt shaker and use while cooking or to finish dishes instead of using salt. The mix will last 6 to 12 months, but you may need to add more lemon zest after a month or two.

Roasted Garlic

MAKES 5 TO 8 TEASPOONS (25–40 ML)

For super easy flavouring of foods without using salt, roast a head of garlic. Roasted garlic is soft and creamy and can be spooned into sauces, soups, stews, vegetable dishes and more.

1 head **garlic**
1½ Tbsp (22 mL) pure **olive oil**

01 Cut off the top of a head of garlic, exposing all the cloves. Discard the top.

02 Place the bottom of the head on a small sheet of aluminum foil. Drizzle oil on top and tightly wrap up garlic in foil.

03 Bake directly on the rack in a 350F (175C) oven for 10 to 15 minutes.

04 Gently squeeze the garlic flesh out of the skins and discard the skins. It gives an earthy base to dishes that would otherwise be pretty bland.

05 Store roasted garlic in the fridge for up to five days.

Spice Bag

MAKES 1 SPICE BAG

Another alternative to using salt to flavour foods is to use a spice bag (herb sachet) made out of cheesecloth (or gauze from a first aid kit). This is a French technique for controlling seasoning when cooking. Spice bags allow you to concentrate other flavours without overpowering a food with herbs and spices. Knowing when to remove the flavouring agents is important, because dried herbs have about two to three times the potency of fresh herbs. The beauty of a spice bag is that you can fish it out once your dish has reached the desired level of flavour. (Just think of how much easier it would be to do this when cooking jumbo batches of soup, stew, sauces or broths). For home use, I happen to find it easier to use a loose tea infuser made of metal, since I can find that easily in the cupboard and use it more quickly than if I made a spice bag.

12 **black peppercorns**, whole or crushed
1 sprig **parsley**, stems only
1 dried or 2 fresh **bay leaves**
1 tsp (5 mL) dried **thyme**

OPTIONAL:
½ tsp (2.5 mL) dried **rosemary**
    or 1½ tsp (7.5 mL) fresh, minced
½ tsp (2.5 mL) dried **tarragon**
    or 1½ tsp (7.5 mL) fresh, minced
1 clove **garlic**
6 **cloves**

01 Place the peppercorns, parsley, bay leaf and thyme in the centre of a doubled square of cheesecloth about 6 inches by 6 inches (15 × 15 cm). These are the standard spice bag ingredients, but feel free to use some or all of the optional ingredients as well. Pull up the four corners and tie spice bag with butcher twine so that no ingredients will slip out, leaving a bit of extra string on it to tie to the pot handle (be careful not to leave any excess string that could catch on fire).

02 If you want to bring out a particular flavour in a dish, you can add more of an ingredient or add other herbs or spices such as star anise, cardamom or dill, for example.

03 Taste the dish to determine when to remove the spice bag. Discard it after using.

Bouquet Garni

MAKES 1 BOUQUET GARNI

Bouquet garni is the French term for a little bundle of herbs and aromatic vegetables tied up together to slip into a stock, soup or sauce to increase flavour. Thinking of it as a bouquet of flowers makes the meaning of the term easy to remember. In the French tradition, tying the herbs together simplifies their removal from the pot once the desired flavour has been reached. There is a lot of flexibility in choosing the ingredients for a bouquet garni. You could use other herbs as you see fit, but parsley stems are customary.

1 dried or 2 fresh **bay leaves**
1 sprig fresh **thyme**
1 sprig fresh **rosemary**
1 sprig fresh **parsley**, with stems
1 **carrot**, chopped into 4 to 6 inch (10–15 cm) lengths
1 **celery stalk**, chopped into 4 to 6 inch (10–15 cm) lengths

01 Place bay leaf in between the herbs and surround with vegetables. Use butcher twine to tightly tie up the bouquet so that nothing will fall out during cooking. Read the Spice Bag recipe (page 34) for tips on using a bouquet garni.

02 Remove and discard the bouquet garni when the dish has reached the desired flavour.

Bouillon

Whereas chicken stock and beef stock are made by simmering bones and vegetables, French *bouillon* (also known as broth) is the clear liquid that you get when you gently simmer meat, vegetables, fish or seafood in water and then strain it. Dehydrated bouillon is sold in cubes for convenience. *Court bouillon* is a French term for a flavoured liquid used for poaching foods, and it's designed to quick cook fish, chicken or vegetables, among other things. Onions, carrots, herbs, salt and peppercorns are added to the water to lightly flavour the food through a low simmer, not a rapid boil, so both the texture and nutritional value of the food are protected.

Poaching foods in a court bouillon is extremely healthy and economical. Before the arrival of Europeans, Indigenous people who lived on the coasts of Alaska and BC used seawater and seaweed for flavouring. Other Indigenous nations used the local resources they could find to season food before simmering it.

Labrador Tea Court Bouillon

MAKES 5 CUPS (1.2 L)

Labrador tea goes by many names: Hudson's Bay tea, Haida tea, swamp tea, trapper's tea and *muskekopukwa* (in Cree). The evergreen Labrador tea shrub produces narrow leaves that are green on one side and turn orange on the other side. It grows from Greenland and Labrador across to Alaska and has lots of medicinal uses that northern peoples such as the Inuit and Gwich'in know well for treating such problems as respiratory infections and stomach and skin disorders. But you have to be cautious—this plant can be toxic if taken in large doses.

My sister-in-law Lorraine Pitawanakwat sent us some Labrador tea she picked when she was living in Kingfisher Lake First Nation, Ontario; that's what I used for this recipe. You can find the slightly spicy Labrador tea online or, if you can't get your hands on any, instead add a second bay leaf to your court bouillon.

4 cups (1 L) **water**
¼ cup (60 mL) **white vinegar**
1 dried **bay leaf**
¼ cup (60 mL) chopped **onion**
2 Tbsp (30 mL) **Labrador tea leaves**
2 Tbsp (30 mL) sliced **carrot**
2 Tbsp (30 mL) sliced **celery**
1 Tbsp (15 mL) kosher **salt** (or sea salt)
½ tsp (2.5 mL) whole **peppercorns**, preferably white

01 Place water, vinegar, bay leaf, onion, Labrador tea leaves, carrot, celery, salt and peppercorns in a stockpot.

02 Simmer mixture for 15 minutes over low heat. Strain before using.

03 For an example of how to use this recipe, see the Labrador Tea Poached Flounder with Saskatoon Berry Drizzle recipe (page 181).

Stocks

In traditional Anishinaabe culture, women are the water carriers. As givers of life, women have the distinct responsibility to care for and protect water, which is recognized as a precious gift from Mother Earth that we all need for survival. Water ceremonies honour the water spirit that Indigenous people consider to be living and breathing and part of us. In fact, Indigenous people who follow cultural traditions consider water to be a sacred medicine. Sadly, drinking water is contaminated in about 20 per cent of First Nations in this country; some communities have had a boil-water advisory in place for 20 years now.

There are few things on this planet more important to our very survival as a species, yet water is still a luxury on many reserves. We were reminded of that a few times when Marlene and I did some cooking demos in communities where boil-water advisories are in effect (and these were not in the remote north). We are not used to living with this kind of hardship, and it really changed our sense of how people approach cooking when they have to boil water or buy bottled water. Water is first and foremost when it comes to making stock, however, and stock is the simple launching pad to many great-tasting foods. I use filtered tap water but some chefs insist on spring water for stock making.

This is a quick guide to the differences between the stock recipes that follow:

· **Vegetable stock** is the prime ingredient in many vegetarian dishes (soups, braised dishes and sauces) and is made with aromatic vegetables that are sautéed or roasted and then simmered in water with seasoning for about an hour.

· **White stock** is made with seasonings, vegetables and bones for additional flavour and gelatin, which are simmered in water for six to eight hours. This stock is used in light coloured soups, stews and sauces.

· **Brown stock** is also made with seasonings, vegetables and bones, but the bones are browned in the oven before being simmered in water (so you can even use chicken bones to make brown stock). Brown stock is used in dark coloured dishes and sauces, and also takes about six to eight hours to make, although some chefs let it simmer overnight.

- **Fish stock** is used specifically in fish and seafood dishes and is made from the heads, tails, bones and skin of fish or shells of crustaceans. It takes from 45 minutes to an hour to make a fish stock.

Two things that all stocks have in common are the use of a *mirepoix* (which is a French term for a rough cut of flavour builders like onion, carrot and celery) and the use of seasonings (typically in a spice bag or bouquet garni). Salt is not used in stock making. All of the recipes in this book that call for stocks assume you are using homemade, unsalted stocks. If you use store-bought stock instead, buy the unsalted variety.

Homemade stock is so much better than anything you can buy in a store; your grandmother would agree! Not only is it cheaper to make your own stock for home cooking, but it's better for you and you can make big batches to freeze for later use.

I remember when Mom made Christmas dinner, she would have a pot on the back of the stove and would add the carrot and onion trimmings, turkey neck, potato peels and other vegetables, and let the mixture cook all day. Then she'd add leftovers to it after dinner to make a healthy soup to enjoy the next day. When I was a cook apprentice, my German chef master who had lived through World War II had all sorts of ways of reducing food costs, too. He used to make us save all the vegetable trimmings for soups—absolutely nothing went to waste in his kitchen.

My "Stock Making Tips" (on this page) will help you to produce stock that is clear, flavourful and balanced in taste. You will find that well-made stocks (from bones) become jelly-like after chilling due to the gelatin produced by cooking raw bones. Even though stocks are unsalted, they give you a head start when you begin to make a dish so you don't have to rely on plain water as your liquid.

After you've made stock a few times, you will find it easy enough to throw together. I like to get it going on the back burner before I head out to cut the grass and trim the hedges, and then I let it cool while I throw in a load of laundry. It's routine.

Stock Making Tips

01
Use cold water to make stock, not hot.

02
Use raw bones.

03
Never put salt into a stock until after you've strained it.

04
Simmer stock, don't boil it.

05
Use a tall, narrow pot for making stock rather than a shallow, wide one.

06
Do not cover the pot or the stock will become cloudy.

07
Never stir stock; let it simmer undisturbed.

08
Remove impurities from the surface of the stock frequently, using a skimmer.

09
Cool the pot of stock quickly in a container of ice water.

10
Strain stock by pouring it through a sieve lined with wet cheesecloth.

11
Pour the cooled stock into food-safe containers, and label and date them before freezing, leaving ¾ inch (2 cm) headspace to allow for expansion.

12
After chilling homemade White, Brown or Fish Stock, remove fat from the surface with a spoon.

13
Heat homemade White, Brown or Fish Stock to the boiling point before using in recipes.

NOTE: Vegetarians can use this version of Vegetable Stock as a substitute in any of my recipes that call for White Stock. The dark stock variation below can be used as a substitute for any recipes that call for Brown Stock.

Vegetable Stock

MAKES 16 CUPS (3.8 L)

Vegetable stock serves as a foundation for any vegetarian dish, but due to the lack of animal protein and fat in it, this stock doesn't have the same gelatinous consistency of white or brown stock. Vegetable stock is still more flavourful and nutritious than using water for making sauces, soups and braised dishes, however. Typically, vegetable stock is made with mirepoix and a few additional vegetables that add flavour, and this stock can be both light coloured (by sautéing vegetables) or a nice brown colour (by roasting vegetables).

2 Tbsp (30 mL) pure **olive oil**
2 cups (475 mL) small-diced **onion**
2 cups (475 mL) small-diced **carrot**
8 cloves **garlic**, peeled
1½ cups (350 mL) small-diced **fennel**
1½ cups (350 mL) quartered button **mushrooms**
5 quarts (5 L) cold **water**
5 sprigs (4 inches/10 cm) fresh **parsley**
2 sprigs (4 inches/10 cm) fresh **thyme**
2 cups (475 mL) diced vine-ripened **tomatoes**
1 cup (250 mL) small-diced **celery**
1 tsp (5 mL) whole black **peppercorns**

01 In a large stockpot, heat olive oil over medium heat and add the onion and carrot. Sauté for two minutes. Add the garlic, fennel and mushrooms, and continue to sauté, stirring frequently, allowing the vegetables to brown slightly. Add the water and bring to a low simmer.

02 Skim off any impurities and add the parsley, thyme, tomatoes, celery and peppercorns. Simmer for 1 to 1½ hours, uncovered, simmering so slowly that only the occasional bubble rises to the surface. Turn off heat and allow stock to sit for 15 minutes.

03 Line a mesh strainer with a wet cheesecloth or coffee filter and place over a large pot.

04 Slowly strain the stock into the new pot, avoiding the gritty parts at the very bottom of the first pot. Then place the newly filled pot in a sink of ice water to chill it quickly—leave there for one hour before refrigerating or freezing for later use. You can refrigerate this stock for up to three days or freeze it and store for up to two months.

Dark Stock Variation: Roast the vegetables (except tomatoes and celery) in a 400F (205C) oven on a lightly oiled baking sheet for 20 to 30 minutes or until golden brown. Pour into stockpot, add water, tomatoes, celery and herbs, and continue recipe as above.

White Stock

MAKES 16 CUPS (3.8 L)

White stock can be made with chicken, turkey, pheasant, veal, beef, ham or lamb bones, although chicken is certainly the most common ingredient, which is why this stock is almost always referred to as "chicken stock." Any of these proteins will produce a light coloured stock with sufficient body and flavour to use as a base for making soups, stews, sauces and more. Ask your butcher for chicken bones (they are not generally on display in stores). If you can debone chicken, then save a few bucks and do it yourself to make stock, like I do.

If I have only a few bones on hand at a time, I freeze them (ideally vacuum sealing them first) until I have enough bones to make a stock. The same goes for parsley stems. For some reason, when you buy herbs you always seem to end up having to buy large quantities even though you need only a little. So freeze the stems for the next time you want to make White Stock.

Tip

For best flavour, match the bones in your stock with the type of dish you intend to make (e.g., use turkey bones for a turkey pot pie, or duck bones for a duck soup).

6.6 lb (3 kg) **bones**
1½ gallons (5.7 L) cold **water**
1 cup (250 mL) medium-diced **onion**
½ cup (120 mL) medium-diced **carrot**
½ cup (120 mL) medium-diced **celery**
½ cup (120 mL) sliced **leek** (white parts only)
3 sprigs fresh **parsley stems**
2 dried or 4 fresh **bay leaves**

½ tsp (2.5 mL) crushed black **peppercorns**
½ tsp (2.5 mL) dried **rosemary**
½ tsp (2.5 mL) dried **thyme**
½ tsp (2.5 mL) dried **tarragon**

01 Cut the chicken carcass into several pieces along with the neck (discard the gizzard and liver if they came with the bones because they may make your stocky cloudy). Place the bones in a large stockpot and cover with the water. Bring water to a simmer—do not boil. Use a skimmer to remove the impurities (scum).

02 Add the mirepoix (onion, carrot and celery) and leek to the pot, and bring back to a simmer.

03 Using cheesecloth and butcher twine, or a metal loose tea infuser, prepare a spice bag containing the parsley, bay leaves, peppercorns, rosemary, thyme and tarragon.

04 Skim the stock once more, add the spice bag and continue to slowly simmer for 1½ to 2 hours, uncovered, simmering so slowly that only the occasional bubble rises to the surface. Then turn off heat and allow stock to sit for 15 minutes.

05 Line a mesh strainer with a wet cheesecloth or coffee filter and place over a large pot.

06 Slowly strain the stock into the new pot, avoiding the gritty parts at the very bottom of the first pot. Then place the newly filled pot into a sink of ice water to chill for one hour before refrigerating or freezing for later use. You can refrigerate this stock for up to three days or store it frozen for up to two months.

Brown Stock

MAKES 16 CUPS (3.8 L)

For this recipe, you can use the bones of large game, chicken, veal, lamb, turkey, pork or beef. Shank, knuckle and neck bones, as well as calf's feet, provide the most collagen and, therefore, the best flavour. Ask your butcher for bones if you don't see them on display. Vacuum seal them and freeze them until you have time to make stock.

6.6 lb (3 kg) **bones**
2 cups (475 mL) large-diced **onion**
1 cup (250 mL) large-diced **carrot**
¼ cup (60 mL) tomato **paste**
2 gallons (7.8 L) cold **water** plus extra if needed
5 crushed **juniper berries**
3 sprigs fresh **parsley** stems
2 dried or 4 fresh **bay leaves**
½ tsp (2.5 mL) crushed black **peppercorns**
½ tsp (2.5 mL) dried **rosemary**
½ tsp (2.5 mL) dried **thyme**
1 cup (250 mL) large-diced **celery**

01 Preheat oven to 400F (205C).

02 Spread bones out on a roasting pan. Roast in oven for one hour. Turn bones over and continue roasting for 30 minutes.

03 Drain off some of the excess oil from the pan (and discard), add the onion and carrot to the bones and continue roasting for another 30 to 45 minutes.

04 Stir the bone and vegetable mixture. Brush bones with tomato paste using a pastry brush. Place the pan back in the oven. Roast for 15 to 20 minutes, or until the tomato paste turns brown.

05 Place the bones, onion and carrot in a large stockpot, discarding excess oil.

06 Place the hot roasting pan on the stovetop over one or two burners. Turn heat to medium and add just enough cold water to cover the bottom of the pan. Scrape off any ingredients stuck on the pan. Then pour the watery mixture into the stockpot.

07 Fill the pot with the remaining cold water and bring to a simmer. As it simmers, remove impurities (scum) with a skimmer.

08 Prepare a spice bag (or a metal loose tea infuser) using the juniper berries, parsley, bay leaves, peppercorns, rosemary and thyme, and add to the pot. Add the celery and bring the mixture back to a slow simmer.

09 Turn down the heat to very low and let the stock simmer uncovered for at least four hours, simmering so slowly that only the occasional bubble rises to the surface. If you want very flavourful stock, add more cold water to raise the level to the top of the pot, and let it continue to simmer an additional six hours.

Tip

If you use all poultry bones to make Brown Stock, then reduce the cooking time by half because the bones are smaller and will cook more quickly than beef or large game bones.

10 Line a mesh strainer with a wet cheesecloth or coffee filter and place over a large pot. Slowly strain the stock into the new pot, avoiding the gritty parts at the very bottom. Then place the newly filled pot into a sink of ice water to chill before refrigerating or freezing for later use. You can refrigerate this stock for up to three days or store it frozen for up to two months.

Fish Stock

MAKES 16 CUPS (3.8 L)

Fish stock takes very little time to make, so the mirepoix vegetables should be sliced thinly rather than chopped into small pieces, for quicker cooking. To preserve the white colour in fish stock, carrots are normally left out and leeks and fennel are included. Flatfish make the best stock and halibut is my all-time favourite, but you can use any kind of mild-tasting whitefish (also called white fish), sole, cod, haddock or even lobster shells. If you intend to make a salmon chowder, on the other hand, then it would make sense to make the stock out of salmon bones. Although salmon makes a flavourful stock, it will be cloudy and its uses are limited because of its strong flavour.

First Nations elders value stock in general but are particularly respectful of fish stock, and they recommend it for anyone who is ill, weak or undernourished. Marlene didn't believe me when I told her she could just drink fish stock straight out of the pot until I made it a few times, and now she is a big fan. All you need to do to make it appetizing enough to drink straight is to add a little bit of salt after it's been made.

6.6 lb (3 kg) **halibut** (heads, tails, skin and bones combined)
1½ gallons (5.7 L) cold **water**
1 cup (250 mL) thinly sliced **onion**
½ cup (120 mL) thinly sliced **celery**
½ cup (120 mL) sliced **leek** (white parts only)

1 cup (250 mL) sliced **fennel** (white parts only)
8 whole white **peppercorns**
2 sprigs (4 inches/10 cm long) fresh flat-leaf **parsley**, with stems
1 sprig (4 inches/10 cm long) fresh **thyme**, with stems
1 dried or 2 fresh **bay leaves**

01 Cut the bones into pieces, making sure to split the backbone open in order to release collagen into the stock. Discard the gills. Place bones and trimmings in a large stockpot and cover with the water.

02 Bring stock to a simmer. Remove impurities (scum) with a skimmer.

03 Add the onion, celery, leek and fennel to the pot, along with the peppercorns, parsley, thyme and bay leaf, and let simmer, uncovered, for 45 minutes to one hour.

04 Strain stock through a wet cheesecloth–lined strainer into a different pot. Then chill that pot rapidly in ice water in a sink for one hour before refrigerating or freezing the stock for later use. You can refrigerate this stock for up to three days or store it frozen for up to two months.

CHAPTER 3

The Little Things: Appetizers, Salads and Snacks

Making "apps" takes me back to the days when I used to speed full tilt down the highways and byways of Toronto with jumbo trays of food and pots of soup rattling and sloshing around in the back of my catering truck. I'm sure I flew through red lights more than I should have in order to serve guests at nightclubs, schools, business offices, churches, parks, convention centres, movie theatres and yacht clubs, and I met people from all walks of life. That was when it was just as easy to make three hundred of an item as it was to make a dozen. (Almost.) Shrimp terrines, venison croquettes and wild rice quenelles...those were my go-to party appetizer recipes, along with cheese trays, cedar tea and puff pastries. I catered so many events and developed so many recipes in those years that I just had to include a number of them in this chapter. More than a few bankers were shocked to gaze upon deer antlers, rabbit skins and hides while nibbling at my banquet tables.

One time I was catering on a large boat cruise on Lake Ontario. I pulled up as close to the boat as I could in my truck and carried on some of the larger trays of appetizers, equipment for keeping foods warm, and so on. After about 15 minutes of getting things organized in the galley, I headed back for a second load only to find we were pulling away from shore. The rest of the food was still in the truck (parked illegally), with the doors wide open and the rest of my equipment lying on the ground! I never told my client what happened, since there was enough food for everyone on board already (luckily), so nobody noticed anything wrong, but I sure learned my lesson that day. I learned to unload everything at once, with help, and ask a few more questions about sailing time! It was nighttime when we returned. I figured I'd be totally cleaned out of gear and would have to work my buns off to replace it all, but somehow everything was still there, and I didn't even get a ticket! It was "Toronto, the Good," as we used to say back in the day.

Notes on Smoked Salmon, Lox and Gravlax

Ah, smoked salmon. Is there anything better? I don't think so. But be careful not to confuse smoked salmon with lox or gravlax, which are prepared differently:

» **Smoked salmon** is made from any part of the fish. It starts with salt-curing or brining the fish, which is then smoked either over low heat for cold-smoking or over higher heat for hot-smoking. The fish becomes silky and smoky at the same time.

» **Lox** is Yiddish for "salmon" and comes from the salmon belly; it's rich and silky and is prepared by salt-curing or brining the fish for several weeks, but never cooking or smoking it. Lox is what you have on bagels with cream cheese.

» **Gravlax** is a Swedish word derived from *grav* ("trench") and *lax* ("salmon"). In Scandinavia, the salmon was traditionally fermented in beach sand with lots of salt, dill and sugar. Today, liquor is often used in the process and gravlax is normally served with lots of dill.

Hot-Smoked Salmon with Sour Cream and Onion Dip

MAKES 8 SERVINGS

My mother's people love salmon in many forms; they love it so much they consider it a sacred food. Long ago, they used to dry and smoke salmon heads on a screen placed over a low flame. Once browned on one side, the heads would be turned over onto the other side. Then they would be soaked for eating in a soup; the cheeks were considered a delicacy. I've never tried that, but my mom talked about it all the time. She said she could smell the fish smoking from miles away; it was a way to bring the family together. Once they smelled the fish, they knew there would be a feast that day, so everyone would visit. Who knows? Maybe you'll get a few surprise visitors too, by making this recipe.

The recipe makes enough brine for a few fish (2 lb/900 g), but they must be completely covered in it before smoking. If you want to use the brine recipe to smoke a smaller batch of fish, then just cut the recipe in half. In case you don't know, you can eat the fish after hot-smoking it without any further processing, as long as it is top-quality fish.

My friend Rob tried this recipe in an electric smoker using whitefish that he caught, and he was very happy with the results. We were happy too, when he gave us a sample.

These recipe instructions apply to an electric smoker. For more information on using a water smoker, charcoal barbecue or propane gas grill, see pages 28–29. Note: Smoked fish is most easily prepared over two days, so allow this extra time in your preparations.

1 fresh coho **salmon** fillet (2 lb/900 g), skin on

BRINE:
8 cups (1.9 L) cold **water**
1 cup (250 mL) brown **sugar**
½ cup (120 mL) kosher **salt** (or sea salt)
½ cup (120 mL) **soya sauce**
2 Tbsp (30 mL) **lemon juice**
2 Tbsp (30 mL) **Worcestershire sauce**

1 tsp (5 mL) ground **black pepper**
1 tsp (5 mL) **onion powder**
½ tsp (2.5 mL) **garlic powder**

Vegetable oil for greasing grate
Alderwood or **cherrywood biscuits**

TO SERVE:
Crackers

01 If working with a whole fish, follow the filleting instructions in "How to Fillet Round Fish" (page 158), leaving the skin on. Rinse.

02 If needed, cut the fish into pieces that will fit into your smoker but not so small that they will fall through the smoker grate.

03 To prepare the brine, mix together the water, brown sugar, salt, soya sauce, lemon juice, Worcestershire sauce, pepper, onion powder and garlic powder until well combined. Pour the brine over the fish in a nonreactive dish (glass, ceramic or stainless steel), making sure to cover it completely; stir the mixture to coat all sides of the fish.

04 Brine the fish for between three and eight hours (or overnight).

05 While the fish is in the brine, prepare the Sour Cream and Onion Dip recipe below and chill it.

06 Rinse the fish very, very thoroughly in cold water and pat dry with paper towel. Place the fish, uncovered, on a rack set over a baking sheet and refrigerate for one hour to air dry (while you prepare the smoker).

07 Clean the smoker racks and set temperature to 150F (65C). Lightly grease the grate with oil. Activate

CONTINUED ...

the smoke biscuits. Once the smoker reaches temperature, place the fish on the grate, skin side down, to smoke. Make sure to leave space between the pieces of fish so that the smoke can circulate evenly. Timing will depend on the outdoor temperature, wind, sun and how hot your smoker can get.

08 You can increase the temperature to 225F (105C) after three hours, but once the fish reaches an internal temperature of 160F (70C), it's done. If you want a super smoky taste, let the fillets smoke for up to 16 hours, but be careful, because they can dry out if the temperature goes too high or if the fish fillets are thin.

09 Remove the fish from the smoker and let cool. Serve with dip and crackers of your choosing.

10 This hot-smoked fish will last up to a week or two in the fridge, or you can freeze it. If you choose to freeze it, remove the skin first.

Sour Cream and Onion Dip

MAKES 2½ CUPS (600 ML)

2 cups (475 mL) sour cream, regular or low-fat
¼ cup (60 mL) lemon juice
2 Tbsp (30 mL) extra-virgin olive oil
2 Tbsp (30 mL) minced red onion
1 Tbsp (15 mL) minced chives
1 tsp (5 mL) table salt
½ tsp (2.5 mL) garlic powder
½ tsp (2.5 mL) ground black pepper

01 Combine the ingredients in a mixing bowl. Blend well.

02 Chill dip for one to two hours before serving.

Cold-Smoked Juniper Salmon

MAKES 10 SERVINGS

My mom is in the spirit world now, but if she were here, she'd probably still lick her fingers clean after having smoked salmon. She said back home in BC, where she grew up, they had a shack filled with dried and smoked salmon that they could enjoy at any time. She talked about how her family smoked it, dried it, pan-fried it and baked it, and she told me about the time her mom sent her just outside their old log cabin to pick berries for baking. Mom snuck a few pieces of salmon out of the shack along the way to snack on with one of her sisters and when she returned, her mom said the berries smelled like smoked salmon for some strange reason. When Marlene and I visited that old log cabin, we found the berry bush she was talking about. It was still there, along with wild horses roaming around and cougar tracks in the mud.

Cold-smoked salmon is a little treat nowadays that goes well in soups, on bread and in salads because of its fine texture, subtle taste and distinct orange colour. Many classic appetizers are made from cold-smoked salmon, but it's just as good served on a bed of greens drizzled in a bit of oil. Once you know how to smoke it yourself, you won't have to wait for special occasions to enjoy it. But be prepared: cold-smoking is a lot harder to do than hot-smoking.

3 lb (1.5 kg) coho **salmon** fillet (previously frozen), skin on

1½ cups (350 mL) kosher **salt** (or sea salt)

1 cup (250 mL) **brown sugar**

½ cup (120 mL) **white sugar**

1 Tbsp (15 mL) black **peppercorns**

1 Tbsp (15 mL) dried **juniper berries**

Alderwood biscuits

Vegetable oil for greasing grate

TO SERVE:

2 cups (475 mL) washed **mixed greens**

1 **lemon**

¼ **red onion**, thinly sliced

1 Tbsp (15 mL) chopped fresh **dill** (optional)

01 If cleaning a whole fish, fillet as in the instructions in "How to Fillet Round Fish" on page 158, leaving the skin on. Rinse and pat dry on both sides with paper towels.

02 If needed, cut the fish into pieces that will fit into your smoker, but not so small that they will fall through the grate.

03 Line a baking sheet (or dish large enough to accommodate the fillet lying flat) with a broad layer of foil, followed by a layer of plastic wrap (enough to generously cover the fillet that will be wrapped up).

NOTE: This recipe could take several days to prepare, so allow this extra time in your preparations before serving. You could use two small fillets instead of one large one, especially if you have a small smoker.

04 Combine salt and sugars in a bowl. Crush the peppercorns and juniper berries in a mortar and pestle and add to the salt and sugar. Spread about half of the mixture down the middle of the wrap. Place the fillet on top of the dry rub, skin side down. Sprinkle the remaining dry rub on top of the fillet, spreading it out a little thicker at the thicker parts of the fish and thinner towards the tail, coating the sides but making sure to leave a layer of about ½ inch (1.5 cm) of rub above and below the fish.

05 Wrap up the fish in the plastic wrap and the foil. Alternatively, if you have two smaller fillets instead of a single large one, divide the rub evenly below, between and above the fillets (with them touching flesh side to flesh side) before wrapping up.

06 Chill fish for 12 hours on the baking sheet (turn it over at the halfway point).

07 Remove fish from the fridge and rinse very, very thoroughly under cold water, letting the water run steadily over the entire fish for at least 10 minutes; longer is better. Pat fish dry on both sides with paper towels.

08 Return fish to the fridge to air dry for 24 hours on a rack set over a baking sheet so that air can get to it on all sides.

09 Clean the smoker racks and set the temperature to 75F (25C). Lightly grease the grate. Activate the biscuits.

10 Once the smoker reaches temperature, place fish in smoker, skin side down, and smoke for between 12 and 16 hours. Alaskan health authorities say it takes up to seven days to cold-smoke salmon, yet I know chefs who serve it after smoking it for under one hour. I have found smoking time to be just right at 12 hours.

11 Remove the fish from the smoker and let cool. Chill fish for at least 30 minutes before serving.

12 Serve salmon in extremely thin slices (cut on the diagonal) on a bed of greens with lemon wedges, red onion and dill if using.

13 Refrigerate leftovers immediately. They will store well for three to four days.

Buttery Bourbon Hot-Smoked Oysters

MAKES 8 SERVINGS

Once word gets out that you know how to smoke oysters, you will get invites to parties from people you don't even know! It's up to you which type of oysters to smoke and which parties to attend, but try to find oysters that are about the same size so that they will smoke evenly. Ask your fishmonger for large ones that are not overly salty.

MARINADE:

3 Tbsp (45 mL) softened unsalted butter

1 tsp (5 mL) minced chives

1 tsp (5 mL) chopped garlic

½ tsp (2.5 mL) prepared horseradish

¼ tsp (1 mL) dry mustard

2 tsp (10 mL) bourbon

1 tsp (5 mL) cider vinegar

Pinch fresh ground black pepper

24 fresh oysters

Applewood or cherrywood biscuits

TO SERVE:

Rock salt

1 lemon, cut into wedges

01 Prepare a marinade by combining the butter, chives, garlic, horseradish, mustard, bourbon, vinegar and pepper in a small bowl. Set aside.

02 Clean the smoker racks and set temperature to 250F (120C). Activate the biscuits. (For information on using other types of smokers, see pages 27-29.)

03 Divide the marinade evenly among the oysters.

04 Scrunch together a small piece of foil under each shell to hold it level in order to catch dripping butter and make it easier to handle.

05 Once the smoker reaches temperature, place the oysters in their bottom shells over foil on the grate and smoke oysters for 10 minutes.

06 The butter should be completely melted by this point, but the oysters will still be soft in the centre. Ten minutes should be the maximum time for smoking oysters at this temperature.

07 Place the oysters in their shells on a plate of rock salt, levelling them. Serve with lemon wedges if using.

HOW TO SHUCK OYSTERS

Examine the oysters and tap any open ones to make sure they close. Throw them out if they don't close and scrub the oysters under cold, running water with a brush to remove sand and other debris. If you are a quick shucker, then prepare the smoker before shucking the oysters; otherwise, shuck them first and keep them on a bed of ice until ready.

The safest way to shuck oysters is to wear a wire-mesh glove. If you don't have one, protect your hand with a kitchen towel at least. You are not training for the North American Indigenous Games here, so take your time. It takes practice to shuck an oyster without stabbing yourself, damaging the shell or spilling the flavourful liquid inside. You will need an oyster knife. These knives have a short blade. Some are rather short and stubby, whereas others are longer and narrower.

Hold each oyster tightly in your palm with the hinge facing away from you, pointed side of the hinge facing down, and insert the tip of the knife into the small gap in the hinge, twisting back and forth until the hinge breaks. Remove any shards of shell from inside and wipe your knife.

Separate the oyster from the shell. Slide the blade above and below the oyster to detach it from the top and bottom shells, but leave the oyster in the bottom shell with the juicy goodness it is sitting in. Remove and discard the top shell along with any shell fragments.

Cod Martinis with Strawberry Peach Salsa

MAKES 8 SERVINGS

Ok, I admit this sounds a little weird. My original name for this recipe was Cod Ceviche, but then you'd need to know what *ceviche* ("se-vee-chay") is and you'd lose the visual image of fish in a martini glass! Ceviche is a dish attributed to the Indigenous peoples of Peru and Ecuador who "cooked" fish and shellfish fresh from the beach by marinating it in the juice of a tombo fruit rather than cooking it over heat. Nowadays lime juice and salt are common fish marinade ingredients, but ceviche marinades vary; chefs worldwide have reinvented ceviche by using diverse vinegars, sauces, herbs and vegetables.

It's generally recommended to use lean saltwater fish for ceviche rather than freshwater fish or oily fish. The freshness of the fish is critical to making this dish, and you need to freeze and marinate it properly to prevent exposure to parasites. See the notes on cold-smoking salmon on page 49 for freezing instructions

Peaches are not indigenous to the Americas, but they were one of many foods that the Spanish introduced to these lands that the Indigenous peoples welcomed (along with lemons and limes). This is an elegant appetizer that will catch the eye of everyone in the room. Consider doubling or tripling the recipe, and for a large crowd use a clear glass bowl set over ice so people can help themselves.

8 oz (225 g) fresh **cod** (previously frozen), skin removed

2 Tbsp (30 mL) fresh **lime juice**

1 tsp (5 mL) minced **jalapeno pepper** (or serrano pepper)

1 Tbsp (15 mL) small diced **tomato**

1 tsp (5 mL) kosher **salt** (or sea salt)

Pinch fresh ground **black pepper**

SALSA:

2 Tbsp (30 mL) minced fresh **mint**

2 Tbsp (30 mL) **grapefruit juice**

1 Tbsp (15 mL) extra-virgin **olive oil**

¼ tsp (1 mL) ground **cumin**

2 tsp (10 mL) minced **garlic**

1 tsp (5 mL) minced fresh **cilantro**

1 cup (250 mL) small-diced fresh **peaches**, skin on (or canned and drained peaches)

1 cup (250 mL) small-diced **strawberries**

OPTIONAL GARNISH:

½ **red onion**, sliced paper thin

01 *If working with a whole fish:* Follow the filleting instructions in "How to Fillet Round Fish" (page 158) for filleting and skinning.

02 Small-dice the fish and place in a nonreactive bowl (glass, ceramic or stainless steel) with the lime juice, jalapeno pepper, tomato, salt and pepper, and allow to briefly marinate in the fridge while you prepare the dressing for the salsa. Set the bowl over ice while you prepare the salsa.

03 In a bowl, whisk together the minced mint with the grapefruit juice, oil, cumin, garlic and cilantro. Add the peaches and strawberries and toss. Set aside.

04 To serve, use a slotted spoon to scoop salsa into martini glasses. Drain the fish and scoop over the salsa. Garnish with the onion if using.

05 Serve chilled, keeping refrigerated in a bowl set over ice until the minute you are ready to use it. Store leftovers in the fridge for up to 24 hours, after draining off excess liquid.

NOTE: If you make the salsa a day ahead, it will taste a lot better but the fish will toughen the longer it sits in the acidic mixture, so you should plan to serve it within one to two hours of making it.

Breaded Cod Tongues

MAKES 6 SERVINGS

This recipe proves that the fillet is not the only part of a fish that is tasty and nutritious. "Cod tongues" aren't tongues at all and are actually a rather large meaty muscle from the throat area of the fish. Many people consider cod tongues (which look like flat chicken nuggets when breaded and fried) to be a Newfoundland party appetizer; but Indigenous people of the New England area traditionally made a similar dish by mashing scraps of fish, including the tongues and cheeks, into a mixture that could be seasoned, rolled into a ball and cooked over the fire. Refer to the Beer-Battered Fish and Chips recipe (page 176) to make the Beer Batter for this recipe.

2 lb (900 g) fresh cod tongues
1 tsp (5 mL) table salt
1 tsp (5 mL) ground black pepper
1 tsp (5 mL) lemon zest
2 cups (475 mL) all-purpose flour
2 cups (475 mL) Beer Batter (see recipe, page 176)
2 cups (475 mL) bread crumbs
3 cups (710 mL) vegetable oil for frying

TO SERVE:
1 lemon, cut into wedges
Flaked or Celtic salt or fleur de sel (optional)

01 Wash the cod tongues, trim off any excess connective tissue and pat dry. Season with the salt, pepper and lemon zest.

02 Set up a three-step breading system: put the flour in one small bowl, the beer batter in a second bowl and the bread crumbs in a third bowl. The secret to getting a good breading on any product is to lightly dust each seasoned piece with flour, shaking off any excess, before placing it in the batter and making sure it gets an even coating. The next step is to remove the fish from the batter, shaking off any excess batter, but keeping an even coating on it and carefully dropping it into the bread crumbs without dripping any extra batter into your bread crumbs. If you can spare a dry hand, toss some extra bread crumbs on top and gently pat so they stay on. Then put a light dusting of bread crumbs on the bottom of a plate. Leave fish on the plate until you are ready to start frying them.

03 Heat oil to 350F (175C) in a medium-sized saucepan, and test the temperature before cooking.

04 Carefully fry cod tongues for one to two minutes per side. Remove them to drain on a mesh wire strainer or rack.

05 Serve with a few wedges of lemon and add a sprinkle of salt if using.

Elk Carpaccio on Salad Greens with Walnut Vinaigrette

MAKES 4 SERVINGS

Carpaccio is the Italian term for thin cuts of meat served raw as an appetizer—not a new thing to Indigenous people, including the Inuit, who commonly ate raw meat and fish.

Many butcher shops sell farmed elk meat now. It's richly flavoured and has a great texture and deep burgundy colour. Beef or any other large game tenderloin could be used in this recipe. If you use beef, get it from a certified butcher and tell him or her that you plan to use it for carpaccio. If you use game for this recipe, check that it was properly field dressed and frozen for at least seven days at -5F (-20C). Read "Preparing Large Game" in Chapter 5 (page 117). For added safety, I sear the meat and then freeze it again briefly; this also makes it easier to slice.

8 oz (225 g) **elk tenderloin**

MARINADE:

1 tsp (5 mL) chopped fresh **thyme**
1 tsp (5 mL) crushed black **peppercorns**
1½ tsp (7.5 mL) **vegetable oil**

WALNUT VINAIGRETTE:

2 Tbsp (30 mL) **red wine vinegar**
Pinch table **salt**
Pinch ground **black pepper**
⅓ cup (80 mL) **walnut oil**

SALAD:

2 Tbsp (30 mL) **raisins**, soaked in warm
    water for 30 minutes
2 cups (475 mL) **arugula**

TO SERVE:

2 Tbsp (30 mL) shaved **Asiago cheese**
2 tsp (10 mL) minced fresh **savory**
¼ tsp (1 mL) **fleur del sel** (or Celtic salt or flaked sea salt)
4 to 8 **edible flowers**—fireweed flowers, rose petals, violets
    or mariposa lily buds (optional)

01 Remove sinew and silver skin from the meat. Combine the thyme, pepper and vegetable oil in a shallow dish. Roll the meat in the marinade mixture. Set aside for at least 15 minutes.

02 Heat a cast iron frying pan for 10 minutes over low heat. Raise the temperature to high. Sear the outside of the meat very quickly—just long enough for the flesh to turn slightly brown, about three minutes. Let cool.

03 Wrap meat in plastic food wrap and freeze for one hour. Chill four plates.

04 Remove meat from freezer and cut (against the grain) into eight slices ¼ inch (1 cm) thick. Place meat slices between two sheets of plastic food wrap and then pound with a mallet to a thickness of ⅛ inch (0.5 cm). Place two slices of meat in the centre of each chilled plate and refrigerate.

05 Prepare the vinaigrette by whisking the vinegar, salt and pepper with walnut oil in a large bowl. Add the raisins and arugula and toss. Place some salad on each chilled plate around the meat. Sprinkle cheese, savory and fleur de sel on top of the meat. Garnish plate with edible flowers if using.

NOTE: This is a fairly complicated recipe suitable for when you have extra time to prepare it and enjoy it afterwards.

Elk and Sea Scallops in a Parmesan Cup with Chili Lime Vinaigrette

MAKES 4 SERVINGS

The "medallion" is a thick-cut round of meat that comes from the narrow end of a tenderloin, which is why it is also known as a tenderloin steak. This is a delicate and tender cut of meat that needs little cooking to show its glory. See "Recommended Venison Cooking Methods" (page 119) in Chapter 5, but remember that it can be served a little pink inside for better texture.

Sea scallops are much bigger than bay scallops, and the largest wild sea scallops come from the cold, deep waters from Newfoundland down to North Carolina. If you buy frozen scallops, defrost them in the fridge and use them the day you thaw them. For this recipe, you can buy either an elk tenderloin or striploin steak and cut it into four.

PARMESAN CUPS:
2 cups (475 mL) grated **Parmesan cheese**

VINAIGRETTE:
3 Tbsp (45 mL) extra-virgin **olive oil**
2 Tbsp (30 mL) **lime juice**
1 tsp (5 mL) chopped fresh flat-leaf **parsley**
1 tsp (5 mL) **chili sauce**
½ tsp (2.5 mL) **honey**
Pinch table **salt**
Pinch fresh ground **black pepper**

SALAD:
½ cup (120 mL) **mustard shoots** (or pea shoots or sprouts)
½ cup (120 mL) **watercress** (or arugula)

ELK:
4 **elk medallions** (1 oz/30 g each)
4 Tbsp (60 mL) pure **olive oil**, divided
1 Tbsp (15 mL) finely chopped fresh **rosemary**
2 tsp (10 mL) crushed **garlic**

Pinch kosher **salt** (or sea salt)
Pinch fresh ground **pepper**

WET SCALLOP BRINE:
2 Tbsp (30 mL) **lemon juice**
1 Tbsp (15 mL) kosher **salt** (or sea salt)
½ cup (120 mL) **hot water**
3½ cups (830 mL) **ice water**

SCALLOPS:
4 sea **scallops** (approximately 1 oz/30 g each)
2 Tbsp (30 mL) **lime juice**
1 tsp (5 mL) **lime zest**
¼ tsp (1 mL) **chili flakes**
Pinch kosher **salt** (or sea salt)
Pinch fresh ground **black pepper**

2 Tbsp (30 mL) **vegetable oil**

01 Preheat oven to 350F (175C).

02 To make the cheese cups, evenly sprinkle the grated cheese in four circles (the size of large pancakes) on a parchment paper–lined baking sheet. Bake for three to four minutes, or until lightly brown. Invert four small glasses or cups on a separate baking sheet. Using tongs, gently remove each round of cheese from the pan and carefully place over the glass bottoms; transfer the baking sheet to the fridge so that the cheese hardens into bowls.

03 Make the vinaigrette by whisking together the oil, lime juice, parsley, chili sauce, honey, and salt and pepper. Toss salad ingredients in the vinaigrette and chill.

04 Combine the elk, half the olive oil, rosemary, garlic, salt and pepper in a bowl and marinate in the fridge while you prepare the scallops.

05 If you bought pricier "dry" scallops, meaning they have never been treated with chemical additives, skip this step. But if you bought "wet" scallops, which always come with a milky white liquid, you will need to soak them in a brine before cooking so that they sear properly.

06 To make the brine, combine the lemon juice, salt and hot water and stir to dissolve the salt. Then add the ice water and stir. Pour brine into a tall bowl. Add the scallops and ensure that the brine covers them. Leave scallops in the fridge for 30 minutes.

07 Rinse scallops and lay them on a baking sheet lined with a couple of layers of paper towel. Put more paper towel on top of the scallops and press down on them to squeeze out moisture. Let them drain for a few minutes.

08 Place the scallops in a bowl and marinate them in lime juice, lime zest, chili flakes, and salt (leave out salt if you brined the scallops) and pepper in the fridge, in a nonreactive dish (glass, ceramic or stainless steel) for 20 minutes.

09 Remove the scallops and elk from the marinades (discard the liquids).

10 Heat a cast iron pan for 10 minutes over low heat. Raise the heat to high and add the vegetable oil. Wait until it starts to smoke before searing the scallops for three minutes on one side, and let cook without disturbing. Check one scallop to see that it has a caramel coloured crust before turning them all over to cook for two minutes on the other side. Remove scallops from the pan and set aside to keep warm.

11 Cook the elk medallions in the same pan over high heat for one minute, using the remainder of the olive oil before turning over to cook for one minute more on the other side. Let meat rest for a few minutes before slicing.

12 To prepare each serving, layer some greens inside a chilled cheese cup, add some meat slices and a scallop, and top with pan drippings.

Nish Kebobs with Birch Balsamic Glaze over Brown Rice

MAKES 4 SERVINGS

"**N**ish" is slang for Anishinaabe, which is the preferred term for a group of culturally related Indigenous nations including the Ojibway, Odawa, Potawatomi, Mississaugas, Nipissing, Algonquin, Oji-Cree and Saulteaux; their traditional territory extends from northern Quebec to eastern Saskatchewan. Venison (deer, moose and caribou) is one of their traditional foods.

You can find deer tenderloin at specialty butcher shops or use beef or pork tenderloin instead. Just remember that beef and pork are much fattier than deer and require a longer cooking time.

Birch syrup has an earthy taste and a little goes a long way; it's made from birch sap and is available in fine food stores, but because it takes so many birch trees to make syrup (a lot more than you would need for making maple syrup), it is a little pricey. You could try making it yourself if you happen to live in birch country, but if you have trouble finding birch syrup, use molasses instead. Serve Nish Kebobs over Brown Rice.

8 wooden skewers (6 inches/15 cm long)
¾ lb (340 g) deer tenderloin

BIRCH BALSAMIC GLAZE:
1½ tsp (7.5 mL) crushed black peppercorns
2 tsp (10 mL) chopped fresh rosemary
1 tsp (5 mL) chopped fresh thyme
2 tsp (10 mL) minced garlic
1 tsp (5 mL) Dijon mustard
2 Tbsp (30 mL) packed brown sugar
3 Tbsp (45 mL) soya sauce (or tamari)
3 Tbsp (45 mL) lime juice
2 Tbsp (30 mL) balsamic vinegar
2 Tbsp (30 mL) pure olive oil, divided

½ tsp (2.5 mL) kosher salt (or sea salt)
1 tsp (5 mL) birch syrup

01 Soak skewers in warm water while preparing the recipe.

02 Slice the deer meat into eight even slices, ½ inch (1.5 cm) wide. Reserve.

03 To make the glaze, mix the peppercorns, rosemary, thyme, garlic, mustard, brown sugar, soya sauce, lime juice, vinegar, half the oil, and the salt and birch syrup in a bowl.

04 Pour half the mixture into a small saucepan (reserve the rest). Simmer on very low heat for 15 minutes. Stir, strain and reserve.

05 Add the meat to the remaining glaze in the bowl and coat evenly. Let meat marinate at room temperature for one hour while you prepare the rice (see below). Then return to this part of the recipe.

06 Drain the meat and discard the marinade. Thread deer strips onto the wooden skewers.

07 Lightly brush the meat with the rest of the olive oil. Grill over medium-high heat in a grill pan or broil in the oven on a baking sheet at 400F (205C) for two minutes per side, turning occasionally. Check that the meat reaches 165F (75C), or 150F (66C) for medium rare.

08 Drizzle the reserved glaze on the Nish Kebobs before serving on rice.

Brown Rice

MAKES 4 TO 6 SERVINGS

Brown rice gets its name from the colour of its outer coating made of bran. Once it is milled, the bran is removed and the grain is polished white, and that's how rice loses some of its fibre and nutrients. Unless you buy organic brown rice, you are probably consuming residual chemical pesticide used in rice production, which stays in the bran layer. I like to get the organic kind for home use. Like white rice, brown rice comes in different forms including short grain, long grain, basmati and parboiled. I used short grain rice in this recipe but included variations for the other forms.

1 cup (250 mL) short grain **brown rice**
1¾ cups (415 mL) **water** (or Vegetable Stock, see recipe, page 38)
½ tsp (2.5 mL) table **salt**
1 Tbsp (15 mL) **butter** or olive oil (optional)

01 Rinse rice in a large bowl under cool water until the water is clear. Drain.

02 In a large saucepan, combine the rice, water, salt and butter if using.

03 Bring to a boil. Reduce heat to low and simmer for 45 minutes with a tight-fitting lid on top. Taste the rice after this time and check to see that all the liquid has been absorbed; if it has not, cook a few minutes longer.

04 Remove pot from heat once rice is cooked and let it steam for an additional 10 minutes with the lid on. Fluff rice with a fork before serving.

Tip

To store cooked rice, make sure it is cool before putting it into food containers and refrigerating it, and consume it within one or two days at the most. Bacteria form on cooked rice very quickly.

Variation for Long Grain or Parboiled Long Grain: Follow instructions above using 1 cup (250 mL) rice, 2 cups (475 mL) water and ½ teaspoon (2.5 mL) salt.

Variation for Basmati: Follow instructions above using 1 cup (250 mL) rice, 2¼ cups (530 mL) water and ½ teaspoon (2.5 mL) salt.

Buffalo Canoes

MAKES 4 SERVINGS

In recent years, beef marrow has become an upscale restaurant trend. It is either roasted in the bone and served with a tiny spoon to scoop it out, or it is removed from the bone, seasoned, cooked and then served resting on roasted bones (mostly for appearance's sake). Bone marrow is not new to Indigenous people or to chefs, for that matter; it's extremely nutritious and great for making stock and just about everything else that stock produces. Marlene's grandmother used to eat the creamy, rich marrow unseasoned, right out of the soup pot.

This recipe requires you to brine the bones so that it's easier to pop the marrow out before roasting, and although it calls for buffalo shanks, you can use thick shanks of beef or venison. If you happen to be buddy-buddy with your butcher, then you might be able to get large straight shanks, ideally split down the middle so you can remove the marrow intact; ask for a "canoe cut." Otherwise, you will end up with an assortment of soup bones of different sizes and shapes and will have to play around with them to remove the marrow from each one as best you can. This won't affect taste, just appearance.

I don't know about you, but in my family, when meat is really good, we like to lick and suck the bones to remove every morsel of goodness. I think yours might do the same with this recipe, especially if you serve it with Lemon and Dill Buttermilk Scones (see recipe, page 231).

BRINE:

8 buffalo **canoes** (4 split buffalo shanks)
4 Tbsp (60 mL) kosher **salt** (or sea salt), divided

TOPPING:

2 cups (475 mL) **bread crumbs**
½ cup (120 mL) finely diced **onion**
1 tsp (5 mL) chopped **garlic**
2 Tbsp (30 mL) **lemon zest**
½ tsp (2.5 mL) chopped fresh **oregano**
¼ tsp (1 mL) ground **black pepper**

OPTIONAL GARNISH:

¼ tsp (1 mL) **fleur del sel**, Celtic salt or flaked sea salt

01 To make the brine, place the canoes in a shallow dish and cover with cold water. Add 1 tablespoon (15 mL) of the salt to the water and refrigerate, covered, for two hours. Rinse the bones, change the water and add 1 tablespoon (15 mL) of the kosher salt. Chill for two hours. Repeat this process two more times.

02 Preheat oven to 400F (205C).

03 Drain the canoes and pat dry. Use your finger or the handle of a wooden spoon to carefully push the marrow out of the bones, keeping the marrow whole as much as possible. Return marrow to the fridge.

04 Place the bones in the oven on a baking sheet and brown for 30 to 40 minutes, turning them periodically, so that they colour evenly. Remove the pan from the oven and drain off the fat drippings into a metal container. Reserve.

05 Combine the bread crumbs with ½ cup (120 mL) fat drippings in a medium-sized bowl. Set aside.

06 In a sauté pan, cook the onion and garlic in 1 tablespoon (15 mL) of the remaining drippings until translucent but not brown. Add garlic and onion mixture to the bread crumb mixture along with the lemon zest, oregano and black pepper. Mix thoroughly.

07 In each canoe (bone cavity), spread ½ teaspoon (2.5 mL) of the bread crumb mixture and top with some chilled marrow. Spoon 1 tablespoon (15 mL) of the bread crumb mixture on top of each serving of marrow.

08 Bake canoes at 375F (190 C) for 10 to 12 minutes. Garnish with a sprinkle of fleur de sel if using, before serving with a small spoon.

Buffalo Egg Rolls with Mango Strawberry Dip (with vegetarian option)

MAKES 12 SERVINGS

Everyone I know loves egg rolls and I love mine with game meat and chili pepper. A good mild chili would be an Anaheim chili or a poblano chili, but if you want something hotter, try a jalapeno or something even hotter, like a serrano pepper. If you like it really hot, use the seeds, but whatever you decide, remove the pepper stem and white ribs (while wearing gloves) before cooking and don't rub your eyes!

Tip: if you use a pot for deep-frying rather than a deep fryer, use a thermometer to gauge the heat of the oil for added safety. Also, make the Mango Strawberry Dip first so that it's ready for when the egg rolls are done.

4 cups (1 L) plus 3 Tbsp (45 mL) **vegetable oil**, divided
4 oz (115 g) ground **buffalo** (or your favourite cooked meat or even firm tofu)
½ cup (120 mL) finely diced **onion**
2 tsp (10 mL) chopped **garlic**
½ cup (120 mL) thinly sliced **red pepper** or green pepper
1 can (5 oz/140 g) sliced **water chestnuts**, drained
¼ cup (60 mL) shredded **carrot**
1 tsp (5 mL) **soya sauce**
1 tsp (5 mL) minced fresh **chili pepper**
¼ tsp (1 mL) ground **black pepper**
1 cup (250 mL) **bean sprouts**
12 egg **roll wrappers**

SLURRY:
¼ cup (60 mL) all-purpose **flour**
½ cup (120 mL) **cold water**

01 Over medium heat in a large sauté pan, heat 2 tablespoons (30 mL) of the oil and cook the buffalo meat for three minutes. Add the onion and garlic and cook for one minute.

02 Add 1 more tablespoon (15 mL) oil to the pan along with red or green pepper, and continue to cook for one minute.

03 Add the water chestnuts, carrot, soya sauce and chili pepper. Season the mixture with the black pepper and cook for one to two minutes.

04 Fold in the bean sprouts. Turn off heat and set aide.

05 Prepare a slurry with the flour and water in a small glass, stirring the mixture with a spoon to remove all lumps.

06 Place one egg roll wrapper on the work surface with a corner of the wrapper pointing towards you. Brush the edges with the slurry using a pastry brush.

07 Place 1 tablespoon (15 mL) of the filling on the corner closest to you and fold the corner up and over the mixture away from you. Fold the left and right corners in towards the centre. Continue to roll the egg roll away from you until you almost reach the end. Brush on more slurry and seal the roll, making sure the filling is contained on all sides.

08 Form the rest of the egg rolls in the same way, and avoid letting them touch one another, or they will stick.

09 Heat remaining oil in deep fryer or medium-sized pot to 350F (175C).

10 Fry egg rolls, one or two at a time, for a minute per side, draining off excess oil on a rack or paper towels. As you fry the egg rolls, adjust heat according to the thermometer. Check that the egg rolls reach an internal temperature of 165F (75C).

11 Serve immediately with chilled dip. You can store cooked egg rolls for one to two days in the refrigerator or freeze them and store for up to two months.

Mango Strawberry Dip

MAKES 1 CUP (250 ML)

The word "strawberry" translates to "heart berry" in Ojibway. Strawberries are one of the first fruits to ripen each year, and in many Indigenous nations in Canada they are celebrated in feasts and ceremonies that bring people together to renew their friendship and connections to one another. Here's a recipe to cool the summer heat as you enjoy your egg rolls with friends.

1 large mango, peeled, seeded and diced
6 strawberries, washed, hulled and cut in half
1 tsp (5 mL) lemon juice
1 Tbsp (15 mL) sugar
¼ tsp (1 mL) ground cinnamon
¼ tsp (1 mL) table salt

01 Blend the mango, strawberries, lemon juice and sugar in a blender.

02 Add the cinnamon and salt and blend until smooth.

03 Chill for 30 minutes before serving. This dip freezes well, too, but not for more than two months.

Curried Caribou in Puff Pastry with Blackberry Dip

MAKES 12 SERVINGS

Wild caribou remains a staple food for many Indigenous families living in Canada's remote north due to the extremely high cost of store-bought foods there. Like all large game, caribou meat is quite versatile and can be used for anything from roasts and ribs, to stews, soups and jerky; Marlene was lucky enough to try some caribou jerky when she visited an elder in Inuvik, Northwest Territories. Oddly enough, caribou is also good in pastry. Use beef or other large game tenderloin or lamb loin as an alternative. Just remember to serve this dish right away, since puff pastry loses its puff before long. For more information on handling wild game, see "Preparing Large Game" in Chapter 5 (page 117).

1 cup (250 mL) medium-diced **sweet potato**

Pinch table **salt**

Pinch ground **black pepper**

MARINADE:

2 Tbsp (30 mL) **molasses**

2 Tbsp (30 mL) **soya sauce**

¼ cup (60 mL) **curry powder**

1 tsp (5 mL) grated peeled fresh **ginger**

1 lb (500 g) small-diced **caribou** tenderloin

2 Tbsp (30 mL) vegetable **oil**, divided

CURRY SAUCE:

2 cups (475 mL) **orange juice**

1 cup (250 mL) **apple juice**

½ cup (120 mL) small-diced **onion**

2 Tbsp (30 mL) chopped fresh **cilantro**

1 Tbsp (15 mL) minced **jalapeno pepper**
   (with seeds too, if you like it hotter)

2 tsp (10 mL) sliced **garlic**

1½ tsp (7.5 mL) ground **cumin**

2 Tbsp (30 mL) grated peeled fresh **ginger**

1 Tbsp (15 mL) **curry powder**

½ tsp (2.5 mL) kosher **salt** (or sea salt)

½ tsp (2.5 mL) ground **black pepper**

OPTIONAL SLURRY:

1 Tbsp (15 mL) **cornstarch**

1 Tbsp (15 mL) **water**

PASTRY:

1 pkg (1 lb/500 g) frozen **puff pastry**, thawed but still cold

2 Tbsp (30 mL) all-purpose **flour** for dusting

EGG WASH:

2 **eggs**, beaten

01 Cook the sweet potato in salted water until soft. Strain, add pepper, combine and set aside.

02 For the marinade, whisk together the molasses, soya sauce, curry powder and ginger, and pour into a large baking dish.

03 Remove sinew and silver skin from the meat. Add caribou to the marinade and turn to coat evenly. Refrigerate for one hour.

04 For the curry sauce, combine the orange juice, apple juice, onion, cilantro, jalapeno, garlic, cumin, ginger, curry powder, kosher salt and pepper in a large, heavy saucepan.

05 Bring curry sauce to a boil over medium-high heat. Lower heat to medium and cook until the sauce reduces by half (about 20 minutes), stirring occasionally.

06 If the sauce hasn't thickened by this point, make the optional slurry by combining the cornstarch and water, stirring to remove all lumps. Add the slurry to the saucepan and continue cooking for several minutes. Set aside.

07 Preheat a frying pan over medium-high heat.

08 Remove caribou from marinade (discard marinade), add 1 tablespoon (15 mL) of the vegetable oil and brown half of the meat lightly in the pan for about two to three minutes, stirring occasionally. Spoon meat into the curry sauce. Use the rest of the oil to cook a second batch. Remove meat from heat and spoon into the curry sauce.

09 Bring the sauce to a simmer. Stir in the sweet potato, mix well and let cool.

10 Preheat oven to 425F (220C).

11 With a rolling pin, gently flatten the puff pastry, on a lightly floured work surface, until the pastry is about ¼ inch (1 cm) thick. Cut the pastry into 12 evenly sized squares with a sharp knife.

12 Fill the centre of each pastry square with a heaping tablespoon (15–20 mL) of the curried meat mixture. Slide one pastry square in front of you with a corner pointing towards you. Brush egg wash on the left and right corners and fold them up towards each other and overlap them over the meat filling to keep it tucked in (some meat will remain exposed). Form the rest of the pastry squares the same way. Completely brush the pastries with egg wash, avoiding the meat.

13 Place the pastries on a parchment paper–lined baking sheet and bake for 15 to 17 minutes. Check that the meat reaches 165F (75C). Serve with warm Blackberry Dip.

Blackberry Dip

MAKES 2 CUPS (475 ML)

3 cups (710 mL) fresh blackberries
½ cup (120 mL) water
1 cup (250 mL) sugar
1 Tbsp (15 mL) cornstarch
1 Tbsp (15 mL) lemon juice

01 In a medium saucepan, simmer the blackberries, water and sugar for five minutes over low heat.

02 Combine the cornstarch and lemon juice in a small bowl and blend well to remove lumps. Add mixture to the blackberries and raise the temperature. Boil for one to two minutes (until mixtures thickens). Stir, remove from heat and serve.

Campfire Bear Onion Balls with Molé Sauce

MAKES 8 SERVINGS

I am not the inventor of stuffed onions, but like the idea for its simplicity, especially when cooked in brown molé sauce over a fire. Traditional Mexican molé sauce dates back to pre-Columbian times and may well have over 30 different ingredients in it, but today molé sauce is possibly best loved for including chocolate. Molé comes from a Nahuatl word that means "concoction" or "sauce."

Bear meat is very strong and can taste a bit like pork but has an earthiness that is complemented by this very basic version of brown molé sauce. If you do use bear meat, just remember that although it's fattier than other large game, it is still drier than beef and has no marbling, and spring bear is even drier than fall bear. Keeping that in mind, you don't want to overcook bear, but if you undercook it, then you risk trichinosis. Bear meat should be cooked to well done (165F/75C), but no more. I combine bear with pork to increase the fat content.

From a cultural perspective, eating bear is not a widespread practice among Indigenous people anymore, and many avoid it entirely now, though First Nations from coast to coast traditionally ate black or brown bear meat and Inuit traditionally ate polar bear, so cooking bear over a smoky fire really makes me feel like I am travelling back in time. If bear is either unavailable or unappealing, go for other large game or lean ground beef. I have included variations for baking or barbecuing the onion balls in case you live in

a condo or don't want to have to run the fire department scanner to make sure firefighters are not on their way to your house! Aim to use onions of the same size for this recipe for even cooking.

4 cooking **onions**
1 lb (500 g) ground **bear** meat
½ lb (225 g) ground **pork**
¼ cup (60 mL) fine **bread crumbs**
1 **egg**, beaten
1 tsp (5 mL) minced **garlic**
½ tsp (2.5 mL) kosher **salt** (or sea salt)
¼ tsp (1 mL) ground **black pepper**
½ cup (120 mL) **water**

MOLÉ SAUCE:
1½ cups (350 mL) **ketchup**
2 Tbsp (30 mL) brown **sugar**
2 Tbsp (30 mL) **unsweetened cocoa**
2 Tbsp (30 mL) **cider vinegar**
2 Tbsp (30 mL) **molasses**
1½ tsp (7.5 mL) **ancho chili pepper**
½ tsp (2.5 mL) **cinnamon**
1 tsp (5 mL) kosher **salt** (or sea salt)
¼ tsp (1 mL) ground **black pepper**

NOTE: This recipe can also be made on a backyard barbecue or in the oven (see variation).

01 Cut roots and tops off onions. Remove outer layer on each onion and cut each onion in half from root to tip. Remove the top two or three layers of each onion and reserve.

02 Dice centres of onions to make ⅓ cup (80 mL) onion.

03 Combine bear and pork meat with diced onion, bread crumbs, egg, garlic, salt, pepper and water. The mixture should be fairly sticky and definitely hold together. Make balls suitable in size to completely fill the onion shells even though the balls will be slightly different sizes. Fill onion shells to form the balls.

04 Whisk sauce ingredients together in a mixing bowl. Lay each onion ball on an individual sheet of aluminum foil. Spoon a couple of tablespoons (30 mL) of sauce on top of each onion ball and wrap up in foil, making sure to make a complete seal.

05 Wait until your wood fire has settled into a bed of red hot coals before cooking the onion balls; or place a grate over a flaming fire, leaving space between the flames and the grate, being careful not to poke the foil, or the juices will run out.

06 Turn the onion balls several times during the cooking process, or the sauce will burn. Use a thermometer to make sure each onion ball reaches an internal temperature of 165F (75C) before serving.

Oven-Baked Variation: Bake the onion balls for 30 minutes on a baking sheet at 350F (175C) or barbecue over medium-high heat for 20 to 30 minutes.

Baked Turkey Wings in a Barbecue Sauce

MAKES 4 SERVINGS (8 PIECES)

Turkeys were domesticated by pre-Columbian Indigenous peoples in 800 BCE; the Pueblo turkey was raised for over a millennium and mostly for their feathers (for ceremonies and clothing) rather than their meat.

I remember the first time I saw actual wild turkey tracks in the snow in Muskoka, Ontario. Not only were they pretty large, but they were right outside our door, around my truck and led into the deep woods. It was amazing to see a flock of wild turkeys walking through the woods; they could stop walking in unison and virtually disappear right before my eyes, totally blending in with the surroundings. These big birds are good eating, judging by the number of people who hunt them. I believe they taste a little stronger than farm-raised turkey (even those allowed to run around in the sunshine), although I've never had the chance to hunt or eat wild turkey myself.

Chicken wings can be used instead of turkey wings in this recipe (see that variation). But why not ask your butcher for a bag of turkey wings for a change? While you are at it, get your butcher to cut up the wings at the joints for you as well.

This recipe is best made over two days. There is a barbecue variation too (see below).

4 turkey wings

BARBECUE SAUCE:
¼ cup (60 mL) **apple cider vinegar**
¼ cup (60 mL) **red wine vinegar**
¼ cup (60 mL) **maple syrup**
¼ cup (60 mL) **molasses**
3 Tbsp (45 mL) **ketchup**
2 Tbsp (30 mL) **chili paste**
1 Tbsp (15 mL) **Dijon mustard**
1 Tbsp (15 mL) **Worcestershire sauce**
1 tsp (5 mL) table **salt**
½ tsp (2.5 mL) ground **cinnamon**
½ tsp (2.5 mL) **paprika**

½ tsp (2.5 mL) ground **black pepper**
4 tsp (20 mL) chopped **garlic**
1 tsp (5 mL) minced fresh **ginger**
Pinch **oregano**

01 Cut wings at joints if still whole, and discard the tips (butchers normally remove them).

02 Mix all sauce ingredients in a nonreactive bowl (glass, ceramic or stainless steel), whisking until well blended.

03 Marinate turkey wings in sauce in the fridge for at least eight hours or overnight, turning periodically.

04 Preheat oven to 375F (190C).

05 Remove wings from marinade, reserving marinade. Place wings in a non-stick roasting pan (or on a parchment paper–lined baking sheet) and bake for 30 minutes.

06 Turn wings and baste with marinade, and continue to cook for another 30 minutes. Check that the internal temperature of the turkey wings reaches 165F (75C). Serve hot.

Barbecue Variation: Heat barbecue to 350F (175C) and cook turkey wings on the upper grill for 15 minutes. Baste wings with marinade. Turn heat down to 325F (160C) and continue to turn and baste wings every 10 minutes until they reach an internal temperature of 165F (75C). Alternatively, if you don't have an upper grill, set the temperature to 325F (160C) for the duration of cooking.

Chicken Variation: Simply replace turkey wings with about 10 chicken wings in the baking recipe above. Bake for 20 minutes. Baste with marinade. Bake for another 10 to 15 minutes, checking that the internal temperature reaches 165F (75C).

NOTE: you will need to make the filling the day before baking or freezing the turnovers; you should also make the dip a day ahead for improved taste.

Spicy Bean Turnover with Orange Mint Yogurt Dip

MAKES 36 SERVINGS

It may be surprising to learn that many beans we all know and love in this part of the world are indigenous to present-day Mexico and the United States: the navy bean, lima bean, kidney bean and pinto bean are some examples. As part of the movement to preserve the use of traditional foods that predate the arrival of Europeans, some Indigenous communities in the American southwest cultivate several types of beans; these people are reviving their cultural connection to the past.

The Zuni gold bean is a mottled brown and white heirloom variety that is very hard to find unless you happen to grow it yourself or be buddy-buddy with someone in the US Southwest who can send some your way. I love the sound of a "Zuni Gold Bean Turnover," don't you? If you can get your hands on some, you will need to soak them overnight in the fridge and simmer them in a good amount of fresh water until soft (before using in this recipe). A good alternative bean for this recipe would be navy or cannellini beans, which are easier to find, especially canned.

There is enough filling in this recipe to make 36 to 40 turnovers, so if this recipe is too large, just bake 12 and freeze the rest to bake and serve later.

1 cup (250 mL) finely chopped onion

1 Tbsp (15 mL) pure olive oil

¼ cup (60 mL) chopped fresh chives

1 Tbsp (15 mL) chopped garlic

½ tsp (2.5 mL) dried thyme

1½ cups (350 mL) canned diced tomatoes, drained

½ cup (120 mL) finely diced celery

½ cup (120 mL) finely chopped red pepper

1 tsp (5 mL) chili powder

1 cup (250 mL) drained and rinsed canned Zuni gold beans
   (or navy or cannellini beans)

½ cup (120 mL) drained and rinsed canned black beans

4 cups (1 L) Vegetable Stock (see recipe, page 38), or water

1 tsp (5 mL) ground turmeric

1 tsp (5 mL) kosher salt (or sea salt)

½ tsp (2.5 mL) fresh ground black pepper

2 Tbsp (30 mL) molasses

2 Tbsp (30 mL) chili paste

1 pkg (1 lb/500 g) phyllo pastry

1 lb (500 g) butter, melted

2 Tbsp (30 mL) ancho chili powder

01 In a stockpot, sauté the onion in the oil. Add the chives, garlic and thyme, and let cook for one minute.

02 Add the tomatoes to the mixture and cook for two minutes at medium heat.

03 Add the celery, red pepper and chili powder, and cook for two minutes.

04 Add the beans to the pot along with the stock, turmeric, salt, black pepper, molasses and chili paste, and bring to a boil. Turn down heat and let simmer. Stir bean mixture frequently to check the consistency and continue to cook until very thick (about 30 to 45 minutes).

05 Let filling cool and chill overnight. Transfer package of phyllo pastry from freezer to fridge to thaw overnight.

06 Preheat oven to 375F (190C).

07 Remove sheets of phyllo from the package and spread out on a baking sheet. Place one sheet on your work surface.

08 Brush melted butter onto the first sheet of pastry and then lay a second sheet of pastry on top. Butter the second sheet and lay a third sheet on top. Butter the third sheet. Cover the remaining sheets of pastry with a damp cloth and return them on the baking sheet to the fridge until you are ready to do the next batch.

09 Cut the layered, buttered sheets lengthwise into six evenly sized rectangles.

10 Spoon 1 tablespoon (15 mL) of the bean mixture onto the bottom of each piece.

11 Fold the bottom of the first piece of pastry diagonally up and over the bean mixture to make a triangle. Next, lift the wrapped bean mixture and turn it over again, retaining the triangle shape. Continue folding it until you reach the end of the pastry. Repeat with the other five pieces.

12 Place turnovers on a parchment paper–lined baking tray and brush the top of each turnover with some more butter. Sprinkle with some ancho chili powder. Repeat these steps to make the rest of the turnovers.

13 Bake the turnovers right away for 15 minutes. Serve hot, with chilled dip.

Variation for Freezing before Baking: Freeze uncooked turnovers on a baking sheet. Once frozen, you can put them in a freezer bag and store them for up to three months in the freezer. When cooking frozen turnovers, add three to five more minutes to the cooking time stated above.

Orange Mint Yogurt Dip

MAKES 2¹/₃ CUPS (550 ML)

Thanks to the citrus in this dip, there is a freshness that lifts the meaty taste of the bean turnovers. I prefer Greek yogurt to other types of yogurt because it holds together well and won't get runny.

1 large **orange**, zested and juiced
2 cups (475 mL) plain **Greek yogurt**
1 Tbsp (15 mL) liquid **honey**
½ tsp (2.5 mL) smoked sea **salt** (see Cold-Smoked Alderwood Salt recipe, page 30) or table salt
2 Tbsp (30 mL) minced fresh **mint**

01 In a bowl, stir to combine the orange juice, yogurt, honey and smoked sea salt.

02 Add three-quarters of the orange zest and three-quarters of the mint and mix together. Spoon into small serving bowls and top with the remaining mint and orange zest for garnish.

Pickled Herring Salad
with Blackberry Vinaigrette

MAKES 4 SERVINGS

Herring is a fish several First Nations in BC are very familiar with. The Heiltsuk have fished herring for over 7,000 years and are well acquainted with caviar as a traditional food, whereas I think most people would consider it a pretty luxurious treat today. The Haida and Coast Tsimshian also have a very long herring history, and they continue the practice of gathering seaweed containing herring spawn to eat either sundried or salted and dried.

Pickling is not the same as cooking, so you must make sure the herring you use is the freshest you can find; it spoils very quickly. When you pickle herring as described below, it's processed in such a way that it will keep in the fridge for up to two weeks, so you need to eat it fairly quickly.

Removing tiny bones from herring fillets is the hardest part of making pickled herring, so I wouldn't blame you if you just skipped this step altogether and went to a fish shop to buy pickled herring. If you are up for it, though, do it yourself but just plan to have your morning coffee *after* you've removed all the tiny bones from the fillets using sterilized tweezers—you need a steady hand.

Pickled herring is popular among northern Europeans; Germans call it *rollmops* and Swedes call it *surströmming*, but Nova Scotians call it Solomon Gundy. Here's my version, used in salad. Try this recipe using smelts if you can't get herring.

12 oz (340 g) whole **herring** (about 3 whole fish or 6 fillets)

OPTIONAL BRINE:

3 Tbsp (45 mL) **pickling salt** (or additive-free kosher salt)
2 cups (475 mL) **water**

PICKLING SOLUTION:

½ cup (120 mL) **sugar**
1 Tbsp (15 mL) **Pickling Spice** (see recipe, page 27), or store-bought pickling spice

1½ cups (375 mL) 7 per cent **pickling vinegar**
1½ cups (375 mL) **water**

TO ASSEMBLE:

2 **dill pickles** (optional)
toothpicks
¼ cup (60 mL) thinly sliced **red onion**

BLACKBERRY VINAIGRETTE:

1 cup (250 mL) **blackberries**
⅓ cup (80 mL) **orange juice**
⅓ cup (80 mL) **water**
3 Tbsp (45 mL) extra-virgin **olive oil**
1 Tbsp (15 mL) red wine **vinegar**
¼ tsp (1 mL) ground **black pepper**
¼ tsp (1 mL) table **salt**

SALAD:

1 cup (250 mL) **sorrel** (or other salad greens)
2 small **tomatoes**
½ tsp (2.5 mL) kosher **salt** (or sea salt)
¼ tsp (1 mL) fresh ground **black pepper**
1 Tbsp (15 mL) vegetable **oil**

GARNISH:

½ cup (120 mL) **sea asparagus** or chopped chives

01 Fillet fish following the instructions in "How to Fillet Round Fish" (page 158), but leave the skin on. Remove all fish bones. Rinse.

02 If you bought pre-salted herring, then skip this step. Otherwise, make the brine by combining the salt and water, and heat on stove until the salt dissolves. Soak fish in the brine for 24 hours in the fridge, covered. If they float to the top, put a clean glass bowl on top of the fish to keep them submerged, or put everything in a food-safe bag.

03 Meanwhile, to prepare the pickling solution, combine the sugar, Pickling Spice, vinegar and water in a saucepan, and heat to the boiling point. Simmer over low heat for five minutes. Let cool. Chill overnight.

04 When the fish-brining period is over, rinse fish in a bowl of cold water for 1 hour. Pat dry with paper towels. If the fillets are more than 1 inch (2.5 cm) wide, I suggest you slice them in half lengthwise.

05 If using pickles, before forming the rolls cut the pickles in quarters lengthwise, and then cut each quarter in half widthwise. Place a piece of pickle at the tail end of each fillet and roll up the fillets, skin side out. Otherwise, skip the pickle and roll up fillets as above. Secure each herring roll with a toothpick.

06 Spoon half of the onion into the bottom of a sterilized glass jar large enough to hold all the herring rolls and the pickling solution and spices, or divide the onion evenly between two or three sterilized jars. Place the herring rolls in next, followed by the rest of the onion and all of the pickling solution. Seal and refrigerate the jar(s) for 48 hours.

07 Meanwhile, prepare the vinaigrette. Rinse and dry the berries. Combine them with the orange juice, water, olive oil, red wine vinegar, salt and black pepper, and blend in a blender (or in a tall container using a hand blender) on low speed for one to two minutes. Chill the vinaigrette until ready to serve.

08 To prepare the salad, rinse and dry the greens. Cut off and discard sorrel stems and chop leaves.

09 Slice the tomatoes, and season with salt and pepper. Brush their tops with oil. Heat a grill pan to medium heat, and grill tomato slices for two minutes on oiled side only. Carefully remove them and reserve on a platter to cool.

10 Drain herring rolls. Assemble the greens on four serving plates. Top greens with tomatoes (grill marks facing up), herring rolls and pickled onions. Garnish with sea asparagus or chives, and serve vinaigrette on the side.

NOTE: It may take up to four days to make this recipe from start to finish. You will need toothpicks to secure the herring rolls.

Pontiac Potato Salad with Hot-Smoked Trout and Creamy Dill Dressing

MAKES 6 SERVINGS

Mom used to make a potato salad that to this day makes my sisters and me laugh when we remember the big chunks of green pepper she put in it. We used to say, "Enough green peppers!" but she kept telling us they were good for us, so in they went. It was actually my sister Jan Wolfman's favourite dish. Green peppers are good for you, but now you know why I don't care for them in my potato salad.

In pre-Columbian times, Indigenous people ate various tubers as a starch food, whether raw, boiled, roasted or dried and pounded into flour to thicken soups or make bread, for example. The swampland wapato tuber was just one such food item that was collected (by using pointed digging sticks) and traded between nations. The Iroquois and Potawatomi ate this tuber, which was also called duck potato and Indian potato. Indigenous people farther south had access to many other types of indigenous potatoes of all colours before the development of the common potato varieties we know and love today, such as red-skins. Pontiac red potatoes, so named in honour of an Odawa chief, are more waxy than airy, which makes them just right for this type of recipe, but any type of new potato will do.

Making hot-smoked trout is easy enough to do yourself when you've got a smoker; just remember to smoke the fish a day in advance of making the salad. To do this, follow the smoking instructions in the Hot-Smoked Salmon with Sour Cream and Onion Dip recipe (page 45), but adjust the brine for only 4 oz (115 g) of fish. For instructions on using various types of smokers, see pages 28–29. Or buy hot-smoked trout at a deli or fine food shop.

SALAD:

¾ lb (340 g) Pontiac potatoes

1 tsp (5 mL) table salt

4 cups (1 L) packed mixed greens

4 oz (115 g) smoked trout, skinned, boned and flaked

4 large hard-boiled eggs, cut into wedges

½ cup (120 mL) grape (or cherry) tomatoes, halved lengthwise

CREAMY DILL DRESSING:

¼ cup (60 mL) plain Greek yogurt

3 Tbsp (45 mL) chopped fresh dill

3 Tbsp (45 mL) white wine vinegar

2 Tbsp (30 mL) extra-virgin olive oil

2 Tbsp (30 mL) Roasted Garlic (see recipe, page 33)

1 tsp (5 mL) Dijon mustard

½ tsp (2.5 mL) ground black pepper

¼ tsp (1 mL) table salt

01 Scrub the potatoes, leaving them whole. Cover potatoes in water in a saucepan, add table salt and bring to a boil. Lower heat to medium and simmer for 12 minutes. Drain and let cool.

02 Rinse and dry the greens. Chill while you prepare the dressing.

03 Whisk together yogurt, dill, vinegar, olive oil, garlic, mustard, pepper and salt in a mixing bowl.

04 Large-dice the cooled potatoes (leaving their skins on), and toss them in the dressing, taking care to avoid mashing them. Chill the potato mixture for at least an hour so that it absorbs the seasonings and liquid.

05 Add smoked trout to the potato mixture. Stir to combine. Drain off excess dressing before serving.

06 Place greens on serving plates and top with potato salad, egg wedges and tomatoes.

Minted Corn and Bean Salad
with Chipotle Cider Vinaigrette

Pinto beans are also known as Navajo beans. I usually use the canned type just to simplify the process of making this salad, but you can certainly use dried beans if you prefer. Follow the manufacturer's instructions on the package for soaking and cooking them.

Even though this is kind of a summery salad, I made it a day or two before Christmas one year to enjoy with turkey and all the trimmings. It was so good it didn't make it to Christmas.

SALAD:

1 cup (250 mL) medium-diced **plum tomato**

1 cup (250 mL) medium-diced peeled seeded **cucumber**

1 cup (250 mL) roasted **corn**

½ cup (120 mL) small-diced **red onion**

3 Tbsp (45 mL) chopped fresh **mint**

1 Tbsp (15 mL) chopped fresh **cilantro**

2 tsp (10 mL) finely chopped **garlic**

1 can (19 fl oz/560 mL) **pinto beans**, drained and rinsed

CHIPOTLE CIDER VINAIGRETTE:

¼ cup (60 mL) **apple cider vinegar**

1 Tbsp (15 mL) **lime juice**

1 tsp (5 mL) ground **chipotle pepper**

½ tsp (2.5 mL) **Dijon mustard**

½ cup (120 mL) sunflower **oil**

½ tsp (2.5 mL) kosher **salt** (or sea salt)

¼ tsp (1 mL) ground **black pepper**

01 In a large bowl, mix the tomato, cucumber, corn, onion, mint, cilantro and garlic, blending well. Add the beans and mix with a rubber spatula, taking care to avoid mashing the beans. Set aside.

02 In a small bowl, prepare the vinaigrette by whisking together the vinegar, lime juice, chipotle pepper and mustard. Slowly whisk in the oil until well blended. Add the salt and pepper.

03 Pour vinaigrette into the bean and corn mixture. Blend well. Chill salad for a minimum of 20 minutes (or overnight for killer flavour). If there is excess vinaigrette in the bowl the next day, drain it out before serving.

NOTE: In this recipe you could either barbecue two cobs of corn or grill them on a grill pan on your stovetop, or use canned niblet corn.

Celeriac and Apple Salad with Honey Vinaigrette

MAKES 6 SERVINGS

On the ugly scale, celeriac scores a full 10. Many times when I've bought it, the grocery store cashier has stared at it and stared back at me and asked what this dirty, hairy, bulbous root was good for. "It's the root of a vegetable that is related to celery," I explained. Celeriac does taste like celery but, once peeled, has a whitish interior and is crispy and firm, like a potato. It is edible raw, boiled and mashed, fried, roasted, or can be used to thicken soups and stews. Celeriac is popular in France, Asia and Peru and is very similar to an indigenous root vegetable, the jicama, but probably easier to find. Use jicama in this recipe if you are lucky enough to find it. The apple, a gift from European colonists, makes a perfect match for this fresh salad that can be made practically all year long.

1 cup (250 mL) julienned peeled **carrot**

½ cup (120 mL) finely diced **celery**

¼ cup (60 mL) dried **cranberries**

¼ cup (60 mL) **raisins**

1 Tbsp (15 mL) **lemon juice**

2 cups (475 mL) diced **apples**, skin on (preferably Granny Smith)

2 cups (475 mL) julienned peeled **celeriac**

HONEY VINAIGRETTE:

⅓ cup (80 mL) extra-virgin **olive oil**

2 Tbsp (30 mL) **rice vinegar**

2 Tbsp (30 mL) liquid **honey**

½ tsp (2.5 mL) table **salt**

½ tsp (2.5 mL) ground **black pepper**

1 tsp (5 mL) **chili paste**

1 tsp (5 mL) **Dijon mustard**

01 In a salad bowl, combine the carrot, celery, cranberries and raisins. Sprinkle lemon juice on the apples and celeriac to keep them from browning, and add them to the mix.

02 In a small bowl, prepare the vinaigrette by whisking together the oil, vinegar, honey, salt, pepper, chili paste and mustard.

03 Pour vinaigrette over the salad and toss. Let marinate for at least one hour before serving. Taste and adjust flavour with honey and salt, draining off excess vinaigrette if needed.

Beet and Mandarin Orange Salad with White Wine Vinaigrette

MAKES 6 SERVINGS

Anyone who knows me knows that I am crazy about beets. Beetroots are not indigenous to Canada, but they are probably the root most like the types of roots Indigenous people ate long ago—sunchokes, potatoes, wapato, jicama, oca, ulluco, manioc (cassava) and mashua to name a few. First Nations in the Okanagan held "first roots" ceremonies to mark the importance of root harvesting season. They cooked taproots mixed with oils and fats and then, after refined sugar was introduced, they used that to take the bitterness out of the roots, whereas the Inuit fermented various root vegetables before consuming them.

Choose beets that are uniform in size (so that they cook evenly) and not too large—the bigger they are, the more likely they are to be woody in texture.

8 oz (225 g) **beets** (about 4 medium-sized beets)

2 dried **bay leaves**

½ tsp (2.5 mL) **black peppercorns**

½ tsp (2.5 mL) **cloves**

2 tsp (10 mL) table **salt**

1 can (10 fl oz/300 mL) **mandarin orange** segments
 (or segments of 1 orange)

1 Tbsp (15 mL) minced fresh **chives**

WHITE WINE VINAIGRETTE:

2 Tbsp (30 mL) **orange juice**

2 Tbsp (30 mL) **walnut oil**

2 Tbsp (30 mL) **white wine vinegar**

1 Tbsp (15 mL) **cider vinegar**

1 Tbsp (15 mL) **corn syrup**

1 Tbsp (15 mL) extra-virgin **olive oil**

¼ tsp (1 mL) minced fresh **thyme**

½ tsp (2.5 mL) table **salt**

¼ tsp (1 mL) ground **black pepper**

01 Remove the leaves and all but 1 inch (2.5 cm) of the stem from the beets, but leave the stringy roots on them. Discard the stems. Scrub beets with a brush to remove dirt. If the green leaves are fresh, chop them up to serve as a base in the salad. Otherwise, discard.

02 In a medium to large saucepan, add the bay leaves, peppercorns, cloves and beets and cover with cold water. Add salt. Bring water to a boil. Lower heat and simmer for about one hour with lid partially on.

03 Let beets cool to room temperature. Strain off seasonings. Remove skin and stringy roots from the beets, and slice them into a mixing bowl.

04 In a small bowl, whisk together vinaigrette ingredients. Pour over the salad and chill for at least an hour before serving (a few hours of chilling would be better).

05 Add orange segments and chives to the salad. Stir salad and strain off excess vinaigrette before serving.

Wild Rice Fruit and Nut Salad
with Balsamic Vinaigrette

MAKES 4 SERVINGS

Wild rice, a cold-weather grass that grows in water, was cultivated by Indigenous communities from Manitoba to the Atlantic Ocean. The traditional way to harvest *manoomin* was to use a long stick to knock the hulls, or kernels, loose from the grass into canoes while paddling through the water. Then the rice was dried in the sun, smoked or toasted over a fire; next it was either stomped or danced on in a pit in a special ceremonial dance. The last step was to winnow it, throwing it into the air from baskets or animal hides to remove the husks in a soft breeze. The rice was then stored for special occasions and use during the winter months. Wild rice stewardship was passed down from one generation to the next, and some nations in Minnesota, Manitoba and Ontario are wild rice producers and exporters even now.

This sweet salad is a colourful, fibrous addition to any meal. It's even better prepared a day or two in advance of serving, allowing the flavours to blend (garnish just before serving).

4 cups (1 L) water
1 cup (250 mL) wild rice, rinsed
2 dried bay leaves
1 tsp (5 mL) table salt, divided
½ cup (120 mL) dried apricots
½ cup (120 mL) dried cranberries
1 tsp (5 mL) orange zest
⅓ cup (80 mL) medium-diced red pepper
⅓ cup (80 mL) medium-diced yellow pepper
¼ cup (60 mL) chopped green onion
2 Tbsp (30 mL) chopped walnuts (or pecans)

BALSAMIC VINAIGRETTE:

⅓ cup (80 mL) balsamic vinegar
2 tsp (10 mL) minced shallots
½ tsp (2.5 mL) Dijon mustard
⅓ cup (80 mL) extra-virgin olive oil
¼ tsp (1 mL) ground black pepper

OPTIONAL GARNISH:

⅔ cup (160 mL) canned mandarin orange segments, drained (or fresh tangerine or orange segments)

01 In a medium saucepan, bring the water to a boil over high heat. Add the rice, bay leaves and ¼ teaspoon (1 mL) of the salt. Cover and reduce heat to medium-low. Cook for 40 to 50 minutes, or until the rice is tender and the water is absorbed.

02 Discard bay leaves. Transfer rice to a large bowl, fluff rice with a fork and chill.

03 Cut dried apricots into small pieces and blanch, along with the cranberries, in a pot of boiling water for three minutes; drain and set aside.

04 Combine the rice, apricots, cranberries, orange zest, peppers, green onion and walnuts together in a large bowl and mix well.

05 Place vinaigrette ingredients in a small bowl with remaining salt and whisk vigorously, or use a hand blender, to combine them.

06 Pour vinaigrette over the salad and mix well. Garnish salad with the mandarin segments, if using.

Back to the Land Salad with Creamy Avocado Dressing

MAKES 4 SERVINGS

It is a tradition of Indigenous people in Canada and the United States to offer tobacco to the Creator, laying a handful of it down on the earth where we pick plants or take anything from nature, as a way of showing respect to the plant spirit and giving thanks. Offering tobacco is customary when hunting or foraging for a meal—although I would go hungry in the woods without the help of an experienced forager so don't attempt it much. Marlene is more adventurous—her exploits have included trying (without any issues) the puffball mushrooms, purslane and sweet woodruff that mysteriously appeared in our yard. To settle the discussion on safety, we compromise and shop at health food stores for organic fruits and veggies when we can. This makes the most sense, since we don't have any experience detoxifying wild plants in the ways that our ancestors did by leaching them, fermenting them, heating them, and so on. We don't need to threaten their sustainability either. You won't have to worry about that with any ingredients in this recipe.

This recipe features some unusual ingredients that are indigenous to North and South America, although the berry, grape, tomato and nut varieties you might find either in the wild now or in regular grocery stores are not the same as those that grew here before the arrival of Europeans. Some indigenous foods died out completely or have been hybridized through selective breeding. For instance, you probably won't be able to find sheep sorrel anywhere anymore, so use the type of sorrel you can find. It's very tart, so you won't need much of it.

If you can find sea asparagus (also called sea pickle, marsh samphire or sea green bean) use it for a salty flavour. It's a really tasty, crunchy vegetable that grows in beachfront marshlands. It goes by other names including beach asparagus, samphire greens, sea beans, glasswort, crow's foot greens or pickle weed. The crunch of the sea asparagus contrasts nicely with the creaminess of the avocado in the dressing. Avocados have been around for 10,000 years, originating in Mexico, and Meso-Americans began to cultivate avocados 5,000 years ago.

Muscadine grapes were a nice surprise to find at the health food store, too, since they are not that common. Long ago the Catawba Native Americans of North Carolina country made drinks from muscadine grapes, which some historians claim was the beginning of Catawba wine—a not so refined drink. Concord grapes originate from a native grape, and various other indigenous grapes can be found growing wild across the Americas, including on Manitoulin Island in Ontario.

In any event, this salad is a good introduction to the bounty of the Americas.

SALAD:

1 **persimmon**, sliced

Handful **blackberries**

Handful **cherries**

Handful **cherry tomatoes**, halved

Handful **muscadine grapes**, halved

Handful **strawberries**, sliced

Handful **sea asparagus** (or a few stalks of steamed salted asparagus)

Handful **sorrel**

Sprinkle of **marigold** (or other edible flower) petals

Handful dried **cranberries**

Handful raw **hazelnuts**, chopped (or pine nuts, walnuts or pecans)

CREAMY AVOCADO DRESSING:

1 **avocado**

1 **garlic** clove

½ tsp (2.5 mL) table **salt**

¼ cup (60 mL) **water**

3 Tbsp (45 mL) **cider vinegar**

2 Tbsp (30 mL) **walnut oil**

2 tsp (10 mL) **maple syrup**

01 Rinse and dry all fresh salad ingredients separately, the sorrel especially since it is probably very sandy (and cut off and discard the sorrel stems). Chill salad ingredients while you prepare the dressing.

02 Blend avocado dressing ingredients in a deep bowl with a hand blender.

03 Space out all salad ingredients in mounds across a large cutting board, or arrange on a serving platter as you like.

04 Pour dressing over the entire salad, or serve dressing on the side.

Variations: For more variety, consider using other indigenous foods such as stewed collard greens, black beans, cape gooseberries, wild rose petals, toasted pumpkin seeds, niblet corn, or peeled and julienned raw sweet potato or jicama.

Iroquois Poutine with Cayenne Hominy

MAKES 4 SERVINGS

I call this dish Iroquois Poutine because of the hominy topping that goes on at the end and because Iroquois still live in Quebec, which is poutine country. Traditionally, the Cayuga, Mohawk, Oneida, Onondaga, Seneca and Tuscarora nations (who self-identify as Haudenosaunee) prepared hominy by soaking corn kernels in lye to remove the hulls; the corn turns white and puffs up in the process. Hominy is now, surprisingly enough, sold in cans in ethnic markets and the international foods section of grocery stores (at least in Toronto, that is).

To make the best fries, you need to use Russet potatoes, and you need to use the right oil; vegetable oil and peanut oil are the best. Frying should be done in two stages: (1) blanching the potatoes in medium-hot oil to partially cook them and soften them, and (2) cooking them again in hotter oil to brown them and make them crispy. I know, I know, "Is that necessary?" That's what my students ask me when I teach them how to make fries. But they don't question the two-stage process after eating them. It's up to you whether you want to leave the potato skins on or not, but scrub the potatoes regardless. This recipe looks complicated (and maybe it is), but it will be worth it in the end.

BROWN SAUCE (GRAVY):

2 Tbsp (30 mL) **vegetable oil**

½ cup (120 mL) chopped **carrot**

½ cup (120 mL) chopped **celery**

½ cup (120 mL) chopped **onion**

1 tsp (5 mL) chopped **garlic**

2 Tbsp (30 mL) all-purpose **flour**

1 tsp (5 mL) **tomato paste**

4 cups (1 L) **Brown Stock** (see recipe, page 40) or store-bought unsalted beef stock

10 crushed black **peppercorns**

1 dried **bay leaf**

½ tsp (2.5 mL) dried **rosemary**

½ tsp (2.5 mL) dried **thyme**

salt and pepper to taste

FRIES:

2½ lb (1 kg) Russet **potatoes**, scrubbed

8 cups (2 L) vegetable **oil**

¼ tsp (1 mL) kosher **salt** (or sea salt)

¼ tsp (1 mL) ground **black pepper**

TOPPINGS:

2 Tbsp (30 mL) **butter**

1 can (14 oz/400 g) **hominy**, drained, rinsed and dried

2 tsp (10 mL) **cayenne pepper**

⅔ cup (160 mL) **cheese curds** (at room temperature)

1 Tbsp (15 mL) chopped **parsley**

01 To make the sauce, heat the oil over medium heat in a saucepan, add the carrot, celery, onion and garlic, and brown for two minutes.

02 Add flour and create what we chefs like to call an "aromatic roux." Keep stirring and allow the roux to become a nice dark brown. Remove pot from heat, stir in the tomato paste and let cool for two minutes.

03 Bring the stock to a boil either in a microwave or on the stovetop.

04 Return the sauce mixture to the stove, add 1 cup (250 mL) of the stock and quickly whisk to remove lumps. Slowly whisk in a second cup (250 mL) of stock. Bring the mixture back to a simmer and add the remaining stock. Simmer for five minutes and add the peppercorns, bay leaf, rosemary and thyme. Continue to simmer for 30 minutes and remove any impurities (scum).

05 Strain brown sauce into a clean saucepan and heat to a simmer. Taste, and add salt and pepper if needed; set sauce aside, but keep warm.

06 For the fries, cut the potatoes into pieces about ½ inch (1.5 cm) by ½ inch (1.5 cm) by 3 inches (7.5 cm) and rinse. Keep them in cold water if you are not ready to continue.

07 Drain the potatoes in a colander, and then thoroughly pat them dry on a baking sheet using paper towel.

Tip

To make great french fries, first you need to blanch the potatoes at a lower temperature (325F/160C) and allow them to drain properly and cool down slightly on a rack or paper towel, and then you need to finish cooking them at a higher temperature (375F/190C) to crisp them up and get a great colour.

---

08 Heat the oil in a deep fryer to 325F (160C). Blanch 1 cup (250 mL) of the potatoes in the oil for two to three minutes. Use a slotted spoon to gently move them around in the oil. Drain them on fresh paper towel before continuing with another batch.

09 When all the potatoes have been blanched, turn up the heat to 375F (190C) and return the potatoes to the oil, cooking them in batches for one to two minutes each. Drain fries.

10 To prepare the toppings, melt butter in a sauté pan over medium heat. Add half the hominy corn and half the cayenne, and cook, tossing gently, for about two minutes. Once the corn has a bit of colour, remove it from the pan and set it aside. Cook the rest of the corn with the rest of the cayenne.

11 For each serving, place fries in the bottom of a bowl and sprinkle with salt and pepper. Top fries with a quarter of each of the Brown Sauce, hominy and cheese curds. Garnish each serving with a sprinkle of parsley.

NOTE: The Three Sisters Relish should be made several days in advance.

Duck Breast Sandwich with Caramelized Onions and Three Sisters Relish

MAKES 4 SANDWICHES

First Nations and Native Americans traditionally roasted whole birds over an open fire. Swampy Cree still cook geese this way, spinning the birds from a rope tied to the centre of their tent. Duck hunting is also a popular pastime among Indigenous hunters in Canada—particularly those living in the north where store-bought foods are very limited and very expensive.

The delicious Muscovy duck is nearly as large as a goose and has been domesticated in South and Central America since the time of the Incan empire, but in Canada and the United States hunters commonly catch the much smaller wild mallard, which has a lean, dark meat. Most domesticated ducks sold in grocery stores are Pekin ducks and are bigger than mallards but smaller than Muscovies. You have lots of duck choices. Regardless, duck breast is best enjoyed medium rare (155F/68C), but for food safety reasons Health Canada says it should be cooked until well done (165F/75C), especially if wild duck is used.

2 boneless **duck breasts** (8 oz/225 g each), skin on

2 tsp (10 mL) **orange zest**

¼ tsp (1 mL) kosher **salt** (or sea salt)

¼ tsp (1 mL) ground **black pepper**

4 Tbsp (60 mL) pure **olive oil**, divided

2 Tbsp (30 mL) **butter**

1 tsp (5 mL) chopped fresh **chervil** (or tarragon)

1 tsp (5 mL) chopped **chives**

1 cup (250 mL) sliced **onion**

2 tsp (10 mL) sliced **garlic**

8 slices sandwich **bread** (see Gluten-Free Potato and Corn Bread recipe, page 243)

01 Using a sharp knife, score the skin of the duck breasts by making a couple of incisions about ½ inch (1.5 cm) deep in a cross pattern, but not so deep as to actually cut the flesh.

02 In a nonreactive dish (glass, ceramic or stainless steel), marinate the duck breasts with the orange zest, salt, pepper and half the oil for 30 minutes to one hour in the fridge. Set aside.

03 In a small bowl, combine the butter with the chervil and chives. Set aside.

04 Preheat the oven to 400F (205C).

05 In a small saucepan, heat the remaining olive oil, and cook the onion and garlic over low heat until caramelized (golden brown), stirring frequently. This should take about 8 to 10 minutes. Set aside.

06 Place the duck breasts in a cold cast iron frying pan, skin side down. Turn heat to medium and brown the meat, without turning it, for about three minutes. Increase the heat to medium-high and continue cooking the meat, without turning it, for another three minutes. Turn the breasts over (skin side up), transfer the pan to the oven and bake for 10 to 12 minutes.

07 Remove the breasts from the pan and set aside on a cutting board, loosely covered with foil to keep them warm.

08 Drain off excess oil and heat cast iron frying pan on stovetop. Lightly toast the bread slices in the hot pan until brown. Brush toast with butter mixture.

09 Slice the duck meat diagonally, place on the bread slices and top with caramelized garlic and onion, and Three Sisters Relish or a condiment of your choice.

Three Sisters Relish

MAKES 3½ CUPS (830 ML)

The Haudenosaunee (Iroquois, or Six Nations) traditionally cultivated corn, beans and squash together, which came to be known as the legendary "three sisters," their staple foods. Corn stalks provide a natural pole for the bean vines to climb. Beans fertilize and strengthen the corn to withstand winds, and the squash (zucchini) acted as a mulch to keep weeds at bay and retain soil moisture. To this day, gardeners find this combination of plants to be practical and sustainable.

1 cob **corn** (with husk)

1 cup (250 mL) diced yellow **onion**

1 cup (250 mL) diced **zucchini**

⅓ cup (80 mL) diced **red pepper**

¼ cup (60 mL) diced **green pepper**

1½ Tbsp (22 mL) kosher **salt**

1 cup (250 mL) canned **black beans**, drained and rinsed

1¼ cups (300 mL) **sugar**

1¼ cups (300 mL) **white vinegar**

½ tsp (2.5 mL) ground **nutmeg**

½ tsp (2.5 mL) ground **turmeric**

1 Tbsp (15 mL) freshly grated **horseradish** (or 2 Tbsp/30 mL prepared horseradish)

1½ tsp (7.5 mL) small-diced **jalapeno pepper** (with seeds)

01 Heat up barbecue to high to get it nice and hot, and then turn it down to medium-high (325F/160C). Barbecue the corncob in its husk for 15 minutes. Let cool. Remove husk and corn silk. Slice corn off cob with a sharp knife.

02 Combine corn, onion, zucchini, peppers and salt in a mixing bowl, stirring well. Cover and let stand for two hours. Strain mixture, rinse and let drain.

03 In a stockpot, combine zucchini mixture with beans, sugar, vinegar, nutmeg, turmeric, horseradish and jalapeno. Bring to a simmer and cook for 30 to 40 minutes, stirring occasionally, but do not let all the liquid evaporate.

04 Serve as is and store excess in fridge. Use within five days.

Sweet Potato Hummus and Herring Roe on Hot Pepper Fry Bread

MAKES 12 SERVINGS

Hummus is a Middle Eastern snack food normally made out of ground chickpeas combined with tahini (an oily paste made out of ground sesame seeds), garlic and olive oil, and topped with toasted nuts. It's served as a spread for pita bread. In my take on hummus, I blend sweet potato, spread it on a deep-fried version of bannock that is called fry bread, and top it with herring roe, but you can use any type of bannock or bread (see Chapter 9) and caviar.

Herring roe was a traditional favourite of Indigenous communities on the east and west coasts. On the Pacific coast, Indigenous people gathered it using hemlock branches and kelp for trading and serving at potlaches. Herring roe was traditionally eaten fresh or air dried, or rehydrated when needed later by steaming. The Heiltsuk are still in the herring business today. Nowadays you can buy roe frozen, fresh (if you are lucky) or canned, which is what I use in this recipe.

2¼ lb (1 kg) **sweet potatoes** (about 3 medium-sized)

½ tsp (2.5 mL) table **salt** plus a pinch for boiling

3 Tbsp (45 mL) extra-virgin **olive oil**

3 Tbsp (45 mL) **tahini**

1 Tbsp (15 mL) minced **garlic**

1 tsp (5 mL) **lemon juice**

¼ tsp (1 mL) **cayenne pepper**

¼ tsp (1 mL) ground **black pepper**

6 pieces **Hot Pepper Fry Bread** (see recipe, page 236) (or crusty bread)

1 cup (250 mL) **sprouts** (beet, onion or sunflower)

2 oz (60 g) hard **herring roe**

01 Peel sweet potatoes and boil in cold water with a pinch of salt.

02 Drain and quickly mash potatoes, and stir in oil, tahini, garlic, lemon juice, cayenne, black pepper and ½ tsp (2.5 mL) salt.

03 Transfer mixture to a blender and process until smooth.

04 Chill before serving. (Store the excess in the fridge for up to a week.)

05 Cut the fry bread pieces in half, open face sandwich style. Spread 1 tablespoon (15 mL) of the hummus on top of each piece.

06 Sprinkle some sprouts on top of each serving, top with ¼ teaspoon (1 mL) of the herring roe and serve.

NOTE: This recipe calls for hard herring roe, which is the tiny eggs (caviar) that come from females rather than the soft herring roe, or "milt," which comes from the males and looks like large shucked oysters.

White Salmon Pizza

MAKES TWO 10 INCH (25 CM) PIZZAS

For those who like a classic, thin-crust white cheese pizza, here it is, but with salmon! White cheese pizzas are generally pretty basic, as the main topping is cheese, hence the name. Most salmon pizzas use smoked salmon; if that's what you want to try, see the Cold-Smoked Juniper Salmon recipe (page 48) to make it yourself, but remove the skin. Personally, I prefer the less salty fresh salmon in this recipe.

PIZZA DOUGH:

2¼ tsp (11 mL) active **dry yeast**

1 tsp (5 mL) **sugar**

¾ cup (180 mL) warm **water** (105–110F/41–43C)

2 cups (475 mL) all-purpose **flour**,
  plus ¼ cup (60 mL) more for dusting

¾ tsp (3 mL) table **salt**

3 Tbsp (45 mL) pure **olive oil**, plus 2 Tbsp (30 mL)
  more for greasing bowl and pans

TOPPINGS:

4 Tbsp (60 mL) pure **olive oil**

2 tsp (10 mL) minced **garlic**

5 oz (140 g) fresh **salmon**, boned, skinned
  and cut into slivers

¼ tsp (1 mL) kosher **salt** (or sea salt)

½ tsp (2.5 mL) ground **white pepper**

4 cups (1 L) shredded **mozzarella** cheese

2 Tbsp (30 mL) minced fresh **basil** (optional)

1 Tbsp (15 mL) minced fresh **parsley** (optional)

01 To make the dough, whisk yeast, sugar and warm water together in a small bowl and let rest for 5 to 10 minutes to allow the yeast to work. Before using the yeast mixture, wait until you see it get foamy. (If it doesn't foam up, start over with a fresh package of yeast.)

02 In a large mixing bowl combine 2 cups (475 mL) flour and the table salt. Add the yeast mixture and mix well using your hands. Add 3 tablespoons (45 mL) olive oil and mix.

03 Lightly dust your work surface with flour and knead the dough for five minutes. Alternatively, use the dough hook on your stand mixer and process according to the appliance instructions. The dough should lose its stickiness and become elastic.

04 Grease a clean bowl with oil and put the dough in it, sliding it around so that it gets coated with oil on all sides. Cover with a damp dish towel and let rest for one hour someplace in your kitchen that is warm and draught free. The dough should double in size.

05 Preheat oven to 450F (230C).

06 Punch down the dough and divide in half to form two balls. On a lightly floured surface, stretch out each piece of dough (starting from the centre) to ⅛ inch (0.5 cm) thickness. I can't help but sing a little Italian—*Figaro!*—like Bugs Bunny when I then fling the dough up in the air to stretch it.

07 Lightly oil your pizza pans. Place dough on pans—either two 10 inch (25 cm) round pans or two 10 by 13 inch (25 × 33 cm) rectangular pans—and brush with olive oil. Sprinkle on minced garlic.

08 Season salmon with kosher salt and pepper.

09 Sprinkle salmon over the pizzas, stopping about 1 inch (2.5 cm) from the edge. Sprinkle cheese all over the pizzas.

10 If using the optional basil and parsley, combine them in a small bowl and sprinkle them over the cheese.

11 Bake for 15 to 17 minutes or until cheese is bubbling and the crust is brown.

NOTE: If making the dough is too time consuming, use store-bought pizza dough, but be sure to roll it out to ½ inch (0.5 cm) thickness; any thicker and it will take too long to bake.

TIPS for using other types of smokers can be found on pages 28–29.

Alderwood Smoked Nuts

MAKES 3 CUPS (710 ML)

Indigenous peoples in the central and eastern United States and the river valleys of Mexico highly valued wild pecan trees in autumn; these people are known to have cultivated indigenous pecan trees as early as the 1500s. Roasted pecans were treasured as snacks on long journeys. The word "pecan" comes from an Algonquin word for "nuts requiring a stone to crack." Some Indigenous nations made nut milk out of shagbark hickory nuts (related to pecans) that was called *powcohicora* and used in making soup; this is how hickory got its name.

To smoke nuts, you need to spread them out on some sort of screen and let the smoke get to them on all sides without letting the nuts fall through the cracks. Whoa, is this an IQ test? I use a 12 inch (30 cm) grease splatter guard (with the plastic handle cut off) for this purpose. I found that tip online and think it's pretty cool for this sort of application. I've read that some people have been successful using disposable aluminum foil pans (presumably the type that has little holes would be best). If you give it some thought, you might come up with an even better device.

As for the nuts, be sure to buy them raw, unroasted and unsalted. As strong as the smoky flavour is when the nuts are done, the taste will tone down after you let them cool overnight, so don't be disappointed if you find the taste too strong at first. Another factor in the smokiness is the venting of your smoker. I tried this recipe in an electric smoker using hickorywood and closed vents but found the flavour too strong. I might try it again some time with the vents open a bit but for now am happy to use alderwood instead.

3 Tbsp (45 mL) **butter**
3 Tbsp (45 mL) **brown sugar**
1 tsp (5 mL) ground **cinnamon**
1 tsp (5 mL) kosher **salt** (or sea salt)
½ tsp (2.5 mL) ground **black pepper**
½ tsp (2.5 mL) ground **allspice**
3 cups (710 mL) shelled **pecan** halves
    (or cashews or whole almonds)
Alderwood biscuits

01 Heat clean smoker to 200F (95C). Activate the biscuits.

02 In a small saucepan, melt the butter. Add the sugar, cinnamon, salt, pepper and allspice, and stir to mix evenly. Add the nuts and stir again until they are fully coated.

03 Drain nuts in a sieve while you wait for the smoker to reach temperature; this will allow excess melted butter to drain so that it doesn't drip through your screen.

04 Spread the nuts on the screen and place inside the smoker. Close the door and let the nuts smoke for 30 to 45 minutes, and taste test them after 20 minutes to ensure that the smoke is completely penetrating the nuts. These nuts will keep for up to three weeks, but if storing them that long, keep them in the fridge so that the butter doesn't go rancid. (They get eaten long before that in our house.)

Buffalo Pemmican

MAKES 10 TO 12 SERVINGS

One of the original Canadian snacks! "Pemmican" comes from the Cree language and is a high protein snack perfect for travelling. Made from sundried, lean meat mixed with berries and animal fat, the dried mixture stored well and provided nourishment for people on the go. On the plains, it was made with buffalo meat for I don't know how many centuries. Unlike the beef jerky sold in gas stations from coast to coast today, traditionally prepared pemmican isn't spicy and it's certainly not available commercially.

Marlene's grandmother made pemmican from time to time when she was in the mood. She pounded chokecherries, seeds and all, with a rock until they broke down into little pieces small enough to swallow. Wild chokecherries were still abundant in Saskatchewan in the 1920s—buffalo, not so much. Then she added strips of thinly sliced dried (raw) beef and continued pounding until the meat broke apart into slivers. She rendered beef suet (the hard, raw fat found around the loins and kidneys) by melting it and simmering it until it liquefied and could be strained and cooled, creating tallow. (She left the crunchy "cracklings" in the pan for Marge and the rest of the kids to chew on.) Then she poured the liquid tallow over the mixture and dried it by the handful on baking trays, like cookies, in the sun on their sod shanty roof, for three or four days before storing it in tins for well over a year or more. Marge's brother, Lorne Wells, was happy to get a package of the stuff mailed to him during World War II when he was fighting in France.

To make pemmican these days, we have dehydrators, ovens and blenders and you can buy beef tallow that you just have to heat before using (and which some butchers provide free). In this recipe, I explain the process of rendering suet to create tallow. Chokecherries are hard to come by, so I use saskatoon berries or blueberries. Since the meat will not be cooked, Health Canada suggests that you freeze your game for at least 30 days at -5F (-20C) before consuming it.

2 cups (475 mL) fresh or frozen saskatoon berries
1½ lb (680 g) previously frozen buffalo round steak
6 oz (170 g) calf suet
¼ cup (60 mL) chopped nuts (optional)
2 Tbsp (30 mL) honey (optional)

01 Wash and dry the berries if fresh, or thaw out and drain if frozen.

02 Slice meat into thin strips about 4 inches (10 cm) long, ½ inch (1.5 cm) wide and no thicker than ¼ inch (1 cm). Spread strips out on a baking sheet and bake in the oven for 10 to 12 hours at 180F (80C), along with the berries (on a separate tray). Alternatively, dry the meat and berries in a dehydrator according to appliance instructions. The meat will be done when it breaks apart easily in your hands.

03 Pulverize the dried meat and berries together in a blender until the mixture gets crumbly and powdery.

04 To render the suet, cook it very slowly in a cast iron frying pan over low heat, stirring occasionally, until the suet liquefies. Keep cooking it until it stops bubbling. Strain the liquid well through either cheesecloth or paper towel layered over a strainer into a container with a spout, leaving the brown bits behind.

05 Gradually pour the warm tallow into the meat and berry mixture and mix it manually until it holds together.

06 Taste the pemmican and adjust the flavour with nuts and honey if using. Press the entire mixture into a loaf pan, chill for several hours and slice before serving, or roll the mixture into balls a little larger than meatballs, wrap them individually in wax paper and store in a tin. I prefer to eat pemmican that's been chilled for a week.

CHAPTER 4

Tastes of Home:
Soups, Stews and Chili

There isn't a culture on the planet that hasn't got its own soup history. For First Nations in Canada's coastal regions, soups were traditionally made with clams, crab, salmon, halibut and flounder and broths were made from salty seaweed. In the Pacific Northwest, some First Nations women wove baskets so tightly they could hold water. By adding heated rocks, they could make soup out of tough vegetables and roots. In the same way, the Mi'kmaq on the east coast hollowed out tree stumps and made soup in them using seawater and hot rocks. Buffalo ribs and joints made for marrow-rich soups on the plains, and in the woodlands, Indigenous people used ground nuts to thicken game and waterfowl soups. Haudenosaunee along the St. Lawrence River made soup from the corn they grew and in the Far North, broths were traditionally made using seal or walrus, seaweed, and muskox bones. My mother's people used ingredients that had been harvested and dried out by sun and wind—fish and roots, for example. Soup has got to be *the* most practical way of using up odd bits of food to make a meal.

Chefs classify soups on the basis of how they are made: clear or thickened. Two things a broth, consommé, bisque, chowder, purée and chowder have in common is that they all involve simmering meat, fish and/or vegetables in liquid, and they are eaten with a spoon! Stews, on the other hand, are made by searing small pieces of meat (tough cuts) or vegetables before completely covering them in liquid and simmering them—and serving them in the sauce or gravy made of the cooking liquid. The Inca, Aztec and Maya were accustomed to combining meat, beans, peppers and herbs in their cooking, which suggests where chili originated, but there are some paranormal Spanish legends associated with its origin, too, so nobody really knows for sure. Don't believe me? Check it out.

Tip
Use a stockpot for making stocks and soups, and a Dutch oven for making stews and chili since the heavy bottom of a Dutch oven conducts the heat more evenly and prevents burning.

Cream of Celery Soup with Red Pepper Purée

MAKES 5 SERVINGS

NOTE: Prepare the Red Pepper Purée before making the soup.

Marge, my mother-in-law, gives this soup two thumbs up, which is saying something! This creamy soup has the layered flavours of celery, celery seeds and celeriac (the strange-looking root of a plant that is related to celery and distantly related to wild celery). Celeriac is best if firm and heavy. Avoid buying very large ones that will probably be too soft to use. If you can't find celeriac for this recipe, use potatoes instead.

Make this when the wind is howling outside and the days are growing shorter. Enjoy this with Salmon Half-Moons (see recipe, page 232).

2 tsp (10 mL) pure **olive oil**
2 cups (475 mL) diced **celery**
2 cups (475 mL) diced peeled **celeriac**
1 cup (250 mL) diced **onion**
1 Tbsp (15 mL) chopped **garlic**
¼ tsp (1 mL) **celery seeds**
6 cups (1.4 L) **White Stock** (see recipe, page 39),
    or store-bought unsalted chicken stock
2 dried **bay leaves**
½ tsp (2.5 mL) kosher **salt** (or sea salt), divided
¼ tsp (1 mL) ground **white pepper**, divided
½ cup (120 mL) 10 per cent **cream**

01 Heat oil in a stockpot over medium-low heat and sauté celery, celeriac and onion for 10 minutes. Add garlic and celery seeds, and cook, stirring, for about one minute.

02 Heat the stock in the microwave or on the stovetop almost to the boiling point. Add stock to the stockpot and turn up heat to medium-high; bring mixture to a boil.

03 Add the bay leaves and half the salt and pepper. Then reduce heat to medium-low and simmer, partially covered, until celery and celeriac are soft (about 30 minutes).

04 Remove bay leaves and blend soup in a blender or with a hand blender until smooth.

05 Just before serving, stir in cream, and the remaining salt and pepper. Heat through, but do not let the soup come to a boil (or the cream will curdle).

06 Strain the soup through a sieve and place 1 teaspoon (5 mL) Red Pepper Purée on each serving.

Red Pepper Purée

MAKES 1 CUP (250 ML)

For those of you who are already experienced at roasting peppers, this is straightforward stuff. But for cooks who have never tried it, here goes! You can roast peppers over the barbecue, over a gas burner flame or in the oven. You can use this purée on top of soups, sandwiches, red meat or even fish. Even though roasted bell peppers are not spicy whatsoever, they add a surprising amount of flavour to a dish.

2 small **red bell peppers** (or 1 large)
1 Tbsp (15 mL) pure **olive oil** for roasting pepper (optional)
1 tsp (5 mL) red wine **vinegar**
1 tsp (5 mL) **sugar**
1 tsp (5 mL) kosher **salt** (or sea salt)
1 tsp (5 mL) ground **black pepper**
1 tsp (5 mL) pure **olive oil**

01 Wash and dry the peppers.

02 Grill the peppers either directly on the burner of a gas stove burner or on the grill of a barbecue; either way you can do this over high heat in less than 10 minutes, but keep an eye on the peppers. Turn them frequently and let them blacken on all sides. Do not be startled by loud popping noises coming from the peppers. Alternatively, if you prefer to roast the peppers in the oven, oil them with 1 tablespoon (15 mL) olive oil,

place them on a baking sheet and roast at 425F (220C) for about 20 to 30 minutes.

03 Once peppers are blackened, place them on a plate for a minute to cool. Remove the skins from the peppers (discard).

04 Cut the peppers in half, lengthwise, and remove all the seeds, white ribs and any stems that may be left on.

05 Process peppers in a food processor with the vinegar, sugar, salt, pepper and olive oil until the mixture reaches a very smooth consistency. Stop the processor and scrape down the sides a few times with a spatula to get the purée to an even consistency.

06 Garnish soup with this purée or spread a little on bread for sandwiches or spoon on top of your favorite fish dish. Leftover purée can be stored for up to four or five days in the refrigerator.

Tip
To easily remove the skin from a roasted pepper, (1) place the pepper in a bowl and cover it with food wrap, or (2) put the pepper into a brown paper bag and tie it closed, or (3) wrap the pepper up in paper towel. Let the pepper rest to steam for 10 minutes and then just rub the roasted skin off.

Hominy Corn and Kidney Bean Soup

MAKES 4 SERVINGS

Hominy is the key ingredient in this soup. But whether you use dry or canned hominy, the soup you end up with will be nothing like the more common creamy yellow corn and potato chowder that you might be imagining. Prized among the Haudenosaunee, this soup is prominent at First Nations functions across the Americas—although *pozole*, the southern version of corn soup, is spicier.

Corn soup is typically flavoured with pork (salt pork being the favourite), but in this recipe I use a smoked ham hock instead, because I like the smoky flavour and the added body the bone gives to the soup. Our niece Teresa Pitawanakwat has only one thing to say about this soup: OMG!

SPICE BAG

(see directions in Spice Bag recipe, page 34):

1 dried **bay leaf**

¼ tsp (1 mL) crushed black **peppercorns**

1 sprig fresh **thyme**

1 sprig fresh **oregano**

SOUP:

1 Tbsp (15 mL) pure **olive oil**

1 small smoked **ham hock**

2 cups (475 mL) diced **onion**

2 tsp (10 mL) chopped **garlic**

8 cups (2 L) **White Stock** (see recipe, page 39), or store-bought unsalted chicken stock

1 can (18 oz/510 g) **kidney beans**, drained and rinsed

½ tsp (2.5 mL) kosher **salt** (or sea salt)

1 can (15 oz/425 g) **hominy**, drained and rinsed

01 Prepare the spice bag and set aside.

02 Heat oil in a stockpot on medium-high.

03 Remove the outer rind from the smoked ham hock and cook both in the pot for about five minutes to release both fat and flavour.

04 Remove the rind from the pot and discard, add the onion and cook in the pot for two to three minutes, stirring frequently.

05 Add the garlic and cook for one minute.

06 Heat the stock in a microwave or on the stovetop almost to the boiling point. Pour stock into the stockpot. Bring to a simmer. Remove any impurities that rise to the surface (scum).

07 Add the spice bag, kidney beans and salt, and simmer for 30 to 35 minutes on low heat. Periodically, remove any scum that floats to the top.

08 Remove the ham hock to a cutting board and let cool slightly. Remove all of the meat from the ham hock; dice it and return it to the soup. Discard the bone.

09 Add the hominy and bring soup to a simmer. Simmer for five minutes.

10 Remove the spice bag before serving.

Métis Boulettes

MAKES 6 SERVINGS

Marlene's grandparents used to enjoy this soup on New Year's Day back in the 1930s and '40s, when it was customary for Métis to hold open houses so that friends and relatives could just drop in to wish a happy new year. In the Métis tradition, the young would bend down on one knee before their male elders, bow their heads and ask for a blessing. Marlene's grandpa went to get his father's blessing on New Year's Day each year, even as an adult, but that Métis tradition is long gone now.

The Métis living on the outskirts of Saskatoon didn't often have much food in those days, so their soups were very simple, even on special occasions. They used whatever meat they could get, and beef was the most common after the buffalo were nearly wiped out. Marlene's grandmother kept this traditional Métis soup hot in a *chodro* (cauldron) that was set inside the back burner (hole) in the top of her black woodstove. The word *boulettes* is French and refers to the meatballs in the soup. To this day my mother-in-law, Marge, doesn't know which words are French and which are Cree when she says things in the Michif language of her childhood.

Although Métis normally used water to make this soup, you could definitely use Brown Stock instead (see recipe, page 40), and I recommend some rosemary for the meatballs and a bay leaf for the broth. Our niece Jenna Johnson made this and her 18-month-old baby got both hands in the bowl to enjoy every last drop!

1 lb (500 g) lean ground **beef**

½ cup (120 mL) small-diced **onion**

½ tsp (2.5 mL) ground **black pepper**

1½ tsp (7.5 mL) kosher **salt**, divided

1 tsp (5 mL) minced fresh **rosemary** (optional)

12 cups (2.8 L) **water**, divided (or combination of water and **Brown Stock**; see recipe, page 40)

¼ cup (60 mL) all-purpose **flour**

2 cups (475 mL) chopped peeled **potatoes**

1 dried **bay leaf** (optional)

Salt and pepper for seasoning at end

01 Mix beef, onion, pepper, half the salt and the optional rosemary (if using) in a bowl. Add up to ¼ cup (60 mL) water—just enough to get the meat to hold together—and mix well.

02 Divide mixture into thirds, then divide each third in two, and then divide those in two to get 12 evenly sized meatballs.

03 Boil 9 cups (2.1 L) of the water in a stockpot.

04 Dust meatballs in flour, shaking off excess. Drop them into the pot of hot water. Simmer for 40 minutes over medium-low heat with a lid partially on.

05 Add potatoes, the rest of the salt and water and the bay leaf (if using). Raise the temperature so that the soup returns to the boiling point, and then lower heat again and simmer the potatoes for 20 minutes or until they are soft.

06 Salt and pepper the soup to taste. Remove the bay leaf before serving.

Hot-Smoked Winnipeg Goldeye Chowder

MAKES 6 TO 8 SERVINGS

If you are fortunate to have access to fresh whole Winnipeg goldeye fish and are eager to try hot-smoking it, follow the smoking instructions in the Hot-Smoked Salmon recipe (page 45) but adjusting to use half the amount of brine. For this chowder, you could also use store-bought hot-smoked trout or smoked salmon, especially since removing all the pin bones from Winnipeg goldeye is a pain in the you-know-what (although it's worth the effort). The beautiful smoked flavour is fabulous. I have to admit, however, that now that I am 50-plus and dependent on glasses, removing the transparent, hair-thin bones isn't easy. I usually call in for backup ("Oh, sweetheart, where are you?"), LOL.

Sea asparagus, the optional garnish in this recipe, is also known as sea pickle, marsh samphire or sea green bean.

SPICE BAG

(see directions in Spice Bag recipe, page 34):
12 crushed black **peppercorns**
2 dried **bay leaves**
1 tsp (5 mL) dried **rosemary**
1 tsp (5 mL) dried **thyme**

CHOWDER:

2 whole (about 7 oz/200 g each) hot-smoked
   Winnipeg goldeye fish
8 cups (2 L) **Fish Stock** (see recipe, page 41)
   or store-bought unsalted fish stock
8 oz (225 g) diced **bacon**
2 cups (475 mL) diced **onion**
1 cup (250 mL) diced **celery**
2 tsp (10 mL) finely chopped **garlic**
2 cups (475 mL) diced **potato**
1 tsp (5 mL) kosher **salt** (or sea salt)
1 cob roasted **corn** (see directions in Three Sisters Relish
   recipe, page 84), or drained canned niblet corn
1 tsp (5 mL) **cornstarch**

2 Tbsp (30 mL) **water**
1 cup (250 mL) 18 per cent **cream**

GARNISH:

Chopped **fresh herbs** or **sea asparagus** (optional)

01 Prepare the spice bag and set aside.

02 Remove skin and bones from fish and reserve. The bones are hard to find, so do this job by a sunny window. Flake the flesh into a small bowl and set aside.

03 Heat stock in a stockpot almost to the boiling point. Add the fish bones, skin, fish head, tail and trimmings, and heat to the boiling point. Lower heat and simmer for 15 minutes. Strain the stock using a fine sieve or strainer into a pitcher.

04 Clean the pot and return to heat. Add the bacon and sauté for five to seven minutes. Add onion and celery, and cook for five more minutes, stirring occasionally. Add the garlic and cook for one minute.

05 Add potato and strained stock, and bring to a simmer. Add the spice bag and salt, and simmer for 20 minutes.

06 Add the corn and simmer for another five minutes. Then add the deboned smoked fish flesh.

07 To thicken the chowder, mix the cornstarch and water thoroughly in a small bowl and pour it into the pot. Bring the chowder back to a simmer and whisk. Add the cream and simmer on medium heat for two minutes.

08 Remove spice bag before serving the chowder with sea asparagus or a garnish of your choice.

Savory-Laced Caribou Stew

MAKES 4 SERVINGS

This recipe will work very well with any kind of large game. Moose, deer, caribou or buffalo, and even lamb, goat or beef—they will all taste great cooked this way. Stew is the most practical use of tougher cuts of meat that come from the shoulder of the animal. See the "Recommended Venison Cooking Methods" illustration in Chapter 5 (page 119). Save your tender cuts for recipes that showcase their finer qualities.

The Métis Bannock: Blueberry Variation (see recipe, page 235) is great for sopping up the juices in this stew.

SPICE BAG

(see directions in Spice Bag recipe, page 34):

1 dried or 2 fresh **bay leaves**

Sprig fresh summer **savory** (or 1 tsp/5 mL dried)

STEW:

1¼ lb (570 g) diced **caribou chuck**

1 Tbsp (15 mL) chopped fresh **thyme**

1½ tsp (7.5 mL) finely crushed mixed **peppercorns**

3 Tbsp (45 mL) pure **olive oil**, divided

1 cup (250 mL) large-diced **onion**

1 cup (250 mL) large-diced **carrot**

2 tsp (10 mL) sliced **garlic**

8 cups (2 L) **Brown Stock** (see recipe, page 40), or store-bought unsalted beef stock

⅔ cup (160 mL) large-diced peeled **white turnip** (or rutabaga)

½ cup (120 mL) large-diced **celery**

1 tsp (5 mL) kosher **salt** (or sea salt)

BEURRE MANIÉ:

1 Tbsp (15 mL) all-purpose **flour**

1 Tbsp (15 mL) soft **butter**

01 Prepare the spice bag and set aside.

02 Season the meat with thyme and pepper and chill in the fridge for one hour.

03 Remove the meat from the fridge and let it reach room temperature. Heat a Dutch oven over very low heat for 10 minutes, and then increase the heat to medium-high before adding 1 tablespoon (15 mL) of the oil. Brown half of the meat on all sides. Remove meat from the pot and set aside. Add another tablespoon (15 mL) oil and brown the rest of the meat. Set aside.

04 Add onion, carrot and garlic to the pot along with remaining oil, and cook for two minutes on medium-high heat.

05 Heat the stock in a microwave or on the stovetop almost to the boiling point.

06 To deglaze the Dutch oven, add around a third of the stock (about 2½ cups/600 mL) and then scrape off all the brown bits from the bottom of the pot. Bring stock to a simmer.

07 Add another third of the stock along with the turnip, celery and salt.

08 Add the spice bag to the pot and let the mixture cook over low heat for one hour, covered.

09 Check the stew after one hour, and remove any floating impurities (scum) with a spoon. Add the remainder of the stock. If the meat is not fork tender at this point, let it stew for up to one more hour, checking every 15 minutes for doneness.

10 To thicken the stew, make a beurre manié (kneaded butter) by mixing flour and butter together in a small bowl and kneading it with your fingers. Whisk a bit of the hot liquid from the stew into the flour mixture to create a slurry. Mix well. Then pour the mixture back into the stew, stir, and let cook for five more minutes.

11 Remove the spice bag before serving.

Applewood Hot-Smoked Turkey Chili

MAKES 6 SERVINGS

Regardless of what type of smoker you use, smoking foods in the summer is a lot easier than in the winter; in summer I can enjoy the sun, cold drinks and chatting with neighbours who've appeared from behind bushes, wondering what I am up to and where that amazing smell is coming from. But when the temperature drops, I make chili. My hands, face and feet got really cold when I made this last time in the dead of winter, and I do mean dead. It was -5F (-20C)! The meat turned out perfectly, but I did have to rig up some plastic sheeting all around our gazebo to break the wind so I could check on the smoker inside it from time to time more comfortably. Did I mention that it was late at night, and a weeknight, and that the neighbours wonder a lot about what goes on at our house? I used an electric smoker, but to help it maintain an even temperature, I even wrapped the door with foil to seal in the heat. Chapter 2 contains some tips on how to use a water smoker, charcoal barbecue or propane gas grill instead (see pages 28–29).

Smoked poultry is just as flavourful as smoked fish and smoked meat, although maybe not so common. If you prefer, you could substitute ground pork or game bird for the turkey so that you don't have to bother chopping it finely. Like all braised entrées, this chili will definitely taste better the day after you make it, so consider chilling it overnight before serving.

NOTE: If you prefer to stay inside and avoid all of the turkey-smoking fun, use store-bought smoked turkey; just remove the skin and bones and chop the meat finely before using.

SMOKED TURKEY:

2 lb (900 g) ground **turkey**

1 tsp (5 mL) **chili flakes**

1 tsp (5 mL) ground **sage**

1 tsp (5 mL) kosher **salt** (or sea salt)

½ tsp (2.5 mL) ground **black pepper**

½ tsp (2.5 mL) ground **allspice**

½ tsp (2.5 mL) dried **rosemary**

Applewood biscuits

CHILI SAUCE:

2 Tbsp (30 mL) pure **olive oil**

2 cups (475 mL) small-diced **onion**

1 cup (250 mL) small-diced **celery**

4 tsp (20 mL) minced **garlic**

1 cup (250 mL) quartered **mushrooms**

3 Tbsp (45 mL) **tomato paste**

2 Tbsp (30 mL) **chili powder**

1 Tbsp (15 mL) **brown sugar**

1 Tbsp (15 mL) **white wine vinegar**

1 can (14 oz/400 g) **pinto beans**, drained and rinsed

1 jar (28 fl oz/830 mL) **tomato sauce** (see sauce in Collard Green Moose Rolls recipe, page 124)

1¾ cups (415 mL) **water**

½ tsp (2.5 mL) kosher **salt** (or sea salt)

¼ tsp (1 mL) **cayenne pepper**

¼ tsp (1 mL) **black pepper**

OPTIONAL TOPPINGS:

½ cup (120 mL) plain **Greek yogurt**

¼ cup (60 mL) sliced **green onion**

01 Set clean smoker to 275F (135C). Activate the biscuits.

02 In a mixing bowl, combine the ground turkey with the chili flakes, sage, salt, pepper, allspice and rosemary. Mix well, spread on a tray and place inside the smoker.

03 Smoking will take between 12 and 15 minutes. Stir the meat once or twice during smoking. Alternatively, if you like a super smoky flavour, turn down the smoker to 225F (105C) and slowly smoke the meat for 25 to 30 minutes. Remove the turkey when done and set aside.

04 Start the chili sauce process by heating a Dutch oven on the stovetop over low heat for 10 minutes. Raise the heat to medium. Add the oil, onion, celery and garlic, and cook for four minutes or until soft.

05 Add the mushrooms and cook for two minutes more. Then add tomato paste and cook for one minute, watching to ensure that the paste does not burn.

06 Add the smoked turkey meat to the mixture and combine well.

07 Then add chili powder, brown sugar, vinegar, beans and tomato sauce. Rinse the jar of sauce with the water and add to the pot.

08 Add salt, cayenne pepper and black pepper, and bring mixture to a simmer, stirring constantly. Let cook over medium heat for one hour, covered.

09 Serve chili in a bowl with a dollop of yogurt and a sprinkle of green onion if using.

Mango and Raisin Curried Elk Stew

MAKES 4 SERVINGS

Large game and curry actually go very well together. I've curried all sorts of game, including camel for a New Year's Eve feast we had at home one year. (No, I am not kidding!) Ostrich, kangaroo, buffalo, pheasant and wild boar were also on the menu that night.

This recipe will work very well with any kind of large game, goat or beef. See the "Recommended Venison Cooking Methods" illustration in Chapter 5 (page 119). Enjoy this stew with Métis Bannock: Pine Nut and Savory Variation (see recipe, page 35).

SPICE BAG

(see directions in Spice Bag recipe, page 34):
6 whole **cloves**
2 dried or 4 fresh **bay leaves**
1 **cinnamon** stick
1 **lime leaf**
¼ tsp (1 mL) dried crushed **red pepper flakes**

STEW:
2 lb (900 g) large-diced **elk**
1 Tbsp (15 mL) kosher **salt** (or sea salt), divided
1½ tsp (7.5 mL) ground **black pepper**, divided
3 Tbsp (45 mL) pure **olive oil**, divided
2 cups (475 mL) large-diced **onion**
3 Tbsp (45 mL) **curry powder**
4 tsp (20 mL) chopped **garlic**
1 cup (250 mL) **apple juice**
1 cup (250 mL) 3.5 percent **milk**
1 can (28 fl oz/830 mL) diced **tomatoes** (with juice)
½ cup (120 mL) **raisins**
3 Tbsp (45 mL) chopped **mango**
3 tsp (15 mL) fresh **lemon juice**
2 tsp (10 mL) minced peeled fresh **ginger**
2–3 cups (475–710 mL) **Brown Stock** (see recipe, page 40), or store-bought unsalted beef stock

OPTIONAL TOPPINGS:
¼ cup (60 mL) diced **mango**
1 Tbsp (15 mL) chopped **chives**

01 Prepare the spice bag and set aside.

02 Season the elk with half the salt and pepper.

03 Heat a Dutch oven gradually over low heat for 10 minutes. Increase the temperature to medium-high. Add 1 tablespoon (15 mL) of the oil. Brown half of the meat on all sides. Remove meat from the pot and set aside. Add a second tablespoon (15 mL) of oil and brown the rest of the meat. Set aside.

04 Add the remaining oil and the onion to the pot, and cook for two minutes. Add the curry powder and garlic and continue to brown for two minutes, taking care not to burn the mixture.

05 Add the apple juice to deglaze the pot by swirling the juice around in the pot and scraping off any brown bits from the bottom of the pot.

06 Return the meat to the pot, add the milk and spice bag, and stir.

07 Bring stew to a boil and add the tomatoes (with juice), raisins, mango, lemon juice, ginger, and remaining salt and pepper.

08 Heat the stock on the stovetop or in the microwave almost to the boiling point. Add 2 cups (475 mL) of the stock to the stew. Lower the heat and simmer the stew for two hours, covered, stirring occasionally.

09 Check that the meat is fork tender; if it's not, add the rest of the stock and continue cooking for 10 to 15 more minutes.

10 Remove the spice bag before serving stew with mango and chives if using.

Lemony Rabbit Succotash

MAKES 4 SERVINGS

We lived on rabbits
for a winter or two
and got paid a dollar a day
for working in the sun.
The farmers called us half-breeds
'cause we spoke both French and Cree
we are Métis.
— From "The Métis Song," by Marlene Finn

Canada's original economy was based on hunting and trapping. If it wasn't for the furs and corn that the explorers found so valuable here in North America, they might have turned around and gone back home! Although European traders were after the furs to satisfy fashion demands overseas, First Nations hunted and trapped animals for food, clothing and shelter. The Métis people, the unique product of the partnerships that formed between the European explorers and the First Nations, made a living as the go-betweens, or trade interpreters. The lines above come from a song Marlene wrote about her poor grandparents who lived on the margins of society in southern Saskatchewan, where, to provide for their families, they relied on trapping and day labouring for farmers. We like singing this song when we have the family over to jam for a few hours.

Succotash contains lima beans and corn (the name comes from the Narragansett word *msiquatash*, meaning boiled corn kernels). Originally it was made by Indigenous peoples of the northeastern United States, but over the years has become better known as a dish from the southern United States. I like succotash with rabbit thrown in to make a simple family-sized meal without breaking the piggy bank. You could use chicken instead of rabbit, but if you do, use skinless chicken. Our nephew Dave Pitawanakwat thinks this dish is "to die for!" and is now showing a little more interest in learning how to trap.

MARINADE:

1 tsp (5 mL) kosher **salt** (or sea salt), divided
½ tsp (2.5 mL) ground **black pepper**, divided
½ tsp (2.5 mL) dried **thyme**
2 tsp (10 mL) minced **garlic**
3 Tbsp (45 mL) **lemon juice**
1 Tbsp (15 mL) **lemon zest**
¼ cup (60 mL) pure **olive oil**, divided

1 **rabbit** (2½ lb/1 kg)
½ lb (225 g) double smoked **bacon**, chopped
1 cup (250 mL) medium-diced **onion**
2 cups (475 mL) **White Stock** (see recipe, page 39),
    or store-bought unsalted chicken stock
2 cups (475 mL) canned diced **tomatoes**, with juice
1¼ cups (300 mL) canned **corn niblets**, drained
    (or frozen corn)
1 cup (250 mL) frozen **lima beans**
2 dried **bay leaves**

OPTIONAL GARNISH:
Chopped fresh **dill**

01 Chop the rabbit into eight pieces. If you use a cleaver, be careful of small bone fragments. I prefer to use a boning knife to disjoint rabbit for that very reason. Or ask your butcher to do it.

02 Combine half the salt and pepper with the thyme, garlic, lemon juice and zest, and a third of the oil, and rub the mixture all over the rabbit. Marinate in the fridge in a nonreactive dish (glass, ceramic or stainless steel) for a minimum of four hours (preferably overnight), covered.

03 Heat a Dutch oven over low heat for 10 minutes. Raise the temperature to medium heat. Add another third of the oil and heat. Brown the bacon in the oil and then place in a large bowl. Set aside.

04 Drain rabbit, reserving marinade. Brown rabbit in the Dutch oven on all sides, in two batches, using up the leftover marinade in the process to keep it from sticking. Remove rabbit from the pot and add to the bowl of bacon.

05 With the remaining oil, brown onion in the pan for three minutes.

06 Heat the stock in a microwave or on the stovetop almost to the boiling point.

07 Add the tomatoes (with juice), corn, lima beans and stock to the succotash, and cook over medium heat for 10 minutes, covered.

08 Preheat oven to 350F (175C).

09 Return the rabbit and bacon to the pot, and add the bay leaves. Bring mixture to a simmer. Add the remaining salt and pepper. Cover the pot, transfer it to the oven and cook for 50 minutes to one hour, stirring occasionally.

10 Remove the rabbit from the pot and keep covered on a warm plate. Discard the bay leaves. Over medium heat, simmer the succotash on the stovetop in the pot, uncovered, and let reduce to a thick consistency.

11 Serve rabbit over the succotash and garnish with fresh dill if using.

NOTE: Wild rabbit can be tougher than farmed rabbit and would taste better if cooked in the oven longer and over lower heat. Follow the recipe as described but cook the rabbit for 1½ hours at 325F/160C.

Stewed Duck with Sage-Infused Dumplings

MAKES 4 SERVINGS

This is a tasty stew to make and is kind of a duck pot pie, but instead of using pie crust on top, you make dumplings out of dough. My mother-in-law, Marge, likes to say that duck is her favourite chicken, except for turkey.

This recipe is in response to all the emails and social media messages I receive asking me for a recipe for small critters, including muskrat, squirrel, porcupine, skunk, raccoon and beaver. Any one of these critters will come out tender and tasty if you cook it this way (instead of using duck). As unusual as it may be to some to even think of cooking these animals, it's still a practice in some rural First Nations communities where food security is an issue. I had muskrat stew in Lovesick Lake First Nation, Ontario, one time that was really good, but I found it strange to eat stew with bones still on the meat. I'd rather make a fortified stock to add flavour to a stew than keep the bones in.

BOUQUET GARNI

(see directions in Bouquet Garni recipe, page 35):

1 dried or 2 fresh **bay leaves**

1 **carrot**, chopped into 4 to 6 inch (10 to 15 cm) lengths

1 **celery stalk**, chopped into 4 to 6 inch (10 to 15 cm) lengths

1 sprig fresh **parsley**, with stem

1 sprig fresh **rosemary**

1 sprig fresh **thyme**

STEW:

8 cups (2 L) **White Stock** (see recipe, page 39), or store-bought unsalted chicken stock

1 **duck** (4½ lb/2 kg), cut into 10 pieces

½ tsp (2.5 mL) kosher **salt** (or sea salt), divided

½ tsp (2.5 mL) ground **black pepper**, divided

1 large or 2 small **carrots**, peeled and cut into batons

½ cup (120 mL) peeled **pearl onions**

3 Tbsp (45 mL) **butter**

1 cup (250 mL) medium-diced **onion**

2 tsp (10 mL) minced **garlic**

3 Tbsp (45 mL) all-purpose **flour**

2 cups (475 mL) quartered **mushrooms**

DUMPLINGS:

1 cup (250 mL) all-purpose **flour**

½ Tbsp (7.5 mL) **baking powder**

¼ tsp (1 mL) table **salt**

1 Tbsp (15 mL) chopped fresh **sage**

1 Tbsp (15 mL) melted **butter**

¾ cup (180 mL) **milk**

01 Prepare the bouquet garni.

02 Heat the stock in a microwave or on the stovetop almost to the boiling point.

03 Place the bouquet garni, stock, duck and half the salt and pepper in a large stockpot, and bring to a boil. Turn the heat down to a low simmer, and cook for 40 to 45 minutes. Remove the duck from the pot and set aside to cool in a bowl.

04 Return the fortified stock and bouquet garni to a boil, and add the carrots and pearl onions. Blanch them for two to three minutes, use a slotted spoon to remove the vegetables, and set them aside in a separate bowl. Allow stock to cool.

05 Carefully separate the duck meat from the fat and bones (discarding fat and bones). Cut meat into 1 inch (2.5 cm) cubes.

06 Heat a Dutch oven over low heat for 10 minutes. Melt the butter in the pot, add the diced onion and cook for two minutes (but do not brown the onion).

07 Add the garlic and continue to cook for two minutes. Add the flour and create a roux (paste), stirring continually while cooking it over medium-low heat for two minutes. Remove the pot from heat.

08 Take 1 cup (250 mL) of the now fortified stock from the separate stockpot and add to the roux in the Dutch oven. Combine stock and roux, using a whisk to remove lumps. Add 1 more cup (250 mL) of the stock and bring sauce to a low simmer. Slowly add another 2 cups (475 mL) of the stock and bring to a simmer.

09 Preheat oven to 350F (175C).

10 Add the mushrooms, duck meat, the remaining salt and pepper to the Dutch oven, and bring back to a simmer. Place Dutch oven in the oven, covered, and cook for 1 hour while you prepare the dumplings.

11 To make the dumplings, combine the flour, baking powder and salt in a mixing bowl with a fork or a wooden spoon. (I don't like making this dough in a stand mixer since the dough can easily be overmixed.)

12 Add the sage and combine. Pour in the melted butter and combine. Add the milk, a little at a time, and mix just until ingredients are combined, being careful not to overmix the dough (or it will toughen). It will be a sticky dough. Let dough rest, covered with a damp cloth.

13 Remove stew from the oven after one hour, and increase oven temperature to 400F (205F). Remove the bouquet garni and discard it. Return the carrot and pearl onions to the stew and gently mix in. Spoon the dumpling dough by the tablespoon (15 mL) on top of the stew, return pot to the oven and bake for 30 minutes.

14 Serve stew hot.

NOTE: You could make this recipe over two days, making the fortified stock on the first day. You will need a stockpot, cast iron frying pan (or casserole dish) and a Dutch oven to make this dish.

Button Mushroom Rabbit Chasseur

MAKES 4 SERVINGS

In Canada, there are still some Indigenous people who set traps and snares to catch squirrel, beaver, groundhog, woodchuck, muskrat, porcupine, frog, raccoon, turtle, rabbit and hare, for food. Of all the small game that Métis and First Nations people eat, rabbit is probably the most palatable to modern tastes and the most easily found in grocery stores (where it has already been skinned for you!). Not only does rabbit have a higher meat-to-bone ratio than chicken (which means there is more edible meat on the carcass), it is as versatile to cook with as chicken.

The French word *chasseur* means "hunter," so this recipe is a traditional hunter-style rabbit stew prepared in the French style. Wild rabbits taste stronger than farmed rabbits, but whether you cook farmed or wild rabbit, this recipe will work. If you don't know how to cut up a rabbit, ask your butcher to do it for you.

This recipe provides a simple way to prepare an affordable family-sized meal. All you need is some boiled potatoes on the side.

1 rabbit (2½ lb/1 kg), cut into 8 pieces
1 tsp (5 mL) kosher salt (or sea salt), divided
½ tsp (2.5 mL) ground black pepper, divided
1 Tbsp (15 mL) chopped fresh tarragon
1 tsp (5 mL) dried rosemary
1 small (14 oz/400 g) smoked pork hock
3 Tbsp (45 mL) pure olive oil, divided
1 Tbsp (15 mL) butter
¼ cup (60 mL) sliced shallots
2 cups (475 mL) whole small button mushrooms
½ cup (120 mL) cognac (or brandy)
1 cup (250 mL) Brown Stock (see recipe, page 40), or store-bought unsalted beef stock
½ cup (120 mL) canned diced tomatoes, with juice
2 dried bay leaves
2 tsp (10 mL) cornstarch
4 tsp (20 mL) cold water

01 Season rabbit with half the salt and pepper, along with the tarragon and rosemary.

02 Heat a Dutch oven over low heat for 10 minutes. Increase the temperature to medium-high. Remove rind from pork hock and cut meat off the bone, but save both the rind and bone. Add 1 tablespoon (15 mL) of the oil and the pork meat, rind and bone to the pot, and brown. Remove everything from the pot once browned, and place in a large bowl. Set aside.

03 Brown the rabbit in the pot, two pieces at a time, using the rest of the oil as needed. Remove rabbit and reserve.

04 Preheat oven to 325F (160C).

05 Add the butter to the pot and brown shallots for two minutes over medium-low heat. Add the mushrooms and continue to cook for two more minutes.

06 Add the cognac and slowly simmer until the liquid has been reduced by half.

07 Heat the stock in a microwave or on the stovetop almost to the boiling point. Add the stock, tomatoes (with juice), bay leaves, and the remaining salt and pepper to the stew, and bring the mixture back up to a simmer.

08 Return the rabbit and pork hock meat and bone to the pot (discard rind), and cover. Place Dutch oven in preheated oven and cook for 1 to 1½ hours.

09 Once the rabbit is fork tender, remove and discard the bay leaves and pork hock bone. Remove the rabbit from the pot and set aside.

10 To thicken the cooking liquid, make a slurry by combining the cornstarch with water in a cup, using a spoon or your fingers to remove any lumps. Add the slurry to the liquid in the pot and bring to a boil. Stir the sauce, blending well.

11 Top servings of rabbit with thickened sauce.

White Bean and Collard Green Ragout

MAKES 4 SERVINGS

Collard greens are kissing cousins to cabbage, broccoli and kale and are considered to be among the world's healthiest foods. They are also native to North America. Indigenous peoples of the southern United States were very familiar with them by the time European settlers arrived and so they were able to teach them how to cook collard greens. If you've never tried them, give them a chance in this easy ragout. Raw, they are too bitter and too rough to eat, but they are delicious when cooked in fat with onion and garlic.

1 Tbsp (15 mL) pure **olive oil**

½ lb (225 g) diced **bacon** (or salt pork)

1 cup (250 mL) diced **onion**

1 Tbsp (15 mL) chopped **garlic**

2 lb (900 g) fresh **collard greens**

3 cups (710 mL) **White Stock** (see recipe, page 39), or store-bought unsalted chicken stock

1 can (19 fl oz/560 mL) **white beans**, drained and rinsed (preferably navy beans, cannellini beans or great northern beans)

1 can (28 fl oz/830 mL) low-sodium stewed **tomatoes**, drained and cut into quarters

1 tsp (5 mL) **sriracha** (or other hot sauce)

½ tsp (2.5 mL) ground **black pepper**

NOTE: If you use salt pork instead of bacon you could end up with few, if any, crispy brown bits at the end. This is okay since it is the liquid fat that will flavour the beans and collard greens.

01 Heat a Dutch oven over very low heat for 10 minutes. Heat oil, and the add bacon, turn up the heat to high and cook for three minutes. Lower heat to medium and cook for five more minutes or longer if necessary, until meat is crispy and brown. Use a slotted spoon to remove the bacon and place on a plate lined with paper towel.

02 Add onion to the pot and sauté until translucent (about five minutes). Add the garlic and sauté for two minutes.

03 Rinse and dry collard greens very thoroughly to remove sand. Remove the white centre ribs with a knife. Chop leaves into bite-sized pieces. Add to the pot and sauté until the greens start to soften (about two minutes).

04 Heat the stock in a microwave or on the stovetop almost to the boiling point. Add the stock, beans, tomatoes, sriracha and pepper to the pot. Let the mixture come to a boil.

05 Lower the heat and return the bacon bits to the pot. Let the mixture simmer over medium to low heat, covered, for 45 minutes.

Lemongrass Quail Broth with Wild Rice

MAKES 4 SERVINGS

When I was an apprentice, my culinary professor, Jacques Marie, an avid hunter, used to say, to anyone cooking game birds, "The animal is already dead. You don't need to kill it again!" He was insistent that game birds might be wild but that doesn't mean they need to be boiled for hour after hour.

Three types of indigenous quails found in North America are good eating: the California quail and mountain quail in the far west, and the northern bobwhite of the central and eastern United States, a species that is now endangered in southern Ontario. Farm-raised quail, which is usually a bit larger than wild quail, is what you would normally find in the freezer section of supermarkets (though they are probably more commonly found in Asian markets).

As tiny birds, quails don't provide a lot of meat or fat, which is why they are usually served whole (roasted and stuffed or pan-fried), but I like them quartered in a delicate soup.

½ cup (120 mL) **wild rice**, rinsed

3 cups (710 mL) **water**

¼ tsp (1 mL) dried **rosemary**

1 tsp (5 mL) table **salt**, divided

½ tsp (2.5 mL) ground **black pepper**, divided

4 **quails** (1–1½ lb/500–680 g in total)

2 Tbsp (30 mL) **vegetable oil**

1 cup (250 mL) diced **onion**

1 Tbsp (15 mL) chopped **garlic**

2 tsp (10 mL) grated **ginger**

1 tsp (5 mL) **lemon zest**

6 cups (1.4 L) **White Stock** (see recipe, page 39), or store-bought unsalted chicken stock

6 inch (15 cm) piece of crushed **lemongrass**

2 Tbsp (30 mL) shredded fresh **basil**

¼ cup (60 mL) sliced **green onion**

01 To cook the wild rice, combine the rice, water, rosemary, and a pinch of the salt and pepper in a small to medium-sized pot. Bring to a boil and then lower heat. Simmer rice, covered, for 45 minutes. Once cooked, remove pot from heat, drain rice (if any excess liquid remains) and keep warm for serving.

02 Cut the quails into quarters as you would with chicken.

03 In a stockpot, heat half of the oil over high heat.

04 Season quails with a pinch of salt and pinch of pepper and brown in two batches using the rest of the oil as necessary. Remove them once browned, and set aside. Turn the heat to medium.

05 Add the onion and garlic to the pot, and brown slightly. Add the ginger and lemon zest.

06 Heat the stock in a microwave or on the stovetop almost to the boiling point. Add 1 cup (250 mL) of the stock to the stockpot, scraping up the browned bits from the bottom of the pan to deglaze.

07 Add the remainder of the stock, the lemongrass, the quails, half of the basil, and the rest of the salt and pepper, and bring to a simmer.

08 Skim off any impurities (scum) floating on top of the soup and cook for 40 to 50 minutes over low heat, uncovered. Check the texture of the quails: if tender enough, remove them from the pot. Otherwise, continue cooking for another 15 minutes. Strain broth through cheesecloth or a fine sieve.

09 Place 1 tablespoon (15 mL) chopped green onion and 2 tablespoons (30 mL) cooked wild rice in each serving bowl. Divide quails and broth among the bowls and finish each serving with a pinch of the remaining basil.

Sumac Squash Soup

MAKES 6 SERVINGS

You've had squash soup, I am sure, but have you had it with sumac? Although sumac is mostly recognized as a Middle Eastern spice, either on its own or as part of the popular seasoning blend known as *za'atar*, First Nations have used sumac for centuries to give foods a citrusy taste. In the summer, they harvested the bright red fruit of the staghorn sumac tree, which is still very common along roadsides (at least in Ontario) and very attractive in fall when the leaves change colour. This plant catches my attention every time I am stuck in traffic on the Don Valley Parkway in Toronto at that time of the year. Ground sumac spice is available in gourmet food shops but can be replaced by other seasonings (see below).

2 Tbsp (30 mL) pure **olive oil**

1 cup (250 mL) medium-diced **onion**

2 tsp (10 mL) chopped **garlic**

1 tsp (5 mL) **sumac spice** (or ½ tsp/2.5 mL lemon zest and ½ tsp/2.5 mL paprika)

2 cups (475 mL) **White Stock** (see recipe, page 39), or store-bought unsalted chicken stock

6 cups (1.4 L) large-diced **butternut squash**

½ tsp (2.5 mL) kosher **salt** (or sea salt)

1⅓ cups (325 mL) chopped peeled **apple** (preferably Ida Red, McIntosh or Honey Crisp)

1 cup (250 mL) 35 per cent **cream**

¼ tsp (1 mL) ground **white pepper**

OPTIONAL GARNISH:

1 Tbsp (15 mL) chopped **hazelnuts**, toasted

01 Heat oil in a stockpot over medium heat. Add the onion and garlic and cook for two minutes. Add sumac spice. Reduce heat and cook, stirring, for two minutes.

02 Heat the stock in a microwave or on the stovetop almost to the boiling point. Add stock, squash and salt. Let simmer for 15 minutes.

03 Add the apple and let simmer for another 10 minutes.

04 Purée the soup in a blender or by using a hand blender in the pot.

05 Add cream and pepper and return to a simmer, but do not let it boil (or the cream will curdle). Garnish soup with toasted nuts if using.

Mountain Goat and Spruce Tip Barley Soup

MAKES 8 SERVINGS

The mountain goat is indigenous to North America and inhabits the Rocky Mountains from Colorado to Alaska and the Yukon. The Chilcotin, Dene and Kootenay in Canada's western provinces and the Wenatchi in Washington State were only a few of the Indigenous nations that used to hunt the large white hump-backed climber for food—boiling the meat to make soup. Antelope or mutton would be good substitutes to use in this recipe, although lamb is probably easier to buy, and more palatable to those who prefer a less gamey flavour.

SPICE BAG

(see directions in Spice Bag recipe, page 34):

2 dried **bay leaves**

¼ cup (60 mL) fresh **spruce tips** (or chopped mint leaves)

2 sprigs **parsley** stems

SOUP:

1½ lb (680 g) trimmed **mountain goat meat**, cut into ½ inch (1.5 cm) cubes

½ tsp (2.5 mL) dried **thyme**

1 tsp (5 mL) kosher **salt** (or sea salt), divided

½ tsp (2.5 mL) ground **black pepper**, divided

¼ cup (60 mL) all-purpose **flour**

4 Tbsp (60 mL) pure **olive oil**

1½ cups (350 mL) diced **carrot**

1½ cups (350 mL) diced **onion**

1½ cups (350 mL) diced **celery**

2 tsp (10 mL) sliced **garlic**

6 cups (1.4 L) **Brown Stock** (page 40), or store-bought unsalted beef stock

½ cup (120 mL) **barley**, rinsed

1 Tbsp (15 mL) **sugar**

2 tsp (10 mL) **Worcestershire sauce**

1 cup (250 mL) brewed **coffee**

1 cup (250 mL) **red wine**

1 Tbsp (15 mL) chopped fresh **parsley** (optional)

01 Prepare the spice bag and set aside.

02 Season the meat with thyme, half the salt and half the pepper. Dust the meat in flour, shaking off excess flour. Heat a Dutch oven for 10 minutes over low heat. Raise heat to medium-high.

03 Heat 1 tablespoon (15 mL) of the oil in the pot. In three batches, sear the meat until it starts to get brown, using two more tablespoons of oil (30 mL) when needed. Remove meat from pot and set aside.

04 Add 1 tablespoon (15 mL) more oil. Lower the heat and cook the carrot and onion for five minutes. Add the celery and garlic and cook one minute.

05 Heat the stock in a microwave or on the stovetop almost to the boiling point. Return the meat to the pot. Deglaze the pot with 1 cup (250 mL) of the stock, scraping the bottom and sides of the pot with a wooden spoon.

06 Add the rest of the stock and the barley, sugar, Worcestershire sauce, spice bag, and remaining salt and pepper. Return meat to the pot and bring to a boil. Lower heat and simmer for one hour, covered. Stir occasionally and remove any impurities that float to the top.

07 Remove the spice bag and discard. Add the coffee and wine, and let soup simmer for one more hour, uncovered. Remove from heat and serve in a bowl with the fresh chopped parsley if using.

CHAPTER 5

The Four Leggeds: Large Game Dishes

Never have I been more aware of deer habitat and behaviour than in the years since we moved to the suburbs. For whatever reason, whitetail deer seem to thrive in a nearby ravine that connects to the shoreline of Lake Ontario. And they don't seem to have any problems hanging out in our yard and sniffing around for interesting things to eat. They aren't tame but are used to people and have surprised me when I was busy fixing the lawn mower or doing some other sort of work outdoors and didn't even notice them coming up behind me. We named one mother Marinara and her male fawn Cacciatore and female fawn Béarnaise. We've watched Cacciatore grow intimidating antlers, but he still perks up his ears like a puppy when I call him. He knows his name but doesn't seem to know that a man in a white chef uniform holding a frying pan is not one to trust. Marlene knows I would never hurt him but she watches me carefully anyway, since she is in the deer clan and is protective of our furry friends.

Deer versus Venison and Buffalo versus Bison

Technically speaking, "venison" refers to any type of edible meat from an animal in the deer family, which includes white-tailed deer, mule deer, moose, elk, caribou and pronghorn (antelope). I tend to specify when I am referring to elk, caribou, antelope or moose, but I've developed the habit of saying "deer" and "venison" interchangeably just to confuse people, so I had to make a special effort to specify deer in my recipes in this cookbook. Similarly, the proper term for our huge roaming beast of the prairies is *bison* (which is Greek, in origin), since *buffalo* (which is French, in origin) technically refers to the giant water and cape buffalos of Asia and Africa. Really, we should be calling bison by their Lakota name, *tatanka*; however, in this cookbook I refer to our hairy friend as "buffalo" just out of habit.

Preparing Large Game

Even before you start cooking game, there are larger issues that affect the end result: the hunt, field dressing and preparation of the meat in the early stages following the kill. I am no hunter, but I know that the skilled hunter who gets a clean shot without stressing the animal or shooting through the organs will end up with better tasting meat than a hunter who is unskilled in these ways.

From a chef's perspective, when it comes to handling food, cleanliness is next to godliness. This is especially important when handling wild game. It must be cleaned, cooled and dry aged *immediately* (i.e., eviscerated within an hour and refrigerated within a couple of hours). These days, it's good practice to wear rubber gloves during the process. Not following these practices properly will leave you with an inferior, highly gamey tasting meat, if not disease. Some parasites can be killed by freezing temperatures, but other parasites will persist unless the meat is cooked to a specific temperature. A nuisance bear with access to a dumping ground, for instance, would probably be infected with all sorts of parasites that other bears or farmed game wouldn't. To kill the parasites, you would have to freeze the meat to -5F (-20C) or lower for a week; but since most people keep their freezers warmer than that, it's only through proper cooking or curing and smoking that it is made safe to eat.

> ### Tip
> Keep meat of any kind chilled and covered in the fridge, preferably on a tray to prevent dripping, for a maximum of three days before cooking, freezing or vacuum sealing it.

One time I made steak for a friend who has travelled the world and dined at some of the world's best restaurants—you could say he has a *very* sophisticated palate. It was a deer steak I had vacuum sealed and thrown into my freezer a year before, but he thought it was the freshest steak he'd ever had, and I hated to tell him the truth (but did anyway). He couldn't believe it had been in the freezer at all. After that, he went out and bought a vacuum packer himself!

Buying Large Game

Large game meat sold in stores in Canada and in the United States is usually farm raised but every once in a while, the government issues culls for muskox or caribou for population control, so this wild game is made available for sale; this happens in Newfoundland and in the Arctic. This meat, like all farmed game, is federally inspected to ensure it is free of parasites. Because farm-raised animals typically eat a corn-based diet and are fattier than their wild cousins that constantly roam the land in search of food and shelter, farm-raised animals are less intense in flavour. Due to its higher iron content, game is also darker in colour than beef and does not have the marbling that beef or pork does, so it almost looks like beef liver when you cut it open.

Large game smells strong when you butcher it or open up a fresh package of it. You might even think the meat has gone bad, but there's a difference between bad meat and strong meat. Bad meat smells sour, or vinegary, whereas fresh game meat just smells really strong.

There are also variations in what types of farmed game are available from province to province, so you may have to make substitutes in game recipes. See the "Meat Substitutions" note on page 121.

Cooking Large Game

Generally speaking, raw cuts of meat are classified as tender, medium-tender or tough (or as some supermarkets like to say in their marketing friendly lingo, *less tender*); these terms apply to beef and large game. These are some examples of cuts of meat:

- **Tender cuts.** Tender cuts of meat come from the softer regions of the animal (back, inside). The more tender the cut of meat is, the quicker it cooks to an appropriate level of doneness and the better suited it would be to dry heat cooking methods such as grilling or broiling. See, for example, the recipes for Elk and Sea Scallops in a Parmesan Cup with Chili Lime Vinaigrette (page 56) and Nish Kebobs with Birch and Balsamic Glaze over Brown Rice (page 58) for information on how I cook tenderloins.
- **Tough cuts.** Tough cuts of meat come from the parts of the animal where the muscles are heavily exercised (front forequarter). Older animals tend to have tougher meat than young animals. Tough cuts of meat take the longest to cook and therefore are better suited to a combination of moist and dry heat cooking methods such as stewing and braising or grinding for use in sausages and burgers. See, for example, the recipes for Slow Cooked Ginger Caribou Shanks (page 138) and Deer Osso Buco (page 135).
- **Medium-tender cuts.** Medium-tender cuts fall in the middle category and are suited to either dry or combination heat cooking methods, depending on the cut.

Another way of looking at this is to differentiate cooking times on the basis of the amount of connective tissue the cut has: the more connective tissue it has, the longer it will take to break it down (through moist heat).

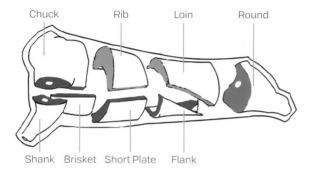

Chuck | Rib | Loin | Round

Shank | Brisket | Short Plate | Flank

Recommended Venison Cooking Methods

PRIMAL CUTS	SUBPRIMAL CUTS	RECOMMENDED COOKING METHODS
TENDER CUTS		
Rib	Chops Rack	Barbecuing Grilling Pan-frying
Loin	Porterhouse Tenderloin Striploin T-bone Rib eye	Grilling Broiling Pan-frying Barbecuing Stir-frying
MEDIUM-TENDER CUTS		
Round	Inside round Outside round Eye of round Rump Sirloin tip	Broiling Barbecuing Pan-frying Stir-frying Braising
TOUGH CUTS		
Chuck	Blade Cross rib Neck Shoulder Stew meat	Stewing Roasting Braising
Shank	Osso buco	Braising
	Ground meat	Broiling Pan-frying Grilling Broiling Barbecuing
Brisket	Stew meat	Stewing Braising
Short Plate	Short ribs	Stewing Braising
Flank	Flank steak	Braising

The Sioux knew what they were doing with moist heat cooking when they used to steam buffalo meat in pits. First, they dug a hole in the ground. Then they lined it with rocks and built a fire on top to heat them. When the fire went out, the Sioux covered the rocks with meat wrapped in leather hides, covered the hides with earth and let the meat steam for several hours. Farmers in Dundurn, Saskatchewan— where Marlene's dad, Joseph Finn, came from—used to do an annual beef summer cookout for large crowds back in the 1960s and '70s using this technique that they learned from local Crees. Indigenous peoples in parts of South America cook meat this way to this day, using plant leaves and earthenware instead of leather hides. Marlene had pork and corn done that way on a gaucho ranch when she travelled to Peru in the late nineties.

The chart "Recommended Venison Cooking Methods" (on this page) shows my recommended cooking techniques for tender, medium-tender and tough cuts of venison, buffalo and beef. The drawing shows the locations of the primal cuts (i.e., large wholesale meat cuts) as well as the names of the subprimal cuts in each of those parts (i.e., small, retail cuts) to help you communicate your wishes to your butcher. For example, in the loin, there are five subprimal cuts, and the recommended cooking methods that apply to these cuts are interchangeable; a porterhouse can be grilled, broiled, pan-fried, and so on. *Bonus:* None of these cooking methods requires digging a hole in your yard (although I am tempted to try pit cooking one of these days and after I buy a tipi).

Doneness

What's the difference between a blue steak and shoe leather? Doneness. What determines doneness?

Temperature and time. How does one learn to control temperature and time? Experience. Lots of it. When cooking large game, a mistake in either temperature or time really affects texture and flavour, especially since game is so lean and can become tough very easily if overcooked. The concept of "doneness" is confusing when cooking any kind of protein for these reasons:

01 "Well done" is actually a range of temperatures, as are "medium" and "rare."

02 Doneness temperatures vary from one country to the next (standards are higher in Canada than in the United States.)

03 Doneness temperatures vary from one species of animal to the next (beef, game and pork each have their own requirements, as do fish and poultry).

04 Doneness temperatures vary from one cut to the next (ground meat, pieces and whole cuts have their own doneness requirements).

05 Game doneness varies depending on where the animal came from, that is, whether it was farm raised or wild.

All of these factors, plus the age of the animal (which is unknown in wild animals), the time of year it was hunted, and its diet will affect the final outcome on your plate. Furthermore, chefs generally remove meat from heat when it is at its best (in terms of texture and juiciness) despite what any government health agency advises. That means removing it from heat even before it reaches the desired serving temperature since it will continue to cook a little afterwards. Chefs also understand the principle of resting. This practice makes for a juicier dish in the end.

Tip

When meat cooks, the juices withdraw to the centre, so when it's done you need to let it rest so that the juices can redistribute before you cut into it; the bigger the piece is, the longer it needs to rest.

The chart below summarizes Health Canada's recommendations for safe internal cooking times for meat. *Note: "Rare" doesn't even appear on their chart.* These temperatures are different than those used for smoking foods, as explained in the smoked foods recipes in this cookbook.

This discussion on doneness reminds me of the story Marlene told me about the time she was studying in Bordeaux, France, and ordered steak and frites (fries) one

Health Canada Doneness Recommendations for Meat

GAME
deer, elk, moose, caribou, pronghorn, bear, buffalo, musk-ox, walrus, rabbit, muskrat, beaver

Chops, steaks and roasts
Burgers, sausages, meatballs, meatloaf, casseroles
165F/74C
Medium well

BEEF, VEAL, LAMB

Pieces and whole cuts
170F/77C
Well done

Pieces and whole cuts
Burgers, sausages, meatballs, meatloaf, casseroles
160F/71C
Medium

Pieces and whole cuts
Mechanically tenderized beef, veal
145F/63C
Medium rare

PORK

Pieces and whole cuts
Burgers, sausages, stuffing, meatballs, meatloaf, casseroles
160F/71C
Medium

time. She wanted the meat well done, but the chef refused and even came out of the kitchen to tell her he wouldn't do it, in front of everyone in the dining room. She refused to eat it any other way, so they had a standoff. She tells me she won, but he made it known to everyone in the restaurant that he was disgusted by dropping the meal in front of her before going off in a huff back to the kitchen. I've had lots of customers who wanted their steak well done too, but I realize there's no point in getting hostile about it if that's what they want. To make matters worse, chefs don't completely agree with levels of doneness, so one's idea of "medium" could be another's idea of "rare."

The Taste of Game

No recipes on game would be complete without some mention of gaminess. The simple truth is if you really do not like any kind of gaminess in your meat at all, then stick to beef, pork or chicken, because there will always be some element of gaminess in game (large or small). On the other hand, if you are interested in dipping your toe into the pool but have skittish friends or family to please, try mixing game with domesticated meat; this will provide more fat and a more familiar taste, and reduce the chance of overcooking.

Tip

Mix game meat with domesticated meat like beef or pork to add fat and prevent overcooking.

In parts of Quebec, classic tourtière is made with deer and pork and is an example of a great combination of lean meat with added fatty meat. You'll notice I add pork to a lot of my game dishes for that reason (see the Smoked Deer Sausage recipe, page 142, for example).

Obviously, I love wild game, but I prefer to eat a plump wild animal hunted at the end of the year rather than a skinny one hunted at the beginning of the year. They say female game is also more tender than male, which may be true, but for sure, the younger the animal, the more tender the meat, although traditionally Indigenous peoples preferred to hunt older animals due to their higher fat content (which was valuable for flavouring and preserving meat). Here's an interesting fact

MEAT SUBSTITUTIONS

Can you substitute beef for large game? People ask me this all the time. The short answer is yes, and no: large game is comparable to high-quality, organic, grass-fed beef more so than run-of-the-mill, cheap cuts of beef, but that is a generalization, since a beef flank steak is never going to be comparable to a buffalo tenderloin, no matter how much grass or fresh air the cow had.

Is one type of large game interchangeable with the next? The short answer is yes, as long as you know how to cook it. Deer, moose, elk, caribou, pronghorn (antelope), buffalo and bear meat are similar in texture and appearance, and they are all higher in protein and *much* lower in fat, pound per pound, than beef; however, large game animals have more in common with one another than they do with small game animals, so you wouldn't want to substitute rabbit in a deer recipe, for instance. For any recipe in this chapter, you could substitute any type of large game meat as long as you use a cut and amount similar to those specified.

for you: the taste of wild game varies throughout the year because, in nature, animals eat different foods at different times of the year. As their diet and level of activity changes over the seasons, the taste of their meat changes. This is why you might eat game one time and find it tastes kind of so-so but at other times find the taste to be fantastic.

Some people like to soak game in brine, vinegar or milk before freezing it to reduce gaminess. Others like to marinate game overnight before cooking. Before doing any cooking, I rinse the meat to remove excess blood (if there's a lot of it) and remove the silver skin and excess fat. Then I focus on the cooking process. In this chapter I have included a few recipes using spice mixes as dry rubs (see Spice Mixes in Chapter 2, page 23), as well as one using buttermilk as a tenderizer for deer (Broiled Ranch Deer Chops, page 145) and several with marinades just for variety.

Cranberry Moose Meatloaf with Mushroom Fig Sauce

MAKES 6 SERVINGS

When I made moose meatloaf on my television show, I used chopped bacon to add flavour and moisture to the moose meat; another way to do it is to cook the meatloaf wrapped in bacon so that the fat drizzles down into the ground meat for the added moisture. And just to make sure the game meat stays moist, I combine it with ground pork. If you happen to have individual (mini) loaf pans, that would shorten your cooking time in half.

1½ cups (350 mL) **water**

⅓ cup (80 mL) wild **rice**, rinsed

2 medium **eggs**, beaten

1½ lb (680 g) ground **moose meat**

¾ lb (340 g) ground **pork**

1 cup (250 mL) small-diced **onion**

¼ cup (60 mL) chopped dried **cranberries**

1 tsp (5 mL) kosher **salt** (or sea salt)

½ tsp (2.5 mL) ground **black pepper**

½ tsp (2.5 mL) dried **thyme**

1 Tbsp (15 mL) **Dijon mustard**

⅓ cup (80 mL) corn flake **cereal** (or bran flake cereal)

½ lb (225 g) **bacon slices**

01 In a small to medium-sized saucepan, combine the water and wild rice. Bring to a boil and then lower heat. Simmer rice, covered, for 40 minutes. Once cooked, remove pot from heat and drain rice (if necessary). Set aside to cool.

02 Preheat oven to 375F (190C).

03 In a large bowl, combine the eggs, moose meat, pork, onion, cranberries, salt, pepper, thyme and mustard, and mix well. Add the cooked rice and mix in.

04 Coarse grind the cereal by using a food processor or a rolling pin.

Tip

To manually grind cereal, pour it into a food storage bag. Partially close the bag. Slowly crush the cereal in the bag using a rolling pin.

05 Add the ground cereal to the meat mixture and mix with your hands until it reaches a smooth consistency. Form into a loaf shape.

06 Place bacon slices widthwise across the bottom of a loaf pan, letting the strips fall over the edges of the pan. Slide the meat mixture into the pan, pressing down firmly so that the meat fills the bottom of the pan evenly. Fold the bacon slices up to cross over the meat mixture.

07 Bake for 60 minutes or until the loaf is well done and reaches 165F (75C) in the centre. While the meatloaf bakes, prepare the sauce.

08 Remove loaf from the oven and let it rest for five minutes before cutting it.

Mushroom Fig Sauce

MAKES APPROXIMATELY 2 CUPS (475 ML)

This sauce goes well on meats of all kinds, but especially red meats.

1 Tbsp (15 mL) **butter**

2 Tbsp (30 mL) chopped **shallots**

1 cup (250 mL) sliced **button mushrooms**

½ cup (120 mL) chopped **chanterelle mushrooms**

4 fresh **figs** (preferably Black Mission)

¼ tsp (1 mL) chopped fresh **thyme**

¼ tsp (1 mL) chopped fresh **rosemary**

½ cup (120 mL) **red wine**

4 cups (1 L) **Brown Stock** (see recipe, page 40), or store-bought unsalted beef stock

½ tsp (2.5 mL) kosher **salt** (or sea salt)

¼ tsp (1 mL) ground **black pepper**

BEURRE MANIÉ:

1 Tbsp (15 mL) **butter**, softened

1 Tbsp (15 mL) all-purpose **flour**

01 In a saucepan over medium heat, melt the butter and cook the shallots for two minutes, making sure they do not brown.

02 Add all the mushrooms and cook for three to four minutes, stirring frequently.

03 Remove the fig stems (discard) and slice the figs into wedges. Reserve one-quarter of them for garnish, and add the rest of the figs, as well as the thyme and rosemary, to the pan and cook for one minute.

04 Deglaze the pan by pouring in the wine, scraping up the brown bits on the bottom and sides of the pan, and swirling the liquid around. Allow the red wine to reduce slightly for three minutes.

05 Heat the stock in a microwave or on the stovetop almost to the boiling point. Add 1 cup (250 mL) of the stock and let the sauce return to a simmer. Add another cup (250 mL) and let the sauce return to a simmer again.

06 Add the rest of the stock along with the salt and pepper, and allow the sauce to simmer for 20 to 25 minutes over low heat. Remove the sauce from heat and let rest for two minutes.

07 Create a beurre manié to thicken the sauce by kneading the butter and flour together with your fingers in a small bowl. Ladle ½ cup (120 mL) of the liquid sauce (without mushrooms) into the butter mixture and whisk to create a slurry. Pour this slurry back into the pot and bring the sauce to a simmer. Then let the sauce cook for three to five minutes.

08 Slice the meatloaf and serve with sauce. Garnish each serving with the reserved fig wedges.

Collard Green Moose Rolls

MAKES 12 SERVINGS

You've heard of cabbage rolls made with beef? Well this recipe uses collard greens with moose meat. Like cabbage, collard greens require a lot of cooking time to soften up, but they retain their bright colour and make for an attractive dish. Native Americans found many uses for this indigenous, extremely nutritious, fibrous vegetable that is normally stewed; they introduced it to early African Americans, and it has since become a *soul food*. Collard greens are not as popular in Canada as in the United States—at least not yet.

You could probably get away with using kale or Swiss chard for this recipe, but if you do, you will definitely have to remove the thick ribs first. *Note:* You could cook the rice a day ahead.

MOOSE ROLLS:

1 lb (500 g) collard greens

2 tsp (10 mL) kosher salt, divided

1 Tbsp (15 mL) pure olive oil

½ lb (225 g) medium-diced bacon

1 cup (250 mL) small-diced onion

4 tsp (20 mL) chopped garlic

½ lb (225 g) ground moose meat

1 cup (250 mL) cooked wild rice (see cooking instructions in Cranberry Moose Meatloaf recipe, page 122)

1 tsp (5 mL) ground black pepper, divided

¼ tsp (1 mL) celery seeds

¼ tsp (1 mL) ground cloves

¼ tsp (1 mL) ground nutmeg

TOMATO SAUCE:

1 tsp (5 mL) pure olive oil

1 cup (250 mL) small-diced onion

2 tsp (10 mL) minced garlic

8 to 10 fresh plum tomatoes

1 tsp (5 mL) dried basil

1 tsp (5 mL) dried oregano

1 dried or 2 fresh bay leaves

01 Remove the stems from the collard greens and discard. In a pot of rapidly boiling water, add 1 teaspoon (5 mL) of the salt and blanch the greens (three leaves at a time) for two minutes. Remove the greens and cool them in a bowl of ice water. Then squeeze the water out of the leaves and let them drain in a colander.

02 Heat the oil in a large sauté pan, and cook the bacon in it for two minutes over medium heat. Add the onion and garlic, and cook for four minutes. Remove pan from heat and set aside.

03 In a large bowl, combine the ground meat, cooked rice, ½ teaspoon (2.5 mL) of the salt, ½ teaspoon (2.5 mL) of the pepper, celery seeds, cloves, nutmeg and the bacon mixture, and mix well. Set aside.

Tip

To check the seasoning of ground meat, make a tiny meatball out of the mixture and pan-fry. Taste and adjust seasoning if necessary, before cooking the rest of the meat.

04 To prepare the tomato sauce, heat oil in a medium-sized saucepan. Add the onion and cook over medium-low heat until soft and translucent. Add the garlic and cook for one minute. Set aside.

05 Bring a pot of water to a boil. Score an X on the bottom of each tomato using a paring knife, and drop them into the boiling water and blanch for one to two minutes. Remove tomatoes from the water and drop them into a bowl of ice water. Peel the skins off, starting from the bottom. Cut tomatoes in half, remove the seeds and discard them, and dice the tomatoes.

06 To the saucepan, add the tomatoes, basil, oregano, bay leaf and remaining salt and pepper (the amounts left over after preparing the rolls). Bring

sauce to a simmer, covered, and cook for 30 to 45 minutes over low heat. Stir sauce from time to time.

07 Remove bay leaf. Pour half of the sauce into a 9 by 13 inch (23 × 33 cm) baking pan. Set aside.

08 To form the rolls, work with one collard green leaf at a time, placing it on your work surface, with the base closest to you. If the centre rib of the leaf is thick, cut it out and pull the cut edges of the leaf inwards towards each other, overlapping them to cover the space. Spoon ¼ cup (60 mL) of the meat mixture onto the bottom of the leaf and roll it away from you, tucking in the sides of the leaf as you go.

09 Place the roll, seam side down, in the baking pan and repeat the process with the remaining leaves and meat mixture until all have been used. Pour the rest of the tomato sauce on top of the rolls. Cover the pan with a layer of parchment paper and a layer of aluminum foil, closing the foil tightly around the edges of the pan.

10 Bake for 80 minutes at 350F (175C). Check that the meat reaches 165F (75C). Just before serving, baste the rolls with the sauce. Serve hot with a bit more sauce.

Moose Burgers with Diablo Pepper Squash Relish

MAKES 8 SERVINGS

Moose is a lean, mean chewing machine, eating up to 60 pounds (27 kg) of plants per day, so it really needs the added fat of pork to become juicy when cooked, especially in a hefty burger. This recipe contains just a little more moose meat than pork, to give you an idea of just how much fat it needs. If you are not crazy about blue cheese, try another type of cheese instead. Think about it while you make the relish; the relish should ideally be made at least a day ahead of serving.

1½ lb (680 g) ground **moose** meat

1 lb (500 g) ground **pork**

2 Tbsp (30 mL) minced **red onion**

1 tsp (5 mL) minced **garlic**

1½ tsp (7.5 mL) kosher **salt** (or sea salt)

½ tsp (2.5 mL) ground **black pepper**

¼ tsp (1 mL) ground **cloves**

3 Tbsp (45 mL) **milk**

¼ cup (60 mL) coarse **bread crumbs**

1 cup (250 mL) medium-diced **blue cheese**

8 **burger buns** (optional)

01 Preheat grill pan or barbecue to medium heat (325F/160C).

02 In a bowl, mix together the moose meat, pork, onion, garlic, salt, pepper, cloves and milk.

03 Add the bread crumbs and cheese, and mix into the meat mixture with your hands until thoroughly combined.

04 Divide mixture in half, then each piece in half, and then each piece in half again to get eight pieces. Roll each piece into a patty using a small amount of water to wet your hands to help form patties about 1 inch (2.5 cm) thick. Try not to compact the burgers too tightly.

05 Grill the patties for three minutes without moving them (and with the lid down if using the barbecue). Then turn them 30 degrees and grill for three more minutes (lid down); this will give you criss-cross marks on one side. Turn patties over and repeat these steps, continuing to grill patties until they are well done and reach an internal temperature of 165F (75C).

06 Toast some buns on the hot grill if you like. Serve burgers with some Diablo Pepper Squash Relish on top.

Half-Baked Variation: After marking the patties with grill marks on one side, move the patties to a baking sheet and bake them in the oven at 350F (175C) for 20 to 23 minutes or until they are well done and reach an internal temperature of 165F (75C). This way you will get the look and flavour of the grill without setting off your smoke alarms inside!

CONTINUED ...

Diablo Pepper Squash Relish

MAKES 1½ CUPS (350 ML)

People don't believe me when I tell them that Wolfman is my real last name. They also find it hard to believe it when I tell them that my mother's maiden name was Diablo ("devil" in Spanish). Therefore, Wolfman + Devil = Me!

If the name doesn't give enough clues about this relish, let me be clear: this is a hot relish! It will clear your sinuses if you are not used to it. (Okay, it's hot in Canadian terms, but not according to our friend Maria from Monterrey, Mexico.) All chilies are native to South America. The diablo grande pepper is rated between 60,000 and 100,000 SHU (Scoville Heat Units) but is not nearly as hot as the ghost pepper used in India or the Scotch bonnet pepper used in the Caribbean. The diablo grande starts out yellow-green and becomes red when it ripens, has a narrow crescent-shape and somewhat thick flesh, and may be harvested while green or red. Adding wasabi paste gives this relish even more punch, but if you want to soften the blow of this relish, you could leave out the wasabi and use a cooler pepper like a fresh serrano (8,000 to 22,000 SHUs), a fresh jalapeno (2,500 to 8,000 SHUs) or a regular sweet red pepper (0 SHUs) instead of the diablo grande.

NOTE: This relish can be made the day before serving and can be kept in the fridge for up to five days.

2 cups (475 mL) small-diced peeled **acorn squash**

4 Tbsp (60 mL) pure **olive oil**, divided

1 Tbsp (15 mL) white **vinegar**

1 Tbsp (15 mL) kosher **salt** (or sea salt), divided

½ tsp (2.5 mL) ground **black pepper**, divided

3 Tbsp (45 mL) minced fresh **parsley**

2 Tbsp (30 mL) finely chopped **green onion**

2 Tbsp (30 mL) finely diced **diablo grande pepper**, with seeds

3 Tbsp (45 mL) **apple cider vinegar**

1 Tbsp (15 mL) **Roasted Garlic** (see recipe, page 33)

½ tsp (2.5 mL) ground **cloves**

¼ tsp (1 mL) ground **nutmeg**

1 tsp (5 mL) **wasabi** paste

1 Tbsp (15 mL) **maple syrup**

01 Preheat oven to 350F (175C).

02 Place the diced squash, one-third of the olive oil, the vinegar, 1 teaspoon (5 mL) of the salt and half of the black pepper in a bowl, and mix thoroughly. Place the mixture on a parchment paper–lined baking sheet and bake for 8 to 10 minutes. Remove from the oven and set aside. Let cool.

03 In a medium-sized bowl, combine the parsley, green onion, diced pepper, cider vinegar, garlic, cloves, nutmeg, wasabi paste and maple syrup with the roasted squash and the remaining salt, pepper and the remaining oil.

04 Mix thoroughly and refrigerate for a minimum of two hours before serving (overnight would be better).

Big Buffalo Pot Roast with Cranberry and Pear Brown Sauce

MAKES 8 TO 10 SERVINGS

Beef pot roast is classic American home cooking at its best, especially with some boiled or baked potatoes, gravy and peas (right, Dad?); its origins are in Europe. Making a pot roast with large game meat is a little trickier. The meat is lean and will easily dry out in the oven, and you can't combine a roast with ground pork for added fat, as in the Moose Burgers with Diablo Pepper Squash Relish recipe (page 126). For pot roast, you need to marinate the meat, and you have to be careful to keep it covered as it roasts at a low oven temperature so that there is a little moist heat action going on. I also put several pieces of bacon across the top of the roast before it goes into the oven. The bacon will drip fat into the meat and give you more fatty drippings for sauce afterwards.

1 **buffalo** inside round (5 lb/2.5 kg)

½ cup (120 mL) **red wine**

7 Tbsp (105 mL) **Big Buffalo Spice Mix** (see recipe, page 24)

½ cup (120 mL) pure **olive oil**

1 cup (250 mL) **Brown Stock** (see recipe, page 40), or store-bought unsalted beef stock

1 cup (250 mL) sliced **onion**

1 head **garlic**

9 strips **bacon**

4 **potatoes**, chopped (optional)

01 Place the roast in a nonreactive dish and pour the wine over it. Rub the roast with the Big Buffalo Spice Mix and coat with the oil. Marinate in the fridge for four hours, turning every hour.

02 Remove roast from fridge and drain off excess marinade (reserve); allow meat to return to room temperature, which will take about an hour.

03 Preheat oven to 300F (150C).

04 Heat the stock to the boiling point in a microwave or on the stovetop. Remove from heat.

05 Heat a Dutch oven over very low heat for 10 minutes. Increase the heat to medium-high. Sear drained roast until brown on all sides (less than five minutes on each side), using reserved marinade as needed. Transfer roast to a plate and set aside.

06 Cook onion and garlic in the pot until soft. Deglaze the pot by pouring in the heated stock, scraping up the brown bits on the bottom and sides of the pot, and swirling the liquid around.

07 Return roast to the Dutch oven. Weave strips of bacon across the top of the roast to keep them from slipping off. Use toothpicks to hold the bacon in place if needed. Add potatoes, if using. Roast the meat for 1½ hours covered and then 1 hour uncovered. Do not attempt to turn the roast over while it cooks, but baste it every 30 minutes. Keep an eye on the bacon; if it starts to get crispy then cover the roast loosely with some foil.

08 To get an accurate reading, test the internal temperature of the roast in several different places. I would take the roast out of the oven when it is medium rare, at 150F (65C) but Health Canada recommends you wait until it is well done (165F/75C). Transfer the roast to a cutting board and allow to rest, covered loosely with a sheet of aluminum foil, for 10 minutes while you make the sauce. Strain and reserve pan drippings for sauce.

09 Before serving, carve the roast very thinly across the grain (after removing any string or toothpicks that were used on the roast).

CONTINUED ...

Cranberry and Pear Brown Sauce

MAKES 2 CUPS (475 ML)

This sauce would go well with any red meat dishes.

¼ cup (60 mL) butter
½ cup (120 mL) chopped onion
1 tsp (5 mL) chopped garlic
½ cup (120 mL) all-purpose flour
2 cups (475 mL) Brown Stock (see recipe, page 40)
   or store-bought unsalted beef stock
¼ cup (60 mL) red wine
¼ cup (60 mL) dried cranberries, soaked in warm water
½ cup (120 mL) diced peeled pears
1 tsp (5 mL) chopped fresh parsley
¼ tsp (1 mL) table salt
Pinch ground black pepper

01 In the Dutch oven used to cook the roast, melt the butter, add the onion and garlic, and cook for two to three minutes over medium heat.

02 Add the flour to the pot and create a roux by stirring the butter mixture vigorously with a wooden spoon; continue to cook the roux over medium heat until it turns slightly brown (about three minutes).

03 Heat the stock in a microwave or on the stovetop almost to the boiling point. Add 1 cup (250 mL) of the stock to the Dutch oven and whisk. Add the wine and whisk some more, bringing the mixture back to a simmer.

04 Add the remainder of the stock and pan drippings that you reserved when you removed the roast from the Dutch oven, and let the sauce simmer for 10 to 15 minutes. Strain the sauce into a clean pot.

05 Drain the cranberries and add to the sauce, along with the pears, parsley, salt and pepper. Simmer sauce for 10 minutes over low heat, stirring constantly.

06 Pour sauce into a gravy boat and serve with the pot roast.

Juniper Buffalo Tomahawk Steak
with Oyster Mushroom Sauce

MAKES 1 LARGE OR 2 MEDIUM SERVINGS

"What was that when it was alive?" Marlene asked me when I brought home a one-and-a-half-pound (680 g) tomahawk steak from the butcher shop one day. The name butchers use for this premium cut from the loin refers to its appearance: it's the size and shape of a tomahawk and it is massive. One steak will easily feed two. It is also called rib steak. All you need is to add potatoes.

Proper technique for preparing a steak of this kind involves marinating it for several hours and then searing it on high heat to lock in flavours without overcooking the inside. You could do the marinating the night before you want to cook and serve the steak. This dish makes a statement when you serve it, but it's an expensive cut, so save it for when you invite your boss over for dinner or for a couple willing to share. This steak would be the equivalent of two 10 ounce (285 g) beef steaks (which you can use as a substitute).

Juniper berries are a traditional seasoning that Indigenous peoples used in the north of Canada as well as in the southern United States on large and small game; on the BC coast juniper berries were used as a flavouring for salmon as well. The dark berries are harvested in fall and are stored whole; crushing them releases very strong flavour, so do that right before cooking with them. If you've ever had gin, then you know the taste of juniper. Look for juniper berries online or in fine food shops.

1½ lb (680 g) buffalo tomahawk steak

DRY RUB:

1 Tbsp (15 mL) dried juniper berries
2 tsp (10 mL) red pepper flakes
2 tsp (10 mL) lime zest
2 tsp (10 mL) minced garlic
1 tsp (5 mL) chopped fresh thyme
1 tsp (5 mL) kosher salt (or sea salt)
½ tsp (2.5 mL) ground black pepper

MARINADE:

¼ cup (60 mL) red wine
¼ cup (60 mL) pure olive oil
2 Tbsp (30 mL) lime juice
2 Tbsp (30 mL) soya sauce
1 Tbsp (15 mL) maple syrup
1 Tbsp (15 mL) sesame oil

01 Place the steak on a large plate or nonreactive dish (glass, ceramic or stainless steel) and dry with paper towels.

02 For the dry rub, crush the juniper berries and red pepper flakes in a mortar and pestle. Transfer to a bowl and combine them with lime zest, garlic, thyme, and salt and pepper. Season both sides of the steak with the dry rub. Set aside for 15 minutes.

03 Whisk together the marinade ingredients, pour the marinade over the steak and marinate for four to six hours, covered, in the fridge, turning periodically.

04 Preheat a gas barbecue to medium-high heat, 350F (175C), using both burners, then turn down one burner to create a lower temperature zone.

05 Remove steak from marinade and discard marinade. Brown the steak for three to four minutes in the high heat zone of the grill, without moving the steak, so that it becomes marked; keep the lid down. Then move it to the lower heat zone and continue cooking, with the lid up, for two minutes, turned 30 degrees from the first position; this will give you criss-cross marks on one side.

06 Turn the steak over and cook in the high heat zone again, with the lid down, for three to four minutes without moving it. Turn it 30 degrees and cook in the low heat zone another one minute to create more grill marks.

07 Since this steak is so large, you will need to continue cooking it in the lower heat zone, with the lid up, until it reaches 150F (65C), which is medium rare for a beef steak, my preferred level of doneness, or the recommended 165F (75C), which is well done. Test the internal temperature of the steak in several different places for an accurate reading.

08 Transfer the steak to a cutting board and allow to rest, lightly covered with foil, for 10 minutes before serving.

Oyster Mushroom Sauce

MAKES 2 CUPS (475 ML)

Oyster mushrooms have a unique appearance; their colour and broad body resemble oysters, hence the name, and they have a slightly sweet flavour (if you get wild organic ones). If none are available, use chanterelle or morel mushrooms instead. Either one will make a beautiful sauce for steak.

Arrowroot is a starch that is used to thicken sauces and soups or stews. Several different varieties of plants in Florida, Central America and the Caribbean have a tuberous root that Indigenous peoples ground to produce arrowroot. Its name might be from the arrow-like appearance of the plant's leaves or because the ancient Mayans used the plant as an antidote for the poison from poison-tipped arrows. Arrowroot is a little pricier than cornstarch but makes for a silkier texture in sauces; you can find it in bulk food stores where it is sold by weight. Arrowroot flour, powder and starch are one in the same. They are also gluten free so are perfect to use when cooking for people with celiac disease or wheat sensitivity.

1 Tbsp (15 mL) pure **olive oil**
½ cup (120 mL) diced **onion**
1½ cups (350 mL) thinly sliced **oyster mushrooms**
　(or chanterelles or morels)

1 Tbsp (15 mL) chopped fresh **rosemary**
1½ tsp (7.5 mL) chopped fresh **thyme**
1 tsp (5 mL) **tomato paste**
¼ cup (60 mL) dry **red wine**
2 cups (475 mL) **Brown Stock** (page 40)
　or store-bought unsalted beef stock
1 dried **bay leaf**
½ tsp (2.5 mL) kosher **salt** (or sea salt)
½ tsp (2.5 mL) crushed black **peppercorns**
1 tsp (5 mL) **arrowroot flour** (or cornstarch)
2 tsp (10 mL) cold **water**

01 Pour the olive oil into a medium-sized saucepan and sauté onion over medium heat until soft (about three minutes).

02 Add the mushrooms, rosemary and thyme, and continue to cook for three minutes.

03 Add tomato paste and cook for one minute. Deglaze the pan by pouring in the wine, scraping up the brown bits on the bottom and sides of the pot, and swirling the liquid around in the pot.

04 Heat the stock in a microwave or on the stovetop almost to the boiling point. Add stock, bay leaf, salt and pepper to the mushrooms and bring to a simmer. Cook for about eight minutes or until the liquid has reduced by half.

05 In a bowl, whisk together the arrowroot flour and water to create a lump-free slurry. Add this to the simmering liquid and continue to whisk the sauce while bringing it back to a low boil for one to two minutes.

06 Remove the pan from the heat and serve in a gravy bowl.

Deer Osso Buco

MAKES 4 SERVINGS

Osso buco, the name of this Italian dish, means "bone with a hole." Traditionally it is made with cross-cut veal shanks, but you can make it with beef shanks or, in this case, deer shanks. Braised this way, tough deer shanks are succulent and so good with just some mashed potatoes or a simple side dish, like Scalloped Rutabaga (see recipe, page 218). Make sure to scoop out the marrow and enjoy it with salt and pepper during the meal.

6 **deer shanks** (3 lb/1.5 kg), each about
   1½ inches (4 cm) thick
1 tsp (5 mL) ground **black pepper**, divided
2 tsp (10 mL) kosher **salt** (or sea salt), divided
¼ cup (60 mL) pure **olive oil**, divided
2 cups (475 mL) **red wine**, divided
1 cup (250 mL) large-diced **carrot**
½ cup (120 mL) large-diced **celery**
1 cup (250 mL) large-diced **onion**
1 Tbsp (15 mL) crushed **garlic**
2 cups (475 mL) **Brown Stock** (see recipe, page 40)
   or store-bought unsalted beef stock
1 can (14.5 fl oz/430 mL) diced **tomatoes**, drained
¼ tsp (1 mL) dried **basil**
¼ tsp (1 mL) dried **thyme**
¼ tsp (1 mL) dried **parsley**
1 dried or 2 fresh **bay leaves**
orange zest (optional)

01   Tie some butcher twine around each shank to keep the meat from separating from the bone while cooking. Dry the shanks with paper towel and season them with half the pepper and salt.

02   Heat a Dutch oven (or heavy bottomed pan large enough to hold the shanks in a single layer) over very low heat for 10 minutes. Add about a third of the oil. Brown half the meat on both sides in one batch. Remove and place in a mixing bowl. Then add another third of the oil to brown the second batch. This should take about 10 minutes per batch.

03   Remove meat from pot and deglaze the pot by pouring in half the red wine, scraping up the brown bits on the bottom and sides of the pot, and swirling the liquid around. Transfer the wine to the mixing bowl and set aside.

04   Add the remaining oil to the pot and let it heat up. Add the carrot, celery and onion, stir, and cook for five minutes. Add the garlic and cook for one minute more.

05   Heat the stock in a microwave or on the stovetop almost to the boiling point. Stir in the stock, tomatoes, herbs, and the remaining salt and pepper and wine. Add the reserved meat and the wine that was used to deglaze the pot. Bring to a boil.

06   Bake shanks in a single layer in the Dutch oven, covered, for two hours at 375F (190C) or until fork tender. Check that the meat reaches 165F (75C).

07   Remove twine and bay leaves before serving shanks with pan drippings. Garnish with orange zest, if using.

Rosemary Tatanka with Sardine Tapenade

MAKES 1 LARGE OR 2 AVERAGE SERVINGS

It wasn't until I was face to face with a buffalo that I realized how big they actually are. Pictures of them charging across the plains do nothing to give a person perspective on their true size. When I visited a friend's buffalo farm to do some videotaping for a segment of my cooking show, I was shocked to see that the hump of a full-grown male buffalo is 6 feet (1.8 m) off the ground—or higher. So, when one starts to show interest in you, and you realize you're a strange male in *his* lot of females, just as he starts making his way over towards you, with flared nostrils, it's hard not to react (even in a fenced lot). (As I recall now, my vegetarian cameraman didn't get a whole lot of footage that day for some reason!)

This recipe is for grilled buffalo steak. When you get down to barbecuing buffalo meat, keep your eyes on the steak! The meat on a buffalo steak is lean since it has no marbling and, without the fat, the meat cooks quickly and gets overdone really easily.

MARINADE:

1 cup (250 mL) sliced onion
2 tsp (10 mL) chopped garlic
2 Tbsp (30 mL) red wine vinegar
1 Tbsp (15 mL) maple syrup
2 Tbsp (30 mL) minced fresh rosemary
2 tsp (10 mL) soya sauce (or tamari)

1 to 1½ lb (500–680 g) buffalo T-bone steak
½ tsp (5 mL) kosher salt (or sea salt)
¼ tsp (15 mL) fresh cracked black pepper
¼ cup (60 mL) pure olive oil

01 Prepare a marinade by mixing together the sliced onion, garlic, vinegar, maple syrup, rosemary and soya sauce in a bowl. Set aside.

02 Season the steak with salt and pepper on both sides and let rest for 10 minutes in a nonreactive (glass, ceramic or stainless steel), shallow dish.

03 Pour the marinade over the steak and coat on both sides; refrigerate, covered, for three hours, turning it over at least once an hour.

04 Drain steak and discard the marinade, reserving the onions. Let steak warm up to room temperature (about 20 minutes).

05 Brush oil on the steak. Heat barbecue to high (450F/230C) and brown meat on one side for three minutes, with the lid down, without moving the steak; then turn it 30 degrees and grill for three more minutes, with the lid down, on the same side to create criss-cross grill marks. Repeat these steps on the other side of the steak, adding reserved onions on top.

06 Due to the thickness of the steak, it will need to continue to cook, but at a lower temperature. Turn the heat down to medium-low (250–300F/120–150C) and cook for about another 10 minutes. Serve it medium rare (150F/65C) or, as recommended, well done (165F/75C). Use a meat thermometer to check the internal temperature of the meat (away from the bone).

07 Let the steak rest on a cutting board with some foil tented above it, for five minutes before carving or serving.

08 Serve steak with the Sardine Tapenade.

Sardine Tapenade

MAKES 1½ CUPS (350 ML)

When I think of tapenade I think of a chunky, salty, chewy spread that's made out of olives and tastes good on crackers or crusty Italian bread, but tapenade is just as good served on main dishes. Olives mix well with oil-packed fish for zing and give tapenade a smoother texture. For the best texture and flavour, I prefer to use canned sardines and anchovies that are packed in oil rather than in water. Sardines and anchovies were among several fish the Nuu-chah-nulth traditionally consumed both fresh and dried.

1 jar (7 oz/200 g) **sundried tomatoes** in oil

6 **anchovy** fillets in oil

2 **sardines** in oil

¾ cup (180 mL) drained pitted **kalamata olives**

2 tsp (10 mL) roughly chopped **garlic**

8 **basil** leaves, roughly chopped (about 2 Tbsp/30 mL)

Table **salt** and ground **black pepper** to taste

01 Drain sundried tomatoes and anchovies in a colander and save the oil. Set aside.

02 Drain the sardines separately and discard the oil. Roughly chop the sardines and transfer to a food processor along with the tomatoes and anchovies.

03 Add the olives, garlic, basil and half of the reserved tomato and anchovy oil, and pulse the food processor until the tapenade reaches a large rough chop—take care not to overprocess the mixture, or it will quickly become a purée, looking and smelling like cat food! (Trust me, I know.)

04 Using a rubber spatula, scrape down the sides of the processor, add more of the reserved tomato and anchovy oil and pulse again. Taste the tapenade and season with salt and pepper and the rest of the reserved oil if desired. Scoop the mixture into a small bowl.

05 Serve at room temperature on the steak.

NOTE: Save leftover tapenade for up to one week in the fridge and experiment by using it in other dishes like pasta or roast chicken.

Slow Cooked Ginger Caribou Shanks

MAKES 4 SERVINGS

This is a recipe for caribou shanks done in a slow cooker, but I included instructions for baking instead (see variation below). People generally associate ginger with Asian cuisine, but Indigenous people in the woodlands of eastern North America traditionally used the spicy Canadian wild ginger root (also known as Canadian snakeroot) for seasoning food and for various medicinal purposes. Even though we grow wild ginger in our backyard, I don't cook with it, because it's toxic if not used properly, so you need to know exactly how much to use and how to process it. Use regular ginger in this flavoured dish (and leave the skin on if you like).

This dish is best served over plain rice or polenta so that you can enjoy the meat as well as the pan drippings and marrow. See the Simply Creamy Polenta recipe (page 220). Don't let the bones' fatty marrow go to waste once the meat is cooked; scoop out the marrow, sprinkle with salt and enjoy! Elders value it for building immunity and supporting digestion, especially in children.

4 Tbsp (60 mL) **coconut oil** (or vegetable oil), divided

2 small cooking **onions** (or 1 large)

1 **cinnamon stick**

2 Tbsp (30 mL) thickly sliced fresh **ginger**

2 fresh **lime leaves** (or a 6 inch/15 cm piece
    of crushed lemongrass)

3 very large (or 4 to 6 small) **caribou shanks**
    with bones (3–4 lb/1.5–2 kg)

½ tsp (2.5 mL) kosher **salt** (or sea salt)

¼ tsp (1 mL) ground **black pepper**

2 cups (475 mL) **Brown Stock** (see recipe, page 40)
    or store-bought unsalted beef stock

½ cup (120 mL) **sherry**

¼ cup (60 mL) **soya sauce**

2 Tbsp (30 mL) **brown sugar**

OPTIONAL GARNISH:

1 **green onion**, sliced (or 1 whole sprig fresh
    coriander, chopped)

01 Turn slow cooker to high heat while you prepare the meat.

02 Heat half the oil in a frying pan over high heat.

03 Cut the onions in half and sear cut side down in the hot oil until dark, along with the cinnamon stick and ginger slices. Once the cut surface of the onion has fully browned, spoon the whole mixture into the slow cooker and add the lime leaves.

04 Tie some butcher twine around each shank to keep the meat from separating from the bone while cooking. Dry the shanks with paper towel and season them with the salt and pepper. Caribou shanks from the tops of the legs can be very large, so if they are too large to fit into your slow cooker, remove the meat from the bone, but cook the bones too, for the added nutrition and body they give to the sauce. The collagen in the bones is what makes this dish so luscious.

05 Pour the remaining oil into the pan. Sear the shanks until brown on both sides (about five minutes per side). Spoon meat and bones into the slow cooker.

06 Heat the stock in a microwave or on the stovetop almost to the boiling point. Deglaze the pan by pouring in the stock, sherry and soya sauce, scraping up the brown bits on the bottom and sides of the pan, and swirling the liquid around in the pan. Bring to a boil, add the brown sugar and whisk out sugar lumps. Pour the liquid over the meat in the slow cooker.

07 Cook the shanks, covered, over high heat for two hours, turning the meat over once or twice during cooking.

08 If meat is not fork tender after this time, continue cooking for one more hour on low heat. Check that the meat reaches 165F (75C).

09 Remove cinnamon stick, onion, lime leaves and butcher twine, and serve dish hot, garnished with sliced green onion if using.

Roasted Variation: If you don't have a slow cooker, follow the recipe above but roast shanks at 325F (160C) in a Dutch oven or casserole dish, covered, for two hours, turning the meat occasionally. Bake an additional hour if meat is not fork tender by this point. Check that the meat reaches 165F (75C) before serving. Remove cinnamon stick, onion, lime leaves and butcher twine, and serve dish hot, garnished with sliced green onion if using.

Garlic Elk Short Ribs in Sour Cherry Sauce

MAKES 4 SERVINGS

Cherries came with English and French settlers, but Indigenous people soon found multiple uses for cherry tree bark, leaves and fruit, including reducing inflammation, relieving pain and aiding sleep. In this recipe, I use canned sour cherries.

Like a lot of city slicker tourists, Marlene and I just had to take pictures of the elk that were wandering in the streets of Banff, Alberta, when we were there. Elk eat flowers and whatever else grows in people's gardens and just carry on despite clicking iPhones. Even though we are now accustomed to seeing the occasional deer in our own backyard, we were shocked to see elk roaming all over Banff on sidewalks. There, they are as common as squirrels and raccoons are to us in Toronto, but I suppose if you are a gardener, the elk would become annoying after a while— but not annoying enough to make anyone turn immediately to this recipe, I hope! (There are plenty of trustworthy sources of elk meat in Canada.)

3 lb (1.5 kg) bone-in **elk short ribs**

1 Tbsp (15 mL) kosher **salt**, divided (or sea salt)

1½ tsp (7.5 mL) ground **black pepper**, divided

¼ cup (60 mL) pure **olive oil**, divided

2 cups (475 mL) chopped **carrot**

2 cups (475 mL) chopped **onion**

1 cup (250 mL) chopped **celery**

2 dried **bay leaves**

1 tsp (5 mL) dried **oregano**

1 tsp (5 mL) dried **rosemary**

5 tsp (25 mL) sliced **garlic**

3 Tbsp (45 mL) all-purpose **flour**

1 Tbsp (15 mL) **tomato paste**

2 cups (475 mL) **red wine**

3 sprigs flat-leaf **parsley**, chopped

4 cups (1 L) **Brown Stock** (see recipe, page 40) or store-bought unsalted beef stock

1 cup (250 mL) canned **sour cherries**, with juice

OPTIONAL GARNISH

Chopped fresh **parsley**

01 Preheat oven to 350F (175C).

02 Season ribs with half of the salt and pepper.

03 Heat a Dutch oven over very low heat for 10 minutes. Add 2 tablespoons (30 mL) of the oil. Raise the heat to medium-high and brown the ribs in two batches, adding another tablespoon (15 mL) of oil as needed. Transfer the ribs to a large bowl.

04 Add the rest of the oil to the Dutch oven and cook the carrot, onion and celery for four minutes. Add the bay leaves, oregano, rosemary and garlic, and cook for two minutes.

05 Dust the pot with the flour and mix well, cook for two minutes. Add the tomato paste and cook for two more minutes.

06 Add the red wine and parsley, and mix well using a whisk.

07 Heat the stock in a microwave or on the stovetop almost to the boiling point. Add the stock, all of the cherry juice and half of the sour cherries, and the remaining salt and pepper (save the other half of the cherries to garnish the dish). Bring mixture to a simmer.

08 Return the reserved ribs to the pot. Cover and bake ribs at 350F (175C) for two hours, stirring periodically.

09 Once the meat is fork tender, check that it has reached 165F (75C). Remove the ribs from the sauce and place them in a serving dish. Keep warm.

10 Strain the sauce into a clean pot and let reduce over medium heat until it thickens (about 5 to 10 minutes).

11 Serve ribs with sauce and reserved sour cherries sprinkled on top, and parsley, if using.

Smoked Deer Sausage

MAKES 5 LB (2.5 KG) OF LINKED SAUSAGES

There are three parts to making sausages: grinding meat, seasoning meat and stuffing sausages. To make the ground meat for the Smoked Deer Sausage recipe yourself, you will need a meat grinder that produces both fine and coarse grinds. A manual meat grinder with a hand crank will do the job, and you might be able to get one that does double duty and stuffs sausages as well. If not, then buy a grinder as well as a sausage stuffer. I use an electric meat grinder that comes with a sausage stuffer attachment, but regardless of the type of grinder you use, you will have to manually combine the ground meat with seasonings. An electric grinder is very helpful for the large-scale recipe variation (see below).

Alternatively, you could use a stand mixer with a meat-grinding attachment for grinding the meat and then a paddle attachment for mixing the ground meat with the seasonings, so that you don't have to do that by hand (it's hard to do manually since the meat has to be kept so cold). But you will still need to buy a sausage stuffer. All of these appliances must be spotlessly clean and sanitized to prevent contamination.

NOTE: It take three days to make these sausages from start to finish, depending on how experienced you are.

The tradition of smoking meat cannot be attributed to any one First Nation, since it was such a widespread practice. The Beothuk of Newfoundland and Labrador coordinated annual caribou drives to obtain an abundance of meat all at once. To preserve the meat, they smoked it in smoke houses made of wood so that it would last throughout the year. This small Indigenous nation perished from conflict with settlers and exposure to tuberculosis; they were no more by the late 1700s. Imagine what the Beothuk would think if they saw people using electric smokers to smoke venison! These sausages were fantastic (thanks to our nephew Dan Finn for providing us with the meat). Refer to Chapter 2, pages 28–29, for tips on using other types of smokers. Despite its name, this recipe gives you two choices other than smoking sausages—cooking the sausages (within 24 hours of making them) or freezing them for cooking later on.

I know people who use deer alone rather than adding any pork when making sausages, and I know people who make sausages out of pork alone, but I prefer to combine the two in my sausages for texture and taste. Leaving pork out altogether makes for an extremely dry sausage that crumbles when you cut it. Not my cup of tea. How much pork to use is up to you, but it should range between 20 per cent and 50 per cent of your total mixture for a good balance. Many people buy ground pork instead of grinding pork themselves, but I prefer to grind up deer meat and pork shoulder at the same time for a good blend of meat to fat. Feel free to use moose meat instead of deer meat. And check your supply of plastic food wrap before starting.

Sausage requires ground meat, fat, salt and added herbs and spices for flavouring. I recommend that you study the "Hardware for Sausage Making" notes before attempting to make sausages. You will also need sausage casings (natural casings made from hog or lamb intestines or artificial casings made from collagen, sold at butcher shops) and a couple of days without distractions. (Sausage making is a good excuse for not being able to house sit for friends, entertain out of town relatives or do your spring cleaning.)

When I make sausages, I like to do it in a meat-cutting room that is kept very cold, between 35F (2C) and 40F (4C), so that means everything in the room is that temperature. But since you probably don't have access to such a setup, you will need to do as directed at the start of the recipe. Follow all the instructions below carefully to prevent contamination.

4 lb (2 kg) **deer meat** (flank, shank or shoulder), cubed

1 lb (500 g) **pork shoulder**, cubed

1 cup (250 mL) cold **water**

3 Tbsp (45 mL) kosher **salt** (or sea salt)

1½ Tbsp (22 mL) crushed black **peppercorns**

3 Tbsp (45 mL) smoked **paprika**

1 Tbsp (15 mL) ground **mustard**

2 tsp (10 mL) ground **nutmeg**

1 Tbsp (15 mL) **garlic powder** (or 3 Tbsp/45 mL minced garlic)

1 Tbsp (15 mL) ground **sage** (or 3 Tbsp/45 mL minced fresh sage)

1 Tbsp (15 mL) **onion powder** (or 3 Tbsp/45 mL diced onion)

15 to 18 feet (4.5–5.5 m) **sausage casings** (preferably dry-packed, tubed, genuine hog or sheep casings)

2 tsp (10 mL) **vegetable oil**

01 The first order of business it to put all the sanitized equipment you need to use for this recipe—including the grinder, the stuffer, mixing bowls, trays, and so on—in the freezer for several hours to chill.

02 If using fresh (or thawed) meat, make sure it is extremely cold when grinding. The last thing you want is for the fat to melt during sausage making.

03 Pour some crushed ice or ice cubes into a large chilled bowl and put a smaller chilled bowl on top of the ice.

04 Remove grinder from the freezer and set to a coarse die. Use a thermometer to check that the meat is 35F (2C) or colder. Push the chilled mixture through the grinder into the chilled bowl.

05 Chill the water in the freezer.

06 Grind the mixture a second time on a fine die.

07 Add the salt, pepper, paprika, mustard, nutmeg, garlic powder, sage and onion powder to the ground mixture, being careful to sprinkle on each spice evenly. Add the chilled water. Using your hands (wear gloves) or a large wooden spoon, mix vigorously for at least five minutes; alternatively, use your stand mixer with a paddle attachment and let it run for two minutes. The meat should stick together when you are done.

08 Make a little meatball and fry it to test the sausage meat flavour. Adjust seasonings as desired.

09 If you want to continue making the sausages, freeze the mixture for 30 to 40 minutes in one or two bowls. Alternatively, cover it with food wrap and refrigerate overnight; that will help to let the spices flavour the meat more intensely.

10 Soak the sausage casings in cold water.

11 To begin the process of making the sausage links, remove the chilled sausage stuffer and a couple of mixing bowls from the freezer. Run cold water through the casings. If you discover holes in the casings, cut the casing at that point (you can do the stuffing in batches). Grease the tube of the sausage stuffer with vegetable oil so that the casing slides onto it easily. Insert a casing onto the tube, leaving about 6 inches (15 cm) hanging off the end, and tie the end of the casing with a double knot.

IF YOU'RE NOT LAUGHING YET . . .
When you start making the sausage links, my sister-in-law Nancy Johnson says you should have the *Seinfeld* episode playing in which Newman and Kramer make sausages in Jerry's apartment to the tune of "Mañana (Is Soon Enough for Me)." That's season 9, episode 4—"The Blood."

Or, you might get more out of watching the *I Love Lucy* episode in which Lucy and Ethel wrap chocolates on a factory conveyor belt (season 2, "Job Switching" episode). That one cracks us up every time.

12 Once everything is set up, remove meat from the freezer or fridge and place in a chilled bowl set over a second bowl containing ice in order to keep the meat cool. Stuff the meat into the sausage stuffer and let the sausage form into a long coil (while tamping the meat down as it goes into the stuffer to remove air pockets). This sounds a *lot* easier than it is, and this is the hardest part of the entire exercise. It takes practice to know how fast to grind to properly fill the casings (not too much and not too little). When you get to the end of the meat, leave an extra 6 to 10 inches (15–25 cm) of casing on the end in order to make it easy to tie off later on.

13 To make the first two links, pinch off the meat at about 8 or 9 inches (20–25 cm) from the knot and squeeze air out and towards the other end of the casing, taking care not to break it. Then pinch the meat in the middle—at about 4 inches (10 cm)—and flip the first link of sausage away from you about five times and the second link of sausage towards you about five times. Repeat this step, pinching off a section of meat about 8 or 9 inches (20–25 cm) long, and then pinching it in half and twisting the links, alternating away from you and towards you. Make a double knot at the end of the sausage or tie off using butcher twine.

14 If you have a huge fridge, you can hang the linked sausages on a drying rack so that they can "bloom" for one to two hours at 35F (2C). Leave space in between them so that they get air on all sides. While they are hanging, you can use a sterilized needle to poke a hole in any visible air bubbles and then spread the meat out with your fingers so that the casing lies flat where the bubbles were.

15 Otherwise, refrigerate coiled sausages overnight on a baking sheet covered in plastic food wrap. The next day, either freeze them, cook or smoke them. I prefer to keep the links attached until I cook them or smoke them.

If freezing: Vacuum seal or wrap sausages in plastic wrap or butcher paper. Write on the packages the date you made the sausages. They usually take about six hours to freeze, but once they're frozen you can store them for six months. If the meat you used to make the sausages was previously frozen, however, you need to poach the sausages (by cooking them for 10 minutes in boiling water over low heat—simmering—in a large saucepan), and let them cool before freezing. Then you can cook them normally later on.

If cooking: Poach, fry or bake sausages until they reach an internal temperature of 165F (75C). Consume within 24 hours.

If smoking: Set the smoker to 140F (60C). Smoke the sausages for one hour, and then turn the heat up to 180F (80C) and smoke until the internal temperature of the sausages reaches 165F (75C)—this will take about one more hour. Then remove the sausages from the smoker and allow them to cool before eating or refrigerating them. Smoked sausages can be stored in the fridge for one week or several months if properly vacuum packed.

Large-Scale Variation: For every 1 lb (500 g) of game meat, use 4 ounces (115 g) of pork shoulder.

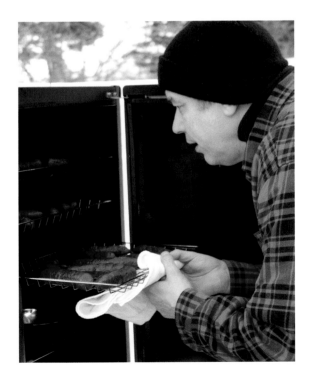

NOTE: You can start this recipe the day before serving.

Broiled Ranch Deer Chops

MAKES 4 SERVINGS

When I cook chops this way, they come out dark and crispy on the outside and pink and soft on the inside and with flavour galore. This recipe is for a small batch of deer chops. I had four that were 1 inch (2.5 cm) thick, but you could double the quantity if you have more people to feed.

Buttermilk helps to reduce the strong flavour of deer, so if you marinate the meat in it, you'll end up with a taste that's more akin to the red meat taste that we are all used to. But, if you don't mind the taste of game, you can go without the buttermilk. It's up to you. This recipe gives you the flavour of ranch style dressing without the dressing.

DRY RUB:

2 Tbsp (30 mL) dried **parsley**

2 tsp (10 mL) dried **onion flakes**

2 tsp (10 mL) **garlic powder**

1½ tsp (7.5 mL) dried **dill**

½ tsp (2.5 mL) kosher **salt** (or sea salt)

¼ tsp (1 mL) ground **black pepper**

4 **deer chops** (2 lb/900 g in total), bone in

2 Tbsp (30 mL) **vegetable oil**

OPTIONAL:

½ cup (120 mL) **buttermilk**

1 chopped **apple** or pear (skin on)

2 Tbsp (30 mL) **jam** (see Wild Blueberry and Rhubarb Jam recipe, page 259)

01 Combine parsley, onion flakes, garlic, dill, salt and pepper in a small bowl using a whisk or fork.

02 Season the chops with the dry rub, coating all sides evenly, in a nonreactive dish (glass, ceramic or stainless steel) large enough to hold the chops in a single layer. If using buttermilk, pour it over the meat now, turning the chops to spread it all over. Cover with plastic wrap and marinate in the fridge for four to six hours, or overnight, turning periodically.

03 Preheat the oven to 500F (260C).

04 Drain buttermilk if used, from the chops. Heat a cast iron frying pan over low heat for 10 minutes. Raise heat to high heat. Heat oil in the pan. Sear the meat for two to three minutes on each side.

05 Add apple or pear, if using, to the pan and coat with pan drippings. Transfer pan to the oven and broil chops for about two minutes on each side.

06 When the chops reach your preferred level of doneness, remove them from the pan. My preference is to cook them until medium rare, at 150F (65C), but Health Canada recommends cooking them until well done, at 165F (75C). Remove chops from the pan, cover lightly with foil and let rest for 10 minutes before serving.

07 Garnish each serving with the cooked fruit, pan drippings and a spoonful of Wild Blueberry and Rhubarb Jam if using.

Métis Deer Tourtière

MAKES 10 SERVINGS (2 PIES)

ourtière is a French Canadian Christmas tradition that goes back over 400 years, although pastry meat pies were enjoyed in Europe even before the birth of Christ. French Canadians debate the origin of the word *tourtière*, as well as whether or not tourtière should have this ingredient or that, but I think they'll all agree it is a dish made of meat encased in pie crust.

I call this a Métis tourtière since so many Métis grew to adopt French traditions. Game meat tourtière is still common in areas in and around Quebec City, even now. If you want, make the pastry a day ahead and chill it so that it's ready to go when you need it; otherwise you will need to make it at least two hours in advance of baking so that it has time to get thoroughly chilled. To make the pastry for this dish, see Marge's Strawberry and Rhubarb Pie dough recipe (page 252). Tourtière goes well with a mushroom sauce (see Oyster Mushroom Sauce recipe, page 134).

Tip

An egg wash that will be brushed on pastry before baking is made by mixing either an egg yolk or white with water, milk, cream or sugar, depending on whether the purpose is to make a seal or to improve the shine, colour or texture of the pastry.

FILLING:

3 Tbsp (45 mL) pure **olive oil**
1½ cups (350 mL) small-diced **onion**
½ tsp (2.5 mL) ground **cinnamon**
½ tsp (2.5 mL) **mace**
½ tsp (2.5 mL) dried **rosemary**
½ tsp (2.5 mL) dried **sage**
½ tsp (2.5 mL) **sumac spice**
2 lb (900 g) ground **deer meat**
1 lb (500 g) ground **pork**
2 cups (475 mL) grated peeled **potatoes**
2 Tbsp (30 mL) minced **garlic**

1 Tbsp (15 mL) **Cold-Smoked Alderwood Salt** (see recipe, page 30) or kosher salt, divided
1½ tsp (7.5 mL) ground **black pepper**, divided
2 cups (475 mL) **Brown Stock** (see recipe, page 40) or store-bought unsalted beef stock

PASTRY:
Pie dough for 2 covered pies, chilled

EGG WASH:
1 **egg yolk**
1 Tbsp (15 mL) **water**

01 To make filling, heat a Dutch oven over very low heat for 10 minutes. Add the oil. Raise heat to medium and cook the onion for three minutes.

02 Add the cinnamon, mace, rosemary, sage and sumac, and cook for two more minutes.

03 Add the deer meat, pork, potatoes, garlic and half of the salt and pepper, and cook until meat is lightly browned, mixing it with a wooden spoon to break up the meat into small pieces.

04 Heat the stock in a microwave or on the stovetop almost to the boiling point. Add the stock to the deer mixture and continue to cook for 10 minutes over medium heat.

05 Add the remaining salt and pepper and cook until the meat mixture has a thick consistency, but be careful not to let it overcook or it will dry out.

06 Transfer the mixture into a shallow bowl and chill in the refrigerator while you prepare the pastry.

07 Divide the chilled dough into four balls. Roll out two of them for the bottom crusts of the pies (to ⅛ inch/0.5 cm thickness) and place in pie dishes. Press down.

08 Divide the chilled meat mixture equally between the two pie dishes, taking care to avoid splashing any on the edges of the pie shells.

09 To make the egg wash, combine the egg yolk and water, and brush the mixture on the edges of the pie shells. This will help the top and bottom layers of dough seal together.

10 Roll out the two remaining balls of dough and cut a small hole in the middle of each (using an apple corer) or make some other cuts with a knife so that steam can escape as the pies bake. Place the pastry lids on top of the filled shells.

11 Use the back of a knife to cut off the excess dough, leaving about ½ inch (1.5 cm) over the edge. Crimp the edges of the pastry with your forefinger and thumb to seal them tightly, or use a fork to do this. Make a few leaf-like shapes out of excess dough and use the remaining egg wash like glue to attach them to the tops of the tourtières.

12 Bake at 375F (190C) for 40 to 45 minutes. Check that the meat reaches 165F (75C). Remove pies from oven and let rest for at least 10 minutes before cutting.

Grilled Deer Rack with Plum and Shallot Compote

MAKES 2 SERVINGS

Deer rack refers to deer rib meat and may be sold "frenched" (meaning the ribs have been trimmed of fat to make a more presentable dish in the end). However, I don't bother to do it if I am going to grill a deer rack to eat at home, since the meat is lean to begin with. If yours has been frenched already, double the amount of olive oil to ensure that the meat doesn't dry out.

Also, from a chef's perspective deer rack is best when served medium rare (150F/65C), although Health Canada advises cooking it until well done (165F/75C). In my opinion, cooking it beyond medium rare will cause it to be dry, so watch it carefully to cook it to your preferred level of doneness.

1 **deer rack** with 6 ribs (1 lb/500 g)
1 Tbsp (15 mL) **Dijon mustard**
1 tsp (5 mL) dried **juniper berries**
3 Tbsp (45 mL) **bread crumbs**
1 tsp (5 mL) **garlic powder**
1 tsp (5 mL) **onion powder**
½ tsp (2.5 mL) ground **black pepper**
½ tsp (2.5 mL) kosher **salt** (or sea salt)
3 Tbsp (45 mL) **apple cider vinegar**
1 Tbsp (15 mL) **Worcestershire sauce**

01 Pat dry the meat with paper towel. Brush meat with the mustard.

02 Crush the juniper berries in a mortar and pestle. Combine juniper berries with remaining ingredients in a shallow nonreactive dish (glass, ceramic or stainless steel) and evenly coat the meat with the mixture, rubbing it in on all sides. Let meat rest for 30 minutes at room temperature, turning over at the halfway point.

03 Heat grill to medium-high (350F/175C) in one zone of the barbecue and low heat (250F/120C) in the other zone.

04 Drain the chops, reserving the marinade, and grill in the high heat zone for two minutes on each side, with the lid down. Brush the marinade on the meat and continue cooking over high heat for another three minutes. Slide meat to the medium heat zone and cook one minute more. Alternatively, heat a grill pan on the stovetop to high. Lower temperature to medium-high to cook the meat for three minutes on each side before adding the marinade; continue cooking on the stove for two more minutes.

05 Remove meat from heat and let rest on cutting board, with tented aluminum foil over it, while you make the compote. Slice the meat into individual chops.

Plum and Shallot Compote

MAKES 2 CUPS (475 ML)

Compotes are a quick meat accompaniment made by boiling whole or chopped fruit in syrup. The best part is compotes are meant for eating right away, not for preserving. Plums and shallots make a good combo for deer meat, but this compote is equally good on pork or chicken.

1 Tbsp (15 mL) **butter**
2 Tbsp (30 mL) minced **shallot**
2 tsp (10 mL) minced fresh **mint**
2 cups (475 mL) thinly sliced **plums**, skins on
½ cup (120 mL) **water**
1 Tbsp (15 mL) **sugar**
¼ tsp (1 mL) ground **cardamom**

01 Melt butter in a small saucepan over low heat.

02 Add the shallot and mint and cook for two minutes over low heat. Add the plums, water, sugar and cardamom. Stir and let cook over low heat for five minutes or until thickened.

03 Serve hot as a garnish for the meat.

Easy Deer Lasagna

MAKES 8 SERVINGS

Who doesn't like to come home from work to the aroma of lasagna fresh out of the oven? When that happens, I've been known to fling my coat across the room, kick off my boots and dig in without a plate.

If you don't have anyone to make lasagna for you, you can do it yourself easily enough by following this recipe and using "oven ready" noodles from the store, jarred marinara sauce and shredded cheese; that cuts out a lot of the work, so you could even double the batch to make two—put one in the freezer (and vacuum seal it for extended freezing time) for some night down the road. What I do is chill leftover lasagna in the fridge overnight, cut it up into several smaller portions and then vacuum seal and freeze them. The dandelion variation is for those of you who want a little extra fibre and nutrition.

2 Tbsp (30 mL) pure olive oil

1⅓ lb (600 g) ground deer meat

1 cup (250 mL) medium-diced onion

2 tsp (10 mL) minced garlic

2 tsp (10 mL) kosher salt (or sea salt), divided

1 tsp (5 mL) ground black pepper, divided

2 jars (22 fl oz/650 mL each) marinara sauce

2 eggs

2 cups (475 mL) ricotta cheese

3 cups (710 mL) grated mixed cheeses (mozzarella, Monterey jack, cheddar)

9 to 12 oven-ready lasagna noodles

01 Preheat oven to 350F (175C).

02 Heat a Dutch oven over very low heat for 10 minutes. Add the oil. Raise the heat to medium and cook the meat until it loses its red colour.

03 Add the onion, garlic and half the salt and pepper, and cook for five minutes over medium-low heat.

04 Stir in the marinara sauce, rinsing the jars with a little water and adding it to the pot, and bring to a boil. Let sauce simmer while you prepare the other ingredients.

05 Beat the eggs in a bowl and combine with the ricotta cheese. Stir in the remaining salt and pepper.

06 Ladle a third of the meat sauce into a 9 by 13 inch (23 × 33 cm) pan. Now, start the layering with three or four noodles, breaking some into smaller pieces if necessary, and slightly overlapping them. Spoon half of the ricotta mixture over the noodles, then top with a third of the shredded cheese.

07 Still with me? Now add a second layer of noodles, then half of the remaining meat sauce, all of the remaining ricotta mixture, and half of the remaining shredded cheese.

08 Add a third layer of noodles, the remaining meat sauce and then the remaining shredded cheese.

09 Bake for 30 minutes, covered with a layer of parchment paper and a layer of aluminum foil. Remove these coverings and continue baking for another 30 minutes. Check that the meat reaches 165F (75C). Let cool for 15 minutes before serving.

Dandelion Variation: Rinse 8 cups (2 L) dandelion leaves and cook in a saucepan over medium heat for two minutes (with no added water). Let cool, drain and squeeze out excess moisture with your hands. Chop dandelion and sprinkle it on top of the ricotta as you form the layers of the lasagna.

CHAPTER 6

The Swimmers: Fish and Shellfish

Not long ago, someone at one of my cooking demonstrations asked Marlene, "What would David's dinner request be if it were to be his last?" (Pretty weird, right?) "Baked salmon fillet with rice and buttered beets," she answered, before walking away from him—quickly. Then he approached me and asked me the same question. I gave the guy the same answer; maybe he wanted to find out if our answers would match, as a test of how well we knew each other. The truth is, I cannot get enough salmon. I eat it all year long in every form possible but never get tired of it, which shouldn't be a surprise, since I come from a First Nation that has been inseparable from fish—salmon in particular—since time immemorial.

My mother's people share a traditional belief that they descended from Coyote, who removed evil and prepared land and food for the people. He created the waterfalls and the fishing spot in the Fraser River in BC where First Nations people still catch salmon from old wooden platforms that jut out over the raging river. Local First Nations authorities collectively manage and monitor the spot. The first salmon caught each year was traditionally celebrated in a community ceremony in Xaxli'p territory, as in many First Nations in BC. This salmon would be dressed, but its skin was left on; sometimes the fish would be wrapped in cedar branches and cooked slowly over hot cedar coals. My friend Art Adolph, the former Xaxli'p chief, explained to me that when the salmon was ready, the drumming and singing would begin, and the salmon would be placed in a ceremonial bowl and passed around so everyone would get a small bite. Then, once everyone had had a taste, the bones and the entrails were returned to the river to honour and give thanks to the salmon spirit. Giving thanks to the Creator for the salmon was a natural way of respecting the animal that the people depended on so heavily. Fish and seafood were staples for a large number of Indigenous nations across Turtle Island, so the connection between humans and fish has always been strong. The connection to fish is central to many First Nations and Inuit creation stories and legends that are passed down through the generations in song, art and dance. Our relationship with fish (and all animals, for that matter) goes beyond simple respect to one of brotherhood, or kin.

Archaeologists in Canada and the United States continue to surprise the world with new evidence of Indigenous communities much older than they were previously believed to be. Some examples are the woven wood and stone fish weirs used to trap freshwater fish on Mnjikaning First Nation, Ontario, and similar weirs for herring in the Boston, Massachusetts, area. These weirs are about 5,300 years old—older than the pyramids of Giza. Ancient salmon fish weirs have been found in the Haida Gwaii archipelago of BC that are estimated to be 13,000 years old.

Arctic char is a relative of salmon that's found in the North.

The settlement there was thought to be the oldest in North America until 2017, when archaeologists discovered fishing hooks and other artifacts in a Heiltsuk village on the coast of BC, a settlement estimated to be 14,000 years old. The discovery of that village confirms the oral history of the First Nation and challenges previously held scientific beliefs about how long Indigenous people have lived (and fished) on this continent. Ancient fish weirs reveal that our ancestors developed sophisticated fishing technologies. Indigenous people invented ingenious methods of preserving fish long before any explorers neared our shores (they were lost explorers, don't forget) and developed practical uses for the flesh, head, eggs, skin and bones, wasting nothing.

Traditionally, Indigenous people highly valued molluscs and developed various means to use their shells for everything from food containers, to jewellery, to clothing decoration, to ceremonies, to tools. Oysters, clams, scallops and mussels all had multiple uses above and beyond nutrition. Eastern woodland nations traditionally used the purple and white shell of the quahog clam to craft beads known as "wampum," which were traded or strung together to make belts that displayed a symbolic recording of history. Cree, Shoshone and Cheyenne women of the plains traditionally wore dresses decorated with cowry (snail) shells received through trade with coastal nations. To this day, the abalone shell is the most commonly used object to hold sacred medicinal plants for ceremonial burning (smudging).

Round versus Flat Fish and Oily versus Lean Fish

There are many ways to classify fish types. Fish have a backbone that runs down the centre of the body, and some have round bodies whereas others have very flat bodies. "Round" fish such as salmon, tuna and trout have two fillets—one on either side of the backbone. In contrast, "flat" fish such as halibut have four fillets and a very flat body, so they require a different type of filleting procedure than round fish. For specific instructions on filleting round fish, see "How to Fillet Round Fish" (page 158); for flat fish, see "How to Fillet Flat Fish" (page 160).

Another way to differentiate between fish types is the oil (fat) content in the flesh. Fish such as herring and mackerel contain a lot of oil and, consequently, have darker coloured flesh than lean fish that are lighter coloured (such as orange roughy and cod). Both types of fish are very good for you, but the cooking methods vary depending on how oily (or lean) a fish is.

Shellfish versus Seafood

Crabs, shrimp (small prawns), lobster and crayfish are classified as crustaceans. Clams, mussels, oysters and scallops are classified as molluscs. "Shellfish" refers to crustaceans, molluscs and cephalopods (octopus and squid) collectively. "Seafood" is a layman's term to represent crustaceans, molluscs, cephalopods and many other types of edible marine animals and plants that I won't get into here—everything but fish, in other words.

| Wind-drying salmon is a beautiful sight.

Preparing Fish and Shellfish

If you have caught your own fish, check for visible signs of disease before storing it, and if you are a newbie, consult an experienced fisher. Health authorities strongly urge that you gut fish, immediately rinse it in cold water and keep it on ice until you can get it into a pan to cook, into the fridge or into the freezer—even though cleaning fish in subzero temperatures is very challenging. When buying fresh fish in the summer, it is a good practice to put ice packs in a cooler in your vehicle (like my sister-in-law Lorraine Pitawanakwat does) before heading off to the grocery store so that your fish stays cold all the way back to the rez. Fish is so delicate you have only 48 hours to cook it before it starts to deteriorate, and that is assuming you store it properly.

When I get home from the store, I put cut pieces of fish in a food-safe plastic bag and place the bag in a metal bowl over a bigger bowl of crushed ice in a drip pan in the coldest part of the fridge; but you can skip the bag and instead put the fish into a covered, perforated pan or colander that drains over ice.

Fresh molluscs should be stored in the fridge in their original sack on a tray, covered with a damp cloth or wet newspapers, to be kept alive, or, if shucked, in their original container in the fridge. Extremely fresh molluscs can be eaten raw, but if planning to cook them, do it the day you get them, or store them for no more than two days (oysters are an exception to this rule and can be chilled for four days).

Fresh crab should be chilled in a bowl covered with seaweed, a damp cloth or wet newspapers. Shrimp should be chilled on ice, and peeled shrimp should be stored in a food-safe plastic bag in a bowl over crushed ice, with a drip pan.

Here are some pointers for freezing fish:

- **Large whole fish.** For freezing, large whole fish should be cleaned, rinsed in cold water and frozen on a baking sheet. Then dip the fish in ice water and return it to the freezer. Rinsing fish in ice water and returning it to the freezer several times will give it a solid ice glaze about a quarter inch (0.6 cm) thick that will help to prevent freezer burn and moisture loss. Then the fish can be wrapped in freezer wrap and a plastic bag. (Never use garbage bags laden with chemicals to store food for any length of time.)
- **Fish fillets and fish steaks.** Fillets and steaks are small enough to be frozen completely surrounded by water in a food-safe freezer bag. Rinse fillets in a salt-water brine (¼ cup/60 mL kosher salt to 4 cups/1 L water) and then put them in freezer bags. Fill the bags with cold water, try to remove any air from the bag and lay the bags flat to freeze. Turn the bags over halfway through freezing to ensure that the fillets are totally encased in ice. Some fishers I know clean fish on the spot and put the fillets in plastic containers filled with lake water for freezing. Then they thaw them and rinse them off before cooking. This is not a practice Health Canada recommends. Avoid freezing fatty fish (like salmon) any longer than two months unless you vacuum seal it first, or the fish's oils may go rancid.

To fillet a fish requires removing the scales, entrails, gills and fins. If planning to pan-fry a fish, you may also need to remove the head and tail to fit in the pan, although with little fish—such as a half-pound (225 g) trout—you can leave them on. Keep in mind that in parts of Asia and France, cooks still like to bake fish with the head and tail intact, but the choice is yours, since *you* are holding the knife!

Before cooking fish that have been frozen, read "Tips on Using Frozen Fish and Seafood" (on this page).

Buying Fish, Crustaceans and Molluscs

Whole fish are normally cheaper to buy, pound per pound, than fillets. The weight of a whole fish is more than the sum of its fillets due to its head, tail, skin, bones and entrails; keep this in mind when shopping for one to fillet for a particular recipe. Lean white fish such as halibut provide the additional benefit of giving you all you need to make fantastic fish stock for soups and sauces. The decision to buy fish whole or filleted depends on your preference, time available, the type of fish you want, and how comfortable your family or friends are with removing skin and bones while eating.

Wild fish is leaner than farm-raised fish. Differences in their taste are not as noticeable as differences in their texture due to the difference in the amount of fat they contain. Nutrition is another issue altogether, since wild-caught seafood is considered healthier in many respects, but also might be more likely to contain higher levels of mercury, depending on where it is caught. Regardless, fish skin should look shiny and moist, and have a nice sheen. Fish secrete a coating that protects the scales and skin; this coating should be transparent. The flesh should be firm and, when pressed, should bounce back. The eyes should also be clear and bright. Fish markets typically leave the skin on fish fillets so that consumers can identify the fish types.

When buying frozen fish, make sure there are no air pockets around the fish in the package; air leads to dryness, discoloration and freezer burn. Also, for the same reason avoid frozen fish with ice crystals inside the package.

Fresh crabs and lobster need to be kept alive until the moment you cook them. Crabs should feel heavy for their size and have hard shells (unless they are soft-shell crabs), without any cracks. Lobster tails should clamp down when you open them up. Shrimp are not sold alive but their shells should still be moist and have no black spots. Strangely enough, frozen raw shrimp in the shell (which are frozen right after being caught), are typically better quality than the fresh shrimp available in some stores, so keep that in mind when shopping.

Fresh oysters, mussels and clams in the shell should have unbroken, moist shells that tightly close up when tapped (which shows that they are still alive). Even if you buy them shucked (as is usually the case with scallops), their flesh should be plump and contain no sand or shell fragments.

Seafood should smell fresh, like the sea, and never have a smell so fishy that it hits you between the eyes and makes you see stars; it is inedible when it reaches that point. If you ask, most fish shops will package your seafood properly so that you can get it home safely.

Tips on Using Frozen Fish and Seafood

Frozen fish and seafood should be completely thawed, rinsed and patted dry before being cooked. Thaw fish in the fridge overnight in a drip tray, not at room temperature.

Cooking Fish

Fish flesh consists of water, proteins, fats, vitamins and minerals. Unlike the protein of land-based animals, however, fish protein has very little connective tissue and, therefore, is less dense and more buoyant, so it is naturally very tender. This is why fish and seafood can quickly lose their juiciness and become dry when cooked (even when cooked at low temperatures).

There are no differences in the density of fish from one end to the other, unlike with large game and birds. Just about any type of cooking method can be used for fish, except boiling, which would cause it to fall apart. These are some general recommendations for cooking fish and seafood:

- **Whole small fish:** grilling, pan-frying, baking *en papillote*, steaming
- **Whole large fish:** baking, roasting, broiling, barbecuing
- **Fish steaks:** baking, roasting (especially meaty cuts such as swordfish, or monkfish tail), barbecuing, steaming
- **Thick fish fillets:** grilling, barbecuing, smoking, steaming, braising
- **Thin fish fillets:** pan-frying, smoking, steaming, poaching, baking *en papillote*

Filleting whole fish takes some practice but it's a useful skill to have, especially if you like to catch your own fish. See "How to Fillet Round Fish" (pages 158–59) and "How to Fillet Flat Fish" (pages 160–63) to learn how.

- **Fish portions:** deep-frying (after coating or battering) poaching, steaming

One of the most difficult skills to grilling fish is keeping it from falling apart. One trick for turning a fillet over intact in your grill pan is to use the proper tool: a fish turner. It looks like any old spatula, but it's not. It has slots to let sauce or pan drippings through but is elongated to get a better hold of a fish fillet. If you cook fish a lot, invest in one of these. The other trick to keeping fish together is to leave the skin on, which holds the delicate flesh together!

Doneness

The terms "rare," "medium" and "well done" do not apply to fish, so chefs generally aim to remove fish from heat when it is still moist and soft; this happens when it reaches an internal temperature between 145F (63C) and 150F (66C) and the flesh just begins to flake. Keep in mind that fish and shellfish, like meat, continue to cook a tiny bit even after they are removed from heat. Health Canada, by contrast, recommends that fish be cooked to 160F (70C) and shellfish be cooked to 165F (75C). Most chefs would never cook shellfish that long, however, since we know they will turn into rubber by that time, so we cook them until they show recognizable signs of being done. These signs of doneness vary from one type of shellfish to another—refer to the shellfish recipes for more information.

Whole fish require more cooking time than fillets. You can definitely use a thermometer to read the internal temperature of fish but this is simply not practical with shellfish.

> ## Tip
> A good guideline for cooking a fish *fillet* is to cook it for five minutes for every ½ inch (1.5 cm) of thickness, measured at the thickest part (including stuffing) at 375F (190C).

Make sure you have your sauces or condiments ready to serve before the fish is cooked, since it doesn't need to rest before being served the way meat does and will get cold fast!

Fish Substitutions

When substituting one kind of fish for another in a recipe, what matters the most is the oil (fat) content of the fish; substitute a lean fish for another lean fish, and an oily fish for another oily fish. Fish with light coloured flesh are almost always much leaner than fish with dark or brightly coloured flesh.

How to Fillet Round Fish (e.g., Salmon)

This filleting method can be used for filleting salmon or any other round fish, such as Arctic char, mackerel, bass, snapper, perch and trout. Some fish, such as trout, mackerel and catfish, don't need scaling.

01 **Scale the fish:** If the fish needs scaling, you can use a fish scaler or the back of either a tablespoon or a knife. Remove the fish scales by scraping the fish from tail to head with the tool (**a**). This is easier if the skin hasn't dried out, so if it has, wet the fish. Be prepared for a huge mess when you remove the scales, as they will fly all over! Spread newspapers or paper towel all around the cutting board before starting. Using a dish towel to hold the fish might help to prevent it slipping as you scale it with your other hand.

02 **Remove fins:** If the fish still has the dorsal fin attached (on the top of the fish's back), cut it off using kitchen shears or a sharp knife.

03 **Gut the fish:** If the fish hasn't been gutted yet, place the fish on a clean cutting board and slit the belly using a sharp fillet or boning knife. Reach inside the cavity with a spoon or your fingers to remove the entrails, and discard them. Rinse the fish under cold water, inside and out. Pat dry.

04 **Fillet the fish:** With the fish lying on its side, and with the belly facing you, get a good grip on the top fillet of the fish. With the other hand, insert your knife (blade facing up) to find the starting point to make a diagonal cut through the top fillet, behind the head and gill (**b**). Continue the diagonal cut from above the fillet (**c**). Lift the top fillet up with one hand in order to position your knife to start cutting through the flesh and rib bones towards the tail (**d** and **e**). Press down on the top fillet to hold the fish in place while you make a smooth sawing motion through the rib cage, following the backbone with your knife (rather than making wide cuts going in and out, which will create rough edges and waste flesh). Cut under and past your hand (**f**). When you get close to the tail, lift the top fillet again and continue cutting to completely separate it from the rest of the fish (**g** and **h**). Flip the fish over and repeat these steps to remove the other fillet.

05 **Remove the ribs:** Using the tip of your knife, score underneath the ribs and lift up the ribs with one hand and slice through to the edge of the fillet on a 20-degree angle (with the blade almost parallel to the fillet) to completely separate the ribs from the flesh (**i** and **j**). Remove the ribs from the other fillet. Scrape off excess flesh from the rib cage and save for other fish recipes (**k** and **l**).

06 **Remove pin bones:** Run your finger along the flesh of the fillets to feel for small pin bones. Using tweezers or needle-nose pliers, pull them out by going with the grain (towards the front of the fish) rather than against the flesh, and discard them (**m**).

07 **Remove the skin:** To remove the skin, place each fillet, skin side down, on the cutting board with the tail end closest to you. Slide the tip of your knife between the flesh and skin on a 20-degree angle, deep enough to make space for you to press down and hold the skin down with one hand (**n**). With your other hand, glide the knife away from you, sliding it gently between the flesh and skin, separating the fillet from the skin underneath in one piece (**o**, **p** and **q**).

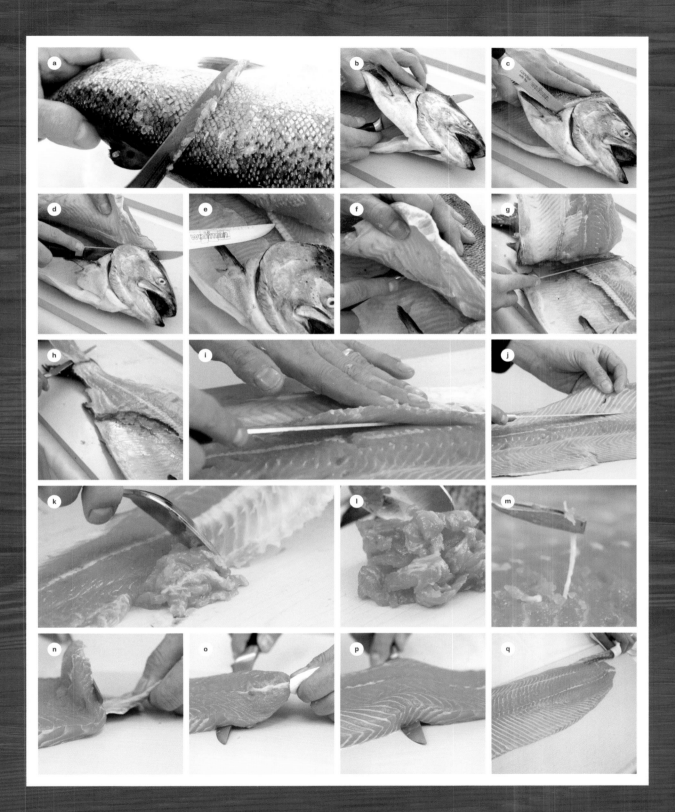

How to Fillet Flat Fish

Most people are surprised to learn that flat fish have eyes on only one side of their body. Flat fish start out with eyes on either side of the brain, but when they mature their eyes slide to one side so that they can better camouflage themselves as they swim, dark side facing up and light side facing down.

Filleting a flat fish is quite different from filleting a round fish: you need more know-how, since a flat fish has four fillets rather than two. In North America, "flounder" includes lemon sole, gray sole and Pacific Dover sole (which are not the same as true Dover sole from England). It is advisable to skin flounder and sole before filleting and cooking, so follow the first filleting method below. Halibut and turbot, on the other hand, typically have their skin left on during filleting and cooking, as in the second filleting method below. Freeze the head, bones and tail to make a fish stock at some other time.

Method 1: Skinning before Filleting, for Fish such as Flounder and Sole

01 **Cut off all fins** using kitchen shears in order to simplify the removal of skin (**a**).

02 **Peel off skin:** Place the fish on your work surface, dark side facing up. Make an incision across the tail just deep enough to get your knife under the skin (**b**).

Scrape a little of the skin back so that you can grasp it with your hand and, once you have a good grip on the skin, slowly peel it back right off the fish (**c**). This action should simultaneously remove the dark flesh (bloodline) down the centre of the fillet while leaving the two top fillets and bones intact.

When you get to the head, the skin will easily tear off (**d**). Repeat this step on the other side of the fish to expose the two bottom fillets.

03 **Fillet the fish:** Starting behind the head, make an incision down along the backbone (**e**).

Then angle the knife at about 20 degrees (blade almost parallel to the fish) and cut the flesh going horizontally from the centre of the backbone to the outer edge of the fish, exposing a row of bones (**f**).

Cut underneath the flesh to separate it from the bone, keeping the flesh intact in one whole fillet. Completely remove the fillet, gently separating it from the backbone with long, smooth strokes. Follow these same steps to remove the other three fillets, which will leave you with four skinless fillets (**g** and **h**).

How to Fillet Flat Fish

Method 2: Filleting before Skinning, for Fish such as Halibut and Turbot

01 **Fillet the fish:** Place the fish on a clean cutting board, light side facing up, with the tail closest to you. Look for the faint line that goes down the centre of the fish, and follow this line with your knife from the shoulder (behind the head, gills and fin) to the tail, making an incision into the skin deep enough to touch the spine (**a**, **b**, **c**, **d**).

Turn the knife to about 20 degrees (almost parallel to the fish) and, starting at the top, cut against the backbone towards the outer edge of the fish; gently cut down the full length of the fish, exposing the row of bones (**e**, **f**, **g**).

Completely remove the fillet by cutting along the outer edge of the fillet (**h**, **i**, **j**). Repeat these same steps to remove the other bottom fillet (**k**). Flip the fish over and repeat the steps to remove the two top fillets.

02 **Remove the skin:** To skin the fish, place one fillet skin side down on the cutting board with the thinner (tail end) closest to you. Slide the tip of your knife between the flesh and skin (on a 20-degree angle) to make space for you to grab hold of the skin with one hand (**l**).

With your other hand, glide the knife away from you, sliding it gently between the flesh and skin, separating the fillet from the skin underneath in one piece (**m**, **n**). Repeat these steps to skin the remaining fillets.

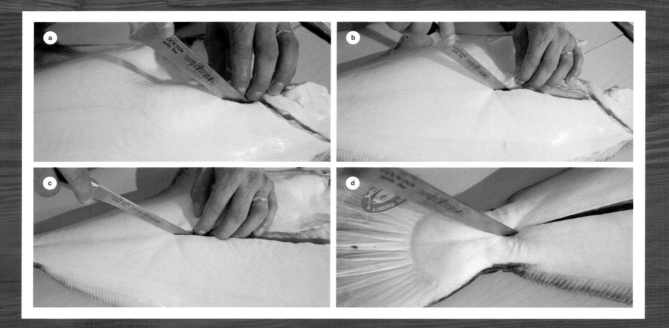

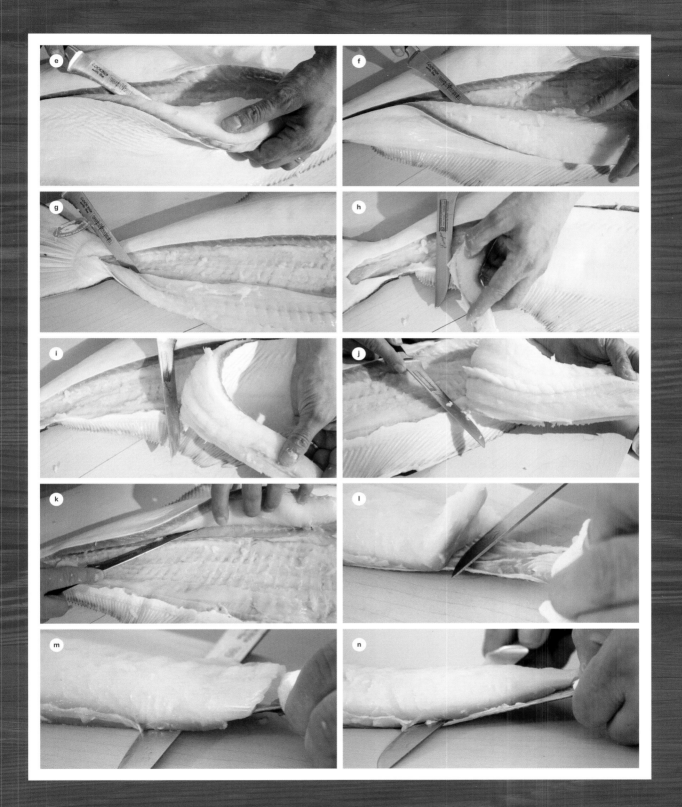

THE SWIMMERS: FISH AND SHELLFISH

Baked Xaxli'p Salmon on Pea Purée

MAKES 4 SERVINGS

This is a salmon recipe inspired by my mom who comes from the Xaxli'p First Nation. I remember her telling me that when she was little, she could hardly wait for the warm weather to arrive because she knew that was when the sockeye would return. When the people heard a particular type of cricket sound (around the end of May or beginning of June), they knew they had two to three days to get down to the river and cast their salmon nets. Some of the elders used to tell this story about how the crickets called the salmon. Noticing the sound of the crickets was their way of listening to the land.

Purple (red) laver seaweed is used in the crust of this recipe to add flavour and dramatic colour. Although my mother's people didn't have direct access to seaweed, they traded with coastal Indigenous nations to get it (as did other First Nations who lived in the interior of BC). *Note:* If working with a whole fish, follow the instructions in "How to Fillet Round Fish" (page 158) and leave the skin on, but you will have to store the excess fish because a whole salmon will be too large for this recipe. Prepare the Pea Purée, which will keep for up to three days in the fridge, before cooking the fish.

1 **salmon** fillet (1 lb/500 g), skin on (or 4 salmon portions ¼ lb/115 g each)

½ tsp (2.5 mL) **Cold-Smoked Alderwood Salt** (see recipe, page 30) or kosher or sea salt

½ tsp (2.5 mL) smoked **paprika**

½ tsp (2.5 mL) crushed black **peppercorns**

Sprig fresh **cedar** (optional)

CRUST:

1 cup (250 mL) **bread crumbs**

2 Tbsp (30 mL) dried **seaweed** (preferably purple/red laver)

1 Tbsp (15 mL) roasted **pine nuts** (or almonds)

¼ tsp (1 mL) kosher **salt** (or sea salt)

1 tsp (5 mL) **lemon zest**

GLAZE:

2 **egg whites**, beaten

1 Tbsp (15 mL) **maple syrup**

2 tsp (10 mL) **Dijon mustard**

2 Tbsp (30 mL) **butter**, melted

01 Preheat oven to 375F (190C).

02 Rinse and pat dry the salmon fillet with paper towels. If still whole, cut the fillet into four equal-sized portions. Season the salmon with the salt, paprika and pepper on a parchment paper–lined baking sheet and let stand for 30 minutes.

03 In a food processor, grind the bread crumbs, seaweed and pine nuts to a fine grind; transfer mixture to a bowl and combine with salt and lemon zest.

04 Prepare the glaze for the salmon by whisking together the egg whites, maple syrup, mustard and butter in a small bowl. Brush glaze over the top of each piece of salmon. Evenly coat the top and sides of each fish portion with the crust mixture.

05 Bake fish for 10 to 15 minutes (depending on the thickness of the portions) while you prepare the Pea Purée (if you have not already done so).

06 Check that the fish reaches 145F (65C), or Health Canada's recommended 160F (70C), before serving.

07 Spread Pea Purée on warmed plates and serve salmon on top. Garnish with a sprig of fresh cedar (which is edible) if desired.

CONTINUED ...

Pea Purée

MAKES 2 CUPS (475 ML)

Pea Purée has a bright green colour, a fresh taste and just the right texture as a base for a fish fillet or steak. You can use fresh or frozen peas, but don't bother with canned peas.

2 Tbsp (30 mL) **butter**
⅓ cup (80 mL) finely diced **onion**
2 tsp (10 mL) chopped **garlic**
½ cup (120 mL) **Vegetable Stock** (see recipe, page 38)
   or store-bought unsalted vegetable stock
2¼ cups (530 mL) **peas**
1 tsp (5 mL) minced fresh **tarragon**
¼ tsp (1 mL) kosher **salt** (or sea salt)
¼ tsp (1 mL) ground **black pepper**
¼ tsp (1 mL) **sugar** (optional)

01 In a medium-sized saucepan, heat the butter over low heat. Add the onion and garlic, and let soften without colouring.

02 Heat the stock in a microwave or on the stovetop almost to the boiling point. Add stock to the pan, along with peas, tarragon, salt and pepper, and bring mixture to a boil. Cook for five minutes over medium heat.

03 Remove mixture from heat, pour into a food processor and blend until smooth.

04 Taste and adjust with sugar if desired.

Quick Pan-Fried Rainbow Trout with Herbed Butter

MAKES 2 SERVINGS

Some fish are known by many different names, which can make shopping a little confusing. "Rainbow trout" refers to inland or freshwater trout, which has a slightly milder taste and lighter colour than seagoing trout, which is also known as steelhead trout and whose flesh colour is similar to that of salmon.

I add a bit of walnut oil to finish this dish and give it a subtle flavour I like, but this oil is not suitable for cooking, since it gets bitter really quickly. If you buy a bottle of walnut oil, get a small one and use the oil in salads or to finish vegetable dishes by sprinkling some on at the end of the cooking.

2 **rainbow trout fillets** (1 lb/500 g in total), skin on
1 tsp (5 mL) **Lemon Pepper Salt** (see recipe, page 21)
1 Tbsp (15 mL) pure **olive oil**
2 Tbsp (30 mL) all-purpose **flour**
½ **lemon**, cut into wedges (optional)

01 Rinse and pat dry the fillets with paper towels. Season the flesh side of the fish with Lemon Pepper Salt.

02 If your frying pan is too small to cook the fillets lying flat, cut them down to size and cook them one at a time if need be.

03 Over medium heat, heat a large frying pan and add the olive oil.

04 In a bowl, dredge the fillets in flour and shake off excess.

05 Brown the fillets in the pan, on the flesh side first, for three minutes. Then turn the fillets over and continue to cook for approximately three more minutes.

06 Check that the fish reaches 145F (65C), or Health Canada's recommended 160F (70C), before serving. Transfer the fish to a warmed serving plate while you prepare the Herbed Butter. Serve with lemon wedges if using.

Herbed Butter

This recipe, quick and easy to make, adds a touch of flavour and colour to any vegetable or fish entrée. I prefer to make this and serve it on fish rather than cook fish in butter, since butter burns very quickly.

2 tsp (10 mL) **butter**
1 Tbsp (15 mL) chopped fresh **dill** (or parsley or chives)
1 tsp (5 mL) **walnut oil**

01 Melt the butter in a sauté pan (clean it out first if you cooked the fish in it). Add the dill and cook for one minute. Remove the pan from heat and stir in the walnut oil. Pour over the fish.

Tangy Bass Fillet with Peanut Sauce

MAKES 4 SERVINGS

Cooking with roasted peanuts is a tradition that goes back 3,500 years to the Indigenous peoples of the Andes mountains in South America. The Mojo and Baure were among those who cultivated peanuts in the valleys of eastern Bolivia and the Tapirape did the same in central Brazil. Arawak living in the Caribbean also farmed peanuts, and over time Native Americans of the southern United States, such as the Cherokee, Choctaw, Creek and Seminole, developed this tradition once peanuts were introduced to the area. Ecuadorians, Bolivians and Peruvians still make peanut sauce flavoured with achiote for various dishes including potato cakes (see Andean Mountain Potato Cakes, page 223). Luckily for us, peanut butter is available, so we don't have to shell, roast and grind nuts anymore.

Achiote is an earthy seed that comes from a bush that grows in the tropical region of the Americas; the Tupi-Garani of the Amazon traditionally used it for cooking, body paint, lipstick and medicine. Look for achiote seed seasoning (it also goes by the name annatto) in Latin American markets. Avoid achiote seeds, which are incredibly difficult to grind (as I found out the hard way). For this recipe, you could use rainbow trout instead of bass, and smooth or chunky peanut butter (but make sure it is the natural, unsweetened type). South Americans would use an aji amarillo pepper (also known as an "aji yellow" or "yellow chile"), which is really hot, but I prefer the less hot jalapeno. Try a poblano if you want just a little bit of heat. This dish would go well over rice (see the Wild Rice Pepper Pilaf recipe, page 217), or served with some bright green steamed veggies. Prepare the peanut sauce before cooking the fish.

4 **bass fillets** (1 lb/500 g in total), boneless and skinless
½ tsp (2.5 mL) kosher **salt** (or sea salt)
¼ tsp (1 mL) **cayenne pepper**
2 Tbsp (30 mL) pure **olive oil**

OPTIONAL GARNISH:
Chopped fresh **cilantro**

01 Rinse and pat dry fish fillets. Season the fish with the Lemon Pepper Salt and cayenne.

02 Heat a frying pan to medium heat. Add the oil and quickly cook the fish on both sides. Check that the fish reaches 145F (65C), or Health Canada's recommended 160F (70C), before serving.

03 Serve fish with Peanut Sauce spooned on top. Garnish with cilantro if using.

Peanut Sauce

MAKES 1½ CUPS (350 ML)

2 Tbsp (30 mL) **butter**
½ cup (120 mL) diced **onion**
1 whole **jalapeno**, minced (with seeds)
1 tsp (5 mL) ground **achiote** seed seasoning (or
    ½ tsp/2.5 mL sweet paprika and ½ tsp/2.5 mL turmeric)
½ tsp (2.5 mL) kosher **salt** (or sea salt)
½ tsp (2.5 mL) ground **coriander**
¼ tsp (1 mL) ground **cumin**
1 Tbsp (15 mL) **tomato paste**
1¼ cups (300 mL) **milk**
⅔ cup (160 mL) natural **peanut butter**
¼ tsp (1 mL) ground **black pepper**

01 Heat a small saucepan to medium heat. Add the butter, onion and jalapeno pepper, and cook for five minutes.

02 Lower heat slightly. Add the achiote, salt, coriander, cumin and tomato paste. Cook mixture until the onion and pepper soften (about five minutes).

03 Slightly heat the milk on the stovetop or in a microwave. Set aside.

04 Add the peanut butter to the onion mixture and cook for one minute. Add half the milk and stir to combine using a whisk. Add the rest of the milk, whisk, and simmer sauce for two to three minutes.

05 Add black pepper and stir. Serve over fish.

Dandelion and Pepper Stuffed Salmon with Clarified Butter

MAKES 6 SERVINGS

This recipe produces a colourfully stuffed fish that will be easy to serve because you will cook two fillets tied together. I think even my sister Marlene Wolfman, who doesn't cook much, might be willing to try making this recipe, since she loves salmon as much as I do.

Though the lowly dandelion that gardeners battle on their lawns each year is not indigenous to the Americas, a wild dandelion is indigenous to the Rocky Mountains, which might explain why dandelion appears frequently in indigenous food cookbooks. Indigenous people also used dandelion roots as a tonic for the blood. Green dandelion leaves are often used in salads (and the yellow petals are edible too), but I like to use the leaves in stuffings (see Easy Deer Lasagna, page 151). Don't eat dandelions from your own yard unless you are positive they are pesticide free.

salmon fillets (3 lb/1.5 kg in total), skin on

DRY RUB:

2 Tbsp (30 mL) **brown sugar**

1 tsp (5 mL) **paprika**

Pinch **cayenne pepper**

½ tsp (2.5 mL) ground **black pepper**, divided

½ tsp (2.5 mL) kosher **salt** (or sea salt), divided

STUFFING:

¼ cup (60 mL) **butter**

2 cups (475 mL) julienned **peppers** (red, orange, yellow or green)

⅔ cup (160 mL) sliced **onion**

1 tsp (5 mL) chopped **garlic**

2 cups (475 mL) **dandelion leaves** (or spinach), washed and chopped

½ tsp (2.5 mL) **lemon zest**

OPTIONAL GARNISH:

Chopped fresh **parsley**

01 Rinse and pat dry fillets. Spread them out on a parchment paper–lined baking sheet. In a bowl, combine the brown sugar, paprika, cayenne, half of the black pepper, and half of the salt, and sprinkle the dry rub on the fillets (flesh side only). Place them in the refrigerator until the stuffing is ready.

02 Preheat oven to 375F (190C).

03 To clarify the butter used in the stuffing, heat the butter in a double boiler. Alternatively, heat a saucepan of water on the stovetop to the boiling point and cover with a metal bowl. Lower the heat to medium, add the butter and let it melt. Skim off and discard the foam that forms on the surface, and simmer until the butterfat that is left becomes clear, separating from the milk solids that sink to the bottom.

04 To make the stuffing, heat a frying pan over low heat. Spoon half of the clarified butter into the pan, and cook the peppers, onion and garlic until soft (about 8 to 10 minutes). Add the dandelion leaves, lemon zest, and the rest of the salt and pepper, and cook for one minute. Remove from heat and let cool.

05 Cut four or five pieces of butcher twine about 8 inches (20 cm) long and place underneath the skin of one fish fillet, widthwise. Spread the stuffing over the fish flesh and cover with the top fillet. Knot the twine to secure the two fillets.

06 Assuming that the fish is 2 inches (5 cm) thick (at the thickest part, including stuffing), bake for 20 minutes. Check that the fish reaches 145F (65C), or Health Canada's recommended 160F (70C), before serving.

07 Spoon the remaining clarified butter into a small ramekin and serve with the fish. Garnish with a sprinkle of parsley if desired.

Crispy Fried Coconut Breaded Smelts

MAKES 6 SERVINGS

Freshwater smelt is quite popular among First Nations in the Great Lakes region, although my mother's people in BC are more familiar with the eulachon (oolichan), which belongs to the smelt family but is an ocean fish that is found along the Pacific coast from northern California to Alaska. Freshwater smelts are small fish that are caught in early spring in nets, by flashlight at night. Follow the instructions in "How to Fillet Round Fish" (page 158) for gutting the fish. Remove the heads, but there is no need to scale them or remove their tails or skin. As you eat the smelts, the fillets will separate from the backbone, which you can toss out.

12 **smelts** (1⅓ lb/600 g in total)

1 tsp (5 mL) kosher **salt** (or sea salt)

1 cup (250 mL) all-purpose **flour**

1 cup (250 mL) unsweetened shredded **coconut**

2 large **eggs**, beaten

Vegetable oil for frying

1 Tbsp (15 mL) chopped fresh **parsley**

01 Lightly season smelts with half of the salt.

02 Combine flour and coconut in a wide shallow dish; a pie dish is ideal.

03 Holding a smelt by the tail, dip it in egg and let excess drip off. Then dredge the smelt in the flour and coconut mixture, on both sides, shaking off any excess. Set aside; repeat steps with the rest of the fish.

04 Pour oil into a large saucepan to a depth of ½ inch (1.5 cm). Heat oil over medium-high heat to 325F (160C).

05 Fry fish until light golden and just cooked through. You may have to turn the fish over and cook them on the other side. This should take about one minute per batch. Let the oil return to 325F (160C) between batches. (Check that the fish reaches 145F (65C), or Health Canada's recommended 160F (70C), before serving.

06 Transfer fish to a paper towel–lined plate or wire rack to drain. Season fish with the rest of the salt and the parsley. If you like, serve smelts on a bed of greens with lemon wedges.

NOTE: Prepare the Pickled Melon before cooking the fish. The melon can be made up to two days in advance and, for best flavour, should be chilled.

Swimming with the Whitefish, Served with Pickled Melon

MAKES 4 SERVINGS

"Whitefish," or "white fish," is a general name for several species of fish that are similar in colour and texture: anything from cod, whiting and haddock, to hake, pollock and Atlantic freshwater fish. The particular fish I am referring to in this recipe, however, is plain ol' "whitefish," a fish that is indigenous to the Great Lakes but can now be found in lakes from Alaska to Newfoundland. It's also known as humpback fish, gizzard fish, Sault whitefish, common whitefish, eastern whitefish, Great Lakes whitefish and inland whitefish; several Ontario reserves are named after the whitefish. You should be able to find whitefish at any Jewish fish market but if you can't, use any other type of lean fish. You will need a 4½ lb (2 kg) fish.

2 Great Lakes whitefish fillets (1½ lb/680 g in total), boneless and skinless
1 Tbsp (15 mL) Swimming with the Fishes Spice Mix (see recipe, page 25)
2 Tbsp (30 mL) pure olive oil
2 Tbsp (30 mL) butter

OPTIONAL GARNISH:
½ lemon, cut into wedges
2 tsp (10 mL) chopped chives

01 Preheat oven to 350F (175C).

02 Rinse and pat dry fillets. Cut fillets into four equal portions. Season both sides of the fish with the spice mix and let rest for five minutes. Drizzle with oil and let rest for five more minutes.

03 Heat a large sauté pan over medium heat and add the butter. Pan-fry the portions for three minutes. Transfer fish to a parchment paper–lined baking sheet and bake in the oven for four minutes. Check that the fish reaches 145F (65C), or Health Canada's recommended 160F (70C).

04 Serve fish with lemon wedges and chives if using, and 1 to 2 tablespoons (15–30 mL) of the Pickled Melon (drained).

Pickled Melon

MAKES 2 CUPS (475 ML)
Pickled melon goes great with any lean grilled or baked fish.

1 tsp (5 mL) Pickling Spice (see recipe, page 27)
1 cup (250 mL) water
1 cup (250 mL) white vinegar
½ firm cantaloupe (or honeydew melon)
1 tsp (5 mL) chopped fresh dill (optional)

01 In a small saucepan, combine the Pickling Spice, water and vinegar, and bring to a simmer. Simmer over low heat to reduce the liquid by half. Strain mixture and allow it to cool in the refrigerator.

02 Cut the melon into small dice. Pour the pickling liquid over the melon, add the dill if using, cover and allow to marinate at least 1 hour in the fridge. Strain melon before serving.

Grilled Halibut with Chili Cucumber Vinaigrette

MAKES 4 SERVINGS

We learned when we visited the Sḵwx̱wú7mesh Lil̓wat7úl Cultural Centre in Whistler, BC, that the Kwagiulth believed Halibut threw off its skin and fins to emerge as the first human after the great flood subsided. Each Indigenous nation seems to have its own creation story, and many begin with a flood and an animal transforming into the first human.

If you have an opportunity to catch a whole halibut, I am jealous. Just kidding. Halibut is a flat fish, so it will require special filleting. Follow the instructions for the second method in "How to Fillet Flat Fish" (page 162), but leave the skin on.

1 **halibut fillet** (1 lb/500 g), skin on (or 4 halibut portions, 4 oz/115 g each, skin on)
½ tsp (1 mL) **Cold-Smoked Alderwood Salt** (see recipe, page 30) or kosher or sea salt
¼ tsp (1 mL) crushed black **peppercorns**
¼ cup (60 mL) pure **olive oil**

OPTIONAL GARNISH:
½ **lemon**, sliced
½ **green onion** (green part only), sliced
Fresh **arugula**

01 Rinse and pat dry fish fillet. Cut into four equal-sized portions. Rub the salt and pepper into the flesh of the fish.

02 Heat a grill pan over medium-high heat.

03 Brush the portions with the olive oil on both sides, and grill them on the skin side first to mark the skin and help them hold together, about three to five minutes, without moving them.

04 Carefully turn the portions over and cook for four minutes on the other side. Do the cooking in batches if your grill pan is not large enough to hold them all with space in between; you don't want to cram them in all together.

05 Total cooking time for a ¾ inch (2 cm) portion should not exceed eight minutes. Check that the fish reaches 145F (65C), or Health Canada's recommended 160F (70C), before serving with the vinaigrette.

06 Grill lemon slices and green onion, if using. Serve with vinaigrette and arugula.

NOTE: It's best if you make the Chili Cucumber Vinaigrette before the halibut dish to give it a little time to work its magic.

Chili Cucumber Vinaigrette

MAKES 1¾ CUPS (415 ML)

1 cup (250 mL) seeded and cubed English cucumber

½ cup (120 mL) small-diced green pepper

¼ cup (60 mL) white wine vinegar

1 tsp (5 mL) extra-virgin olive oil

¼ tsp (1 mL) chili flakes

¼ tsp (1 mL) table salt

¼ tsp (1 mL) ground black pepper

1 tsp (5 mL) prepared horseradish

1 tsp (5 mL) maple syrup

Extra salt and pepper to taste

01 Place the cucumber, green pepper, vinegar and olive oil in a bowl, and mix well.

02 Add the chili flakes, salt and pepper, horseradish and maple syrup. Blend well.

03 Refrigerate the mixture for a minimum of 10 to 15 minutes in a nonreactive dish. Taste and adjust the flavour with more salt or pepper if needed.

Beer-Battered Fish and Chips

MAKES 4 SERVINGS

Fish play a key role in the traditional diet and culture of Indigenous people. Halibut fishing has been a tradition among the Haida in Haida Gwaii, BC, for thousands of years. The Haida devised ivory fishing hooks and, like the neighbouring Tlingit nation, in more recent times would use wooden halibut hooks made of intricately carved wood. Fishing for halibut was preceded by ceremonial singing to the fish to let them know a battle was upon them.

Halibut just happens to be one of the best fishes for fish and chips due to its dense, firm texture, although haddock and cod are a close second and third, in my opinion. No surprises there. If you are working with a whole fish, follow the instructions in the second method for filleting and skinning fish in "How to Fillet a Flat Fish" (page 162) before starting the recipe below.

There's a trick to great fries, and that is to fry them in two stages. However, since you are using the same oil to also cook the fish, there's a sequence to follow carefully. The oil is the key to the whole recipe. Beef tallow is what a lot of people in Britain used for making fish and chips (a near staple there, I hear), but vegetable oil is preferred now because it costs less and may be better for your health.

BEER BATTER:

1 cup (250 mL) all-purpose flour
1 Tbsp (15 mL) paprika
1½ tsp (7.5 mL) table salt
1 tsp (5 mL) ground black pepper
1 tsp (5 mL) onion powder
1 egg, beaten
1 bottle (12 oz/355 mL) beer

FRIES:

5 large Russet potatoes
11 cups (2.6 L) vegetable oil for deep frying
¼ tsp (1 mL) kosher salt (or sea salt)
¼ tsp (1 mL) ground black pepper

FISH:

1 halibut fillet (1 lb/500 g), skinless and boneless
1½ tsp (7.5 mL) kosher salt (or sea salt)
1 tsp (5 mL) ground black pepper
½ cup (120 mL) all-purpose flour

TO SERVE:

1 lemon, cut into wedges
Malt vinegar

01 To make the batter, in a bowl combine 1 cup (250 mL) flour with the paprika, salt, pepper and onion powder. Blend mixture well. Add the egg and beer, and use a whisk to slowly blend the ingredients together. Let batter rest for 10 minutes before using.

02 For the fries, you can leave the potato skins on or peel them off, but scrub the potatoes regardless. Cut them into pieces about ½ inch (1.5 cm) by ½ inch (1.5 cm) by 3 inches (8 cm) and rinse. Keep them in cold water if you are not ready to continue.

03 Drain the potatoes in a colander, and then thoroughly pat them dry on a baking sheet using a paper towel.

04 Heat the oil in a deep fryer to 325F (160C). Blanch 1 cup (250 mL) of potatoes at a time for two to three minutes per batch. Use a slotted spoon to gently move them around in the oil. Drain them on fresh paper towel before continuing. Allow the potatoes to cool.

05 Rinse and pat the fish dry with paper towels. Cut fillet into eight equal-sized portions. Season both sides of fish with salt and pepper.

06 Place ½ cup (120 mL) flour in a shallow dish. One at a time, dredge each piece of fish in the flour, shake off the excess and dip the fish into the batter, letting excess batter drip off before carefully placing the fish in the fryer. Turn each piece of fish over after

two minutes of frying so that they are cooked evenly brown on both sides. Check that the fish reaches 145F (65C), or Health Canada's recommended 160F (70C), before serving. Remove fish from the deep fryer and place on a wire rack to allow excess oil to drain off. You can place the fish on a warm tray in the oven until your fries are ready.

07 Turn up the heat to 375F (190C) and return the potatoes to the oil, cooking them in batches for one to two minutes. Drain the fries and season with salt and pepper.

08 Serve fish and chips with lemon wedges and vinegar. Fish without lemon is like a hug without a kiss!

NOTE: Make the pesto before steaming the mussels so it's ready to add while the shellfish are hot.

Steamed Mussels in Hazelnut Pesto

MAKES 4 SERVINGS

The pesto sauce goes a long way towards giving an inviting aroma and taste to the broth of this mussel dish. Italian-style pesto is made with pine nuts and served on pasta, but here I use hazelnuts and serve the pesto over shellfish in the Algonquin tradition of thickening broths with nut meal, combined with the Malecite tradition of steaming mussels.

Trees and tree nuts were incredibly valuable to Indigenous peoples across North America, providing food that could be eaten raw, toasted or ground into meal. Hazelnuts, walnuts, hickory nuts and pecans, as well as peanuts (which are legumes that develop underground), were used for making soups, stews and dried foods to eat when travelling. Some BC First Nations regarded hazelnut bushes as so important that they burned them to the ground in controlled fires to improve nut yield—an example of natural resource management in action.

This recipe is the closest I get to smelling the sea in Toronto! And a word to the wise: have some crusty garlic bread with this dish to sop up every last drop.

12 cups (2.8 L) cold **water** (optional)

2 Tbsp (30 mL) kosher **salt** (or sea salt, optional)

3½ to 4 lb (1.5–2 kg) fresh **mussels**

2 Tbsp (30 mL) pure **olive oil**

1 Tbsp (15 mL) **butter**

4 tsp (20 mL) thinly sliced **shallot**

¼ cup (60 mL) chopped fresh flat-leaf **parsley**, divided

1½ cups (350 mL) dry **white wine**

1 tsp (5 mL) **lemon zest** (optional)

01 Brining mussels before cooking them is optional. The purpose of soaking mussels in a cold saltwater brine is to remove sand—grit is the last thing you want in your mouth when you eat mussels. The cold brine simulates their natural environment in seawater so that they keep breathing and expelling impurities (toxins) before you cook them. Combine the water and salt in a stockpot or large bowl. Add the mussels, ensuring that they are covered. Chill for 15 minutes. Rinse mussels after brining.

02 Examine the mussel shells very carefully under good light to make sure there are no cracks or chips. Scrub the mussels under cold running water with a scrub brush to remove sand, barnacles and other debris. When you tap on them, they should close up. Discard any mussels that don't immediately tighten up.

03 Remove mussel "beards" by yanking them off towards the hinge of the shell, and discard the shells. Try to do this *just* before moving on to the next instruction (because removing their beards will effectively kill them, and you don't want to kill them until you cook them).

04 Heat the oil and butter in a stockpot over medium heat. Add the shallot and half the parsley and cook until softened (about two minutes). Do not allow shallots to colour.

05 Deglaze the pot by pouring in the wine and scraping up bits of sediment, swirling the liquid around in the pot. Drop the mussels into the pot, cover with a lid and steam for two minutes.

06 Stir the mussels and add 2 tablespoons (30 mL) of the pesto to the pot, along with the remaining parsley, cover and steam for two more minutes.

07 Remove the pot from heat and add the lemon zest if using. Stir the pot. Carefully remove mussels from the pot and divide between serving bowls, throwing out any that have not opened.

08 Divide sauce into serving bowls and enjoy.

CONTINUED ...

Hazelnut Pesto

MAKES 1½ CUPS (350 ML)

We make our pesto from the basil we grow in the backyard. Each spring we buy a basil plant and pop it into the earth; it provides us with fresh leaves to cook with for nearly six months. If the climate where you live is not suitable for basil, try growing it on your windowsill instead. This recipe makes a lot, but you can store excess pesto in the fridge for up to five days (although it will discolour); use it in sandwiches or toss with cooked pasta.

⅓ cup (80 mL) hazelnuts
2 cups (475 mL) packed fresh basil leaves
½ cup (120 mL) extra-virgin olive oil
½ cup (120 mL) grated Parmesan cheese
1 tsp (5 mL) lemon zest
1 tsp (5 mL) kosher salt (or sea salt)
¼ tsp (1 mL) ground black pepper
1 Tbsp (15 mL) chopped garlic
Salt to taste
¼ tsp (1 mL) lemon juice (optional)

01 Toast hazelnuts in a dry frying pan over very low heat for up to five minutes, shaking the pan every minute so that they don't burn. Let cool, and rub nuts with a wet paper towel to remove their skins. Let cool and roughly chop.

02 Shred basil with a sharp knife. Then combine all of the pesto ingredients in a food processor, pulsing for 30 seconds at a time. Scrape down the sides of the food processor between pulses.

03 Adjust to taste with extra salt and lemon juice if using.

Labrador Tea Poached Flounder with Saskatoon Berry Drizzle

MAKES 4 SERVINGS

"Flounder" refers to a number of saltwater flat fish, which traditionally were caught using a spear in shallow waters off the Pacific and Alaskan coasts, as well as along the coast of Newfoundland, at different times of the year. Inuit typically boiled flounder and flavoured it with eulachon oil and wild onion, whereas Pacific Coast First Nations preferred to barbecue it and use the bones for making chowder.

In this recipe, I poach the small flounder fillets in a *court bouillon* made with onions and the leaves of a shrub that grows in the Far North but south of the tree line. Then I serve them rolled up and pierced with tiny skewers to emulate spears. You will end up with three fillets per serving.

If you are buying fillets, you are off to the races. Alternatively, you will need three whole fish and will need to follow the first method in the filleting instructions in "How to Fillet Flat Fish" (page 160). Prepare the Saskatoon Berry Drizzle before cooking the fish.

10 cups (2.4 L) **Labrador Tea Court Bouillon** (double recipe, see page 36)
12 **flounder** fillets (1½ lb/680 g in total), boneless and skinless (or 3 whole flounder, 4½ lb/2 kg in total)
12 **wooden skewers**
2 **cucumbers**, julienned
1 **carrot**, julienned

01 Strain the heated Labrador Tea Court Bouillon into a shallow pot. Roll the fillets up and skewer them.

02 Gently poach the fillets in the court bouillon over very low heat, uncovered.

03 Check that the fish reaches 145F (65C), or Health Canada's recommended 160F (70C), before serving. Use a slotted spoon to move the poached fillets onto a paper towel–lined plate and cover loosely with a small piece of foil until ready to serve.

04 Divide the cucumber and carrot between the servings and top with two to three fillets each. Serve with Saskatoon Berry Drizzle.

Saskatoon Berry Drizzle

MAKES 1½ CUPS (350 ML)

2 cups (475 mL) **saskatoon berries** (fresh or frozen)
¼ cup (60 mL) **sugar**
¼ tsp (1 mL) table **salt**
1 Tbsp (15 mL) **red wine vinegar**

01 In a small to medium-sized saucepan, combine the saskatoon berries with the sugar, salt and vinegar. Bring mixture to a boil, lower heat and simmer for four to five minutes. Simmer a little longer if you are using frozen berries, until they thicken.

02 Use a hand blender to blend the mixture until smooth. Remove from heat and serve in a bowl with a serving spoon for drizzling.

Steamed Littleneck Clams in Garlic Butter

MAKES 2 SERVINGS

The Kwakiutl are one Indigenous nation that traditionally consumed clams in a big way. Women used woven baskets to collect clams, which were steamed or skewered onto sticks and smoked.

For generations, Vancouver Island First Nations operated clam gardens in terraces they built on the shoreline, and First Nations still cultivate littleneck clams in these areas of BC. Along the eastern US coast, Mohegans held clambakes in the beach sand by digging holes that they filled with hot rocks and then covered with seaweed. Clams were placed on top, covered with more seaweed and steamed in the hole. The shells were so plentiful they came to be used to pave paths.

You can store fresh clams in your fridge for up to two days in their original sack, on a tray, covered with a damp cloth. If the clams are already shucked, chill them in their original container.

Littlenecks are really tender and great for eating raw, but I generally steam them. They are also among the smallest of the clams, so eating them doesn't require a fork and knife, as eating the odd-looking jumbo quahog ("co-hog") clams does. Because of their tenderness, littleneck clams are better appreciated steamed or baked rather than cooked in a clam chowder.

BRINE (SEE PAGE 178)

2 cups (475 mL) Fish Stock (see recipe, page 41)
   or store-bought unsalted fish stock
1 tsp (5 mL) chopped fresh sage
1 tsp (5 mL) minced garlic
2 lb (900 g) fresh littleneck clams (about 16)
1 Tbsp (15 mL) butter
¼ tsp (1 mL) ground sumac spice (or lemon zest)

OPTIONAL GARNISH:
Chopped fresh parsley or basil

01 Littleneck clams are likely to be quite sandy, so brine them by following the instructions in the Steamed Mussels with Hazelnut Pesto recipe (page 178), using half the amount of brine for this quantity of clams. Rinse and scrub the clams as directed in the Steamed Mussels recipe. Tap them to make sure they "clam" shut!

02 Bring the stock to a boil in a large stockpot. Reduce the heat, add the sage and garlic, and stir. Add the clams, cover the pot with a tight-fitting lid and steam for three to five minutes.

03 The shells of live molluscs open when they are cooked, and that is generally how you can be sure they are done. Their meat quickly becomes like rubber if you overcook them, which you will discover with a little experience.

04 Take off the lid and give the clams a gentle stir. As they open, remove them from the pot one by one and place them in a hot serving bowl. Give the remaining clams still in the pot another minute to steam. If they don't open, discard them.

05 Drop the butter into the pot and add the sumac. Stir mixture to melt butter.

06 Serve the sauce over the clams and garnish with a sprinkle of minced parsley or basil if using.

Flame-Kissed Pineapple Shrimp Kebobs

MAKES 4 SERVINGS

The Onondaga were big time crayfish eaters long ago, even though crayfish don't have a lot of meat on them. They cooked them in various ways, including threading them onto sticks that were then stuck into the ground in such a way that the meat roasted while leaning over an open fire; they also skinned them and fried their tails and stewed them with wild onions.

Shrimp kebobs done on the barbie are the next best thing. Pineapple, indigenous to Central and South America, adds a little sweetness and freshness to balance out the flavours of the seasoned shrimp. Shrimp doesn't need any salting but does need seasoning. (It has more sodium than fish.)

Wooden or metal skewers
½ fresh pineapple
1 lb (500 g) medium shrimp (abut 16 to 20)
1 tsp (5 mL) Salt Alternative (see recipe, page 32)
¼ cup (60 mL) melted butter

01 If using wooden skewers, first soak them in water for 30 minutes.

02 Cut pineapple into slices, remove the centre core and cut each slice into quarters, leaving the rind on for easier handling when eating.

03 To prepare fresh shrimp, pull off the legs with your fingers. Cut off the heads if still attached, using a paring knife. Peel back the shells to remove. Pull off the tail section of the shell. Use the knife to make a shallow cut down the curved back of the shrimp from top to bottom to expose the dark intestinal vein just below the surface. Pull out the vein and discard it. You can freeze the shells to make shrimp stock for another recipe (see Fish Stock recipe, page 41).

04 Thread shrimp and pineapple pieces onto skewers. Place the skewers in a single layer in a flat nonreactive dish (glass, ceramic or stainless steel). Sprinkle the skewers with the Salt Alternative. Chill for one to two hours, covered with plastic food wrap.

05 Preheat your barbecue to medium heat, 350F (175C).

06 Grill shrimp for two minutes, turning each skewer over once or twice only to get some colour on both sides. Brush skewers with the melted butter, using a pastry brush, several times during the cooking process.

07 Cooking shrimp doesn't take long, so keep an eye on them. Shrimp should be pink, firm and cooked through when done; you could check to make sure that the internal temperature of the shrimp reaches 165F (75C).

08 Place skewers on serving platters and serve hot with melted butter.

Stovetop Variation: Heat a greased grilling pan on the stovetop. Grill skewers for 4 minutes over medium-high heat (2 minutes on each side).

Sea Asparagus Crab Cakes

MAKES 4 SERVINGS

If I lived near the sea, I think I'd probably overdo it on sea asparagus and crab. But in the big city where I live, sea asparagus is hard to find (I really treasure it when I get it), and Marlene is allergic to crustaceans, so we don't make crab dishes at home. If you can't find sea asparagus in a nearby health food store or farmers' market, try using some lightly steamed asparagus instead. Since it's not salty like sea asparagus, add a pinch of extra salt to the cakes before cooking.

When purchasing crab meat for this recipe, I recommend buying canned crab since it is cooked already and is easier to use than crab you have to shell. All you have to do is squeeze all the water out of the canned crab before using. Frozen cooked king crab legs are excellent, of course, if you have access to them. Just thaw them out, crack the shells with a mallet or the back of a heavy knife, remove the meat with a skewer or lobster pick and dice it up (but these shells are not good for stock making since they've been cooked and frozen, IMHO). Because of the high moisture content in crab, a little flour is needed to bind the cakes.

King crabs are usually found in Alaskan waters. They weigh an average of 6 pounds (2.5 kg) but can weigh up to 10 pounds (4.5 kg) and are sold mainly for the meat in the legs and claws. Queen crabs (snow crabs) are usually fished in the North Atlantic and North Pacific, where they have been known to weigh up to five pounds (2.5 kg). They are sold mainly in claw or leg clusters, with some body meat attached. It's debatable which kind of crab is better for this type of recipe, but if you use king crabs, then leave out the salt.

1 can (4 oz/115 g) **crab** meat (or 4 oz/115 g cooked crab leg meat, finely diced)
⅔ cup (150 g) shredded peeled Yukon Gold **potatoes**
1 Tbsp (15 mL) small-diced **red pepper**
1 Tbsp (15 mL) small-diced **yellow pepper**
2 Tbsp (30 mL) finely chopped **sea asparagus**
1 Tbsp (15 mL) finely chopped **cilantro**
1 Tbsp (15 mL) finely chopped fresh **parsley**
1 Tbsp (15 mL) finely diced **shallot**
½ tsp (2.5 mL) finely chopped **garlic**
Pinch **Cold-Smoked Alderwood Salt** (see recipe, page 31) or kosher salt or sea salt
Pinch ground **black pepper**
1 Tbsp (15 mL) all-purpose **flour**
¼ cup (60 mL) pure **olive oil**, divided

OPTIONAL:
Sour Cream and Onion Dip (see recipe, page 47)

01 Squeeze moisture out of crab meat whether using canned or thawed from frozen.

02 In a mixing bowl, combine the crab meat, potatoes, peppers, sea asparagus, cilantro, parsley, shallot, garlic, salt and pepper, and mix well.

03 Add flour and blend well (with your hands), and form mixture into four evenly sized patties about ½ inch (1.5 cm) thick.

04 Flatten and chill patties in the fridge for 30 minutes.

05 Heat a dish in the oven to hold the patties as they are cooked.

06 In a heavy cast iron pan, heat half of the oil over medium heat. Brown the cakes (two at a time) for two to three minutes on one side. Turn patties over carefully and brown them on the other side. Use the remainder of the oil to cook the rest of the cakes. Check that the internal temperature reaches 165F (75C).

07 Transfer cakes to the dish in the oven to stay warm as you continue to cook the rest. Serve with the optional Sour Cream and Onion Dip, or another dip of your choosing.

Blackened Sea Scallops
with Cream of Pumpkin

MAKES 3 TO 4 SERVINGS

Big, juicy sea scallops make a great dish when fried in a pan with a little butter and seasoning. The thing about searing scallops is you need very high heat and perfect timing, and most home cooks just don't have a hot enough grill to make the kind of blackened crust you get in restaurants, so you have to do a few things to compensate.

A cast iron pan is the preferred utensil for cooking scallops. Non-stick pans simply don't allow scallops to blacken the way they should for this type of dish. In the industry, we use aluminum sauté pans but cook with gas over open flames at a higher temperature than residential stoves can reach, so the cooking takes less time and produces a more dramatic contrast between the crust and soft centre of the scallop. So now you know. The Cream of Pumpkin can be prepared before cooking the scallops.

WET SCALLOP BRINE:

4 Tbsp (45 mL) lemon juice

2 Tbsp (30 mL) kosher salt (or sea salt)

1 cup (250 mL) hot water

7 cups (1.6 L) ice water

SCALLOPS:

1 lb (500 g) sea scallops (about 12)

¼ tsp (1 mL) cracked black pepper

¼ tsp (1 mL) kosher salt (or sea salt)

1 Tbsp (15 mL) vegetable oil

1 Tbsp (15 mL) butter

Pinch nutmeg (optional)

BEET GREENS VARIATION:

1 cup (250 mL) beet greens, thoroughly rinsed

Salt and pepper

01 If you bought "dry" scallops, meaning they have never been treated with chemical additives, skip this step; otherwise follow the instructions in the Elk and Sea Scallops in a Parmesan Cup with Chili Lime Vinaigrette recipe (page 56) for soaking "wet" scallops in a brine for 30 minutes, using twice as much brine for the number of scallops in this recipe. Wet scallops are sold in a milky white liquid. Follow the instructions for rinsing and drying the scallops in the same Elk and Sea Scallops recipe.

02 Season scallops with pepper and salt (if you brined the scallops, leave out the salt). Since all the scallops probably won't fit in your pan at once, you should do the searing in two batches. Don't crowd them in the pan, because that will cool down the pan too much.

03 Heat oil in a large cast iron pan over high heat. Wait until it starts to smoke before searing the scallops for three minutes on one side, and let cook without disturbing. Add butter and turn the scallops over once to cook for two minutes on the other side. Spoon some of the melted butter over the scallops while they sizzle. Remove scallops from the pan immediately to prevent them from becoming rubbery.

04 Serve scallops in a warmed dish with Cream of Pumpkin and a sprinkle of nutmeg if using.

Beet Greens Variation: Cooked beet greens make a colourful base on which to serve scallops or fish. After rinsing the greens, chiffonade them (chop in long, thin strips). In a saucepan, boil 2 tablespoons (30 mL) water and toss in the greens. Cook them only until they wilt—about one minute. Turn the leaves over quickly, place them in a strainer and squeeze out the water; season them with salt and pepper. If you want to get fancy, pour some of the pumpkin sauce on a plate and stuff the beet greens into a round mould or small ramekin. Invert it onto the plate and place scallops on top of the beet greens.

Cream of Pumpkin

MAKES 1½ CUPS (350 ML)

1 Tbsp (15 mL) **butter**

1 Tbsp (15 mL) minced **shallot**

1 tsp (5 mL) minced **ginger**

1 Tbsp (15 mL) all-purpose **flour**

½ cup (120 mL) 35 per cent **cream**, divided

1½ cups (350 mL) **Fish Stock** (see recipe, page 41) or store-bought unsalted fish stock

2 Tbsp (30 mL) **pumpkin purée**

2 tsp (10 mL) **Worcestershire sauce**

Salt and **pepper** to taste

01 Heat a cast iron pan over low heat for 10 minutes. Raise the heat to medium and add the butter. Sauté the shallot and ginger for one to two minutes, stirring frequently.

02 Sprinkle in the flour and stir with a wooden spoon. Add half of the cream and continue stirring to remove lumps. Heat the cream but do not allow it to boil. The creamy mixture will thicken, but keep cooking it for one minute.

03 Heat the Fish Stock to the boiling point in a microwave or on the stovetop. Remove from heat.

04 Add the stock, pumpkin, Worcestershire sauce, remaining cream, and salt and pepper to the pan. Cook for two more minutes and stir before serving.

CHAPTER 7
The Fliers: Poultry, Game Birds and Waterfowl

My brother-in-law Jim Chum lives in Moose Factory First Nation in James Bay, Ontario, and you could say he knows geese. He grew up on goose and moose and, when he was a younger man, used to join the annual hunting parties that the entire community took part in. In his community, he says, if they couldn't call the geese, then there'd be nothing to eat at times. They still hunt snow geese and Canada geese every year and make good use of the meat, feathers and down (for duvets). Some community members still slowly roast geese in tipis over an open fire, dangling the birds by rope attached to the tipi poles in the centre to keep them from overbrowning on any given side as the fat drips below. The cooking process hasn't changed much in generations but, in this day and age, their tipis are generally made from waterproof tarps.

When Marlene's sister Pat Chum moved up there she learned first-hand how much work is involved in cleaning birds and plucking goose and duck feathers, especially when the hunt has brought in enough to fill a freezer. No time for Facebook when the hunters come home! That reminds me of the time Mom was excited to be able to help me with a big catering function I had planned. Chicken liver pâté was on the menu, and I had collected a lot of chicken livers and needed help peeling off their membranes. There we sat in the basement kitchen of the Native Canadian Centre of Toronto, peeling liver after liver after liver. At first she enjoyed the work, but after we were all done, she said she never wanted to see chicken livers *ever* again. That's the thing about catering: you get so used to large quantities of food that your perception of things changes—and you eventually forget that even you took time to adjust to working in bulk.

One time Pat and Jim were at the cottage we had in Muskoka, helping us to cut up fallen trees and stack the wood (a never-ending, backbreaking job for us), when I heard a goose honking close by. I wouldn't have even noticed except that it sounded really close. Then I looked up and saw that it was Jim making the sound; he was calling the geese. He must have heard some geese flying overhead along the river, and out of habit he called them over like he does when hunting. Within seconds the first Canada goose swooped down and landed in the water in front of us, and then a second one and a third and, in no time, there were at least a dozen geese there swimming in formation. Cottagers on the other side of the river saw this and stood still, mouths gaping wide. Jim just laughed and called over to them, asking if anyone had a gun handy. They didn't answer but took off running!

Jim said the geese would come back from that point on because they thought there were other geese there, which I didn't really believe since we never once had

Vanilla Salted Maple Duck Breast · **194**

Duck Parmesan with Wild Rice Fusilli Pasta · **196**

Sexy Duck Legs with Balsamic Glaze · **198**

Chestnut and Prune Turkey Roulade with Saskatoon Berry Compote · **199**

Apple Cider Brined and Roasted Turkey with Cranberry Sauce · **202**

Cedar Pheasant with Apricot and Plum Pan Drippings · **204**

Roasted Goose with Hazelnut Stuffing and Giblet Sauce · **206**

geese land there before, but he was right, and every year after that, the geese came and landed in front of our place and waded by the riverbank for hours at a time. I always think of Jim now when I hear geese flying overhead.

Poultry versus Game Birds versus Waterfowl

"Waterfowl" refers to swimming birds. Ducks, geese and swans caught in the wild are not sold in supermarkets (and swans are protected by law). "Game birds" are upland birds and shoreline birds that are hunted for sport. Currently, the most common edible game birds in Canada include grouse (ptarmigan), pheasant, pigeon, wild turkey and quail. Unfortunately, the prairie chicken, a game bird that Marlene's mom grew up eating in Saskatchewan, has become extinct. You can't buy "wild" game birds in supermarkets, but consumer demand for them is on the rise in Canada; consequently, more farmers are turning to raising and selling domesticated game birds. "Poultry" refers to domesticated birds raised specifically for their meat, feathers and/or eggs: chicken, turkey, goose, duck, pigeon (squab), guinea fowl, pheasant and, more recently, quail, ostrich and emu. I refer to all of these as "birds" for simplicity.

Preparing Birds

First Nations people are not generally in the habit of dry aging game birds as they did long ago by hanging them up with feathers and intestines intact for days at a time—a practice that started before there were fridges and freezers. That traditional way of dry aging is effective at tenderizing meat enzymes, thus removing any gamey flavour by draining excess blood and breaking down highly developed muscle tissue. The finest restaurants prize such meat; however, Health Canada recommends that if meat or game birds are to be aged, it be done very carefully and under ideal temperature and humidity conditions to prevent bacterial growth.

The recommended practice now is that if you can't field dress your freshly killed bird, then you need to chill it over ice immediately (especially if the weather is warm) until you can clean it at home, which you should do within a few hours (take a cooler when you go hunting). Then the bird can be cooked, stored in the fridge (on a tray in the coldest part of the fridge for up to three days) or frozen. Generally, whole poultry from the market will have the neck and giblets (liver, heart and gizzard) inside the cavity, and you can use these to make sauces. These also need to be stored in a food-safe plastic bag on ice until they can be cooked or frozen; personally, I wouldn't keep the liver unless I had a plan to collect enough of them to make pâté.

I know some hunters swear the best thing to do with birds is to clean and defeather them, soak them in a saltwater brine overnight, rinse them in fresh water and then freeze them. Brining helps to dilute some of the excess blood in the flesh, and some people even claim it is more effective than using a vacuum sealer for preventing freezer burn. See the Apple Cider Brined and Roasted Turkey with Cranberry Sauce recipe on page 202, and the Basic Brine recipe on page 204, which you can use for any whole wild bird. In reality, a lot of First Nations people, particularly in Ontario, freeze cleaned ducks and geese with feathers intact; they say the feathers don't affect the meat all that much.

From a chef's point of view, cleaning birds before freezing them makes it easier to thaw them out later (in the fridge) for cooking. It also means the birds will take up less space in your freezer. Game birds and poultry can be frozen whole or in parts, wrapped in freezer-weight food-safe plastic bags, with as much air removed as possible. Generally speaking, birds will keep for up to six months in the freezer without deteriorating; vacuum sealing them can double that time, so that's what I do.

Poultry, waterfowl and game birds often carry the salmonella bacterium that can spread to counters, cutting boards, knives, sinks, bowls, taps, fridge shelves, and so on—basically anything the bird touches. So when thawing frozen poultry, store it in the fridge to thaw gradually in its original wrapper or covered in food-safe plastic wrap (on a tray to contain drips), allowing one to two days for chickens, or up to four days for turkeys or geese. Previously frozen birds need to be either cooked or brined immediately after thawing. Thawing birds at room temperature is a very bad idea. Rinsing them in the sink after they thaw out is also a bad idea and just increases the risk of spreading bacteria all over the kitchen. Cleaning the kitchen after handling poultry is critical to preventing food poisoning. That means going over surfaces with a weak bleach solution. The other sure way to prevent poisoning is to follow safe cooking temperature guidelines.

Chicken available for purchase in grocery stores is brought to market at a very young (and tender) age. Backyard hens tend to get more exercise and take longer to mature, so their meat is more flavourful but also leaner and tougher, more like wild poultry.

Buying Birds

In Canada, poultry, like beef, is federally inspected for human consumption and graded for size and condition, so when you shop in supermarkets, you can choose the grade you want. Mom used to look for "utility" grade chickens and turkeys when I was growing up, because the meat was just as good as Canada Grade A poultry but less expensive. She used to say that ugly birds taste better! We didn't mind if a wing or leg was missing. Marlene's mom did the same thing when she shopped for groceries.

If you know in advance how you want to cook a bird, then your grocery shopping will be easy; otherwise you will be left trying to figure out how to cook the bird you have. When it comes to poultry, there are different classes to choose from. The older the bird, the less desirable it is, the cheaper it is to buy and the longer it will take to cook.

Yield is another consideration. You will get more for your money by buying certain bird parts rather than others. One reason so many bar restaurants can afford to serve half-price chicken wings at happy hour is because wings have a low yield to start off with—much lower than any other part of a chicken—so they are cheaper to buy than legs or breasts, pound per pound. In addition, edible weight varies from species to species. Duck has a small yield, so a four-and-a-half-pound (2 kg) whole duck will make two to four servings, whereas chicken of the same weight has a higher yield and will make up to twice the number of servings. Goose also has a low yield compared with chicken or turkey.

Whether factory-raised, farm-raised or hunted in the wild, birds should smell fresh when you get them, and game birds and waterfowl should have a slight gamey smell.

There's a reason why turkey phone hotlines are so busy at Thanksgiving with calls from all the people who want to roast turkeys but don't know where to begin.

Tip
To decide how large a turkey to buy for a large meal, allow 1 pound (500 g) of turkey per serving (or 1½ lb/680 g) per person, and you will have enough for leftovers.

Cooking Birds

Bone structure, connective tissue and fat content are the three most important factors involved in cooking birds. Waterfowl and game birds fly, so they have strong connective tissues and less fat than birds that can't fly. Whereas beef and pork fat is distributed throughout the meat, much of the fat in poultry is in the skin, and on game birds it's in a layer under the skin. In the case of goose and duck, the fat is so thick you need to prick or score it so that it will render during cooking. The melted fat drains off the bird, leaving it very dry if overcooked and very greasy if not drained, especially if it's not roasted on a rack. See the Roasted Goose with Hazelnut Stuffing and Giblet Sauce recipe (page 206) for information on how to deal with these challenges. Compare the differences between wild and farm-raised birds in the "Differences between Wild and Domesticated Birds" sidebar on this page.

Poultry is generally consumed at a younger age than birds you would catch in the wild. A young chicken—called a fryer, roaster or broiler—in the supermarket, is tender and can be cooked at a high temperature for a short period of time, unlike a mature female chicken, called a fowl or hen. The same guideline applies to turkey. Old birds have darker, hard-skinned legs, more brittle breastbones and tougher beaks than young birds (not unlike their human counterparts!) and are better suited to braising, stewing and "barding" (which means cooking with some fat, such as bacon, on top). All of these factors affect what you end up with for dinner on your plate.

After turkey dinner, a lot of home cooks save the carcass to use in making other meals. We've had discussions at our

Differences between Wild and Domesticated Birds

Characteristic	Wild	Domesticated
Height	Taller	Shorter
Weight	Lighter	Heavier
Muscle tissue	More	Less
Leg length	Longer	Shorter
Breast size	Smaller	Larger
Age	Older	Younger
Fat	Leaner	Fatter

Cooking Notes:
- On average, wild birds need to cook more slowly and at a lower temperature than domesticated
- Since wild birds are tougher, it is recommended to brine the whole bird before roasting, or use them to make soup or confit
- Domestic birds can be roasted whole, without brining, because they have more fat

---

table at Thanksgiving as to whose turn it is to take the turkey carcass home after dinner! What I like to do is refrigerate it immediately after the meal and then debone it the next day when it's cold and the leftover meat is easier to cut. If I know I won't have time to do it the next day, then I freeze it until I can. The carcass provides meat for sandwiches and pot pies. Some like to make soup from the carcass, but I prefer to use raw turkey bones.

Testing for Doneness

To test whole roasted birds for doneness, some people poke a hole with a knife into the leg joint to see if the juices run clear rather than pink. That is not a recommended practice, because you will lose flavourful juices and it's not as reliable as using a digital thermometer. Shaking the leg will

Health Canada Doneness Recommendations for Poultry, Game Birds and Waterfowl

180F/82C	Whole birds
165F/74C	Breasts Roasts Thighs Wings Stuffing

Reference: Health Canada

help indicate if a small bird is done, as will pressing down on it with a finger to see how dense it is, but the best way to test for doneness is to insert a thermometer into the inner thigh, away from the bone. Keep in mind that stuffed birds take longer to cook than unstuffed birds so you need to test the internal cooking temperature of a bird in various spots before serving.

Health Canada recommends that bird parts be cooked to 165F (75C) and whole birds to 180F (80C); some cooks even go so far as to cook them to 185F (85C). Duck breast is possibly the only type of bird dish I would ever serve at 155F (70C), since that degree of doneness is a standard among chefs.

Poultry and game birds, like red meat, should be allowed to rest, loosely tented with foil, for 15 minutes before carving. Doing that not only makes cutting easier, but also makes the meat juicier.

Bird Substitutions

The primary differences between the many types of edible birds are meat texture and appearance. Unlike large game and beef, poultry has both light and dark meat. Light meat, which is found in the breast and wings, has less fat than the dark meat found in legs; however, parts with bones take longer to cook. Ducks and geese are a little unusual since they have dark meat throughout. So, can you substitute chicken for quail, or turkey for duck? Sometimes.

Wild birds are higher in protein and leaner than domesticated birds pound per pound, so they require more attention when cooking or they will dry out. For any poultry recipe in this chapter, you could substitute any other type of poultry meat as long as you use a cut and amount similar to those specified. Similarly, for any game bird recipe in this chapter, you could substitute any other type of game bird as long as you use a cut and amount similar to those specified.

Vanilla Salted Maple Duck Breast

MAKES 2 SERVINGS

Duck Lake, Saskatchewan, a famous battleground where the Métis fought the Canadian government at the start of the 1885 North-West Rebellion, was named for the large number of ducks that used to migrate through this area in early spring and late fall. The Cree in Saskatchewan, who called Duck Lake *See-Seep-Sakayegan*, traditionally cooked duck over a fire or in soups. Duck hunting is still common among Indigenous people even today, particularly for those living in the north of Canada where store-bought foods are extremely expensive.

Duck breast has a lot of fat in it, which gives it such nice flavour that you don't need to oil the pan before cooking it, and the texture of the skin is lovely after it's been crisped up in the frying pan and served with pan drippings. Here is an extremely simple way to prepare duck breasts. Consider serving this with the Fiddleheads and Carrots in Sesame Birch Sauce recipe (page 227).

2 **duck breasts** (1 lb/500 g in total)
1 tsp (5 mL) **Vanilla Salt** (see recipe, page 22)
    or kosher salt, divided
½ tsp (2.5 mL) ground **black pepper**, divided
2 Tbsp (30 mL) **maple syrup**
2 Tbsp (30 mL) **red wine vinegar**
2 minced cloves of **garlic**

OPTIONAL GARNISH:
Fresh flat-leaf **parsley**, chopped

01 Using a sharp knife, score the duck skin by making a couple of incisions about ½ inch (1.5 cm) deep in a criss-cross pattern, but do not cut down into the flesh.

02 Season the skin side of the breasts with half the Vanilla Salt and half the pepper, rubbing it in. Set aside for five minutes. Turn the breasts over and repeat on the flesh side using the remaining salt and pepper. Set aside for five minutes.

03 Whisk together the maple syrup, red wine vinegar and garlic, and pour the mixture over the duck, coating it.

04 Allow the duck to marinate for 30 minutes to one hour in the fridge in a nonreactive dish (ceramic, glass or stainless steel). Drain duck, and discard marinade.

05 Preheat oven to 400F (205C).

06 Place the duck breasts in a cold cast iron frying pan, skin side down. Turn heat to medium and brown the meat without turning it (about three minutes). Increase the heat to medium-high and continue cooking without turning the meat.

07 After three more minutes, turn the breasts over, skin side up, and cook for two more minutes.

08 Turn the breasts over again, skin side down, and bake duck in the same pan for 10 minutes in the oven. I would serve the duck at 155F (70C), but you could wait until it reaches the temperature Health Canada recommends, 165F (75C).

09 Remove the duck from the pan and set aside on a cutting board with a little foil on top to rest for a couple of minutes before serving.

10 Slice and garnish duck with pan drippings and chopped parsley if using.

Duck Parmesan with Wild Rice Fusilli Pasta

MAKES 4 SERVINGS

One time when I served moist, tender duck breast entrées to a ballroom full of Manitoban First Nations chiefs, many refused to touch it. Apparently, the meat was too rare for them and they could not be swayed to even try it. Marlene just laughed when I phoned her from Winnipeg to tell her about it. She too grew up eating everything cooked to well done. Like most chefs, I still prefer duck breast, even the duck scallopine in this recipe, quite pink inside.

Wild rice fusilli isn't the only type of pasta you could use for this recipe; we happen to like it because of the wild rice, but you could use regular wheat pasta instead. Penne and rigatoni pasta are suitable substitutes in this dish. Another choice is whether to use pine nuts instead of bread crumbs to give the breading a little more crunch; see the Pine Nut Variation below.

2 cups (475 mL) wild rice **fusilli pasta**

½ tsp (2.5 mL) table **salt**

1 tsp (5 mL) finely chopped fresh **thyme**

1½ tsp (7.5 mL) kosher **salt** (or sea salt), divided

½ tsp (2.5 mL) fresh ground **black pepper**, divided

4 boneless **duck breasts** (1½ lb/680 g in total), skin and fat removed

1 cup (250 mL) all-purpose **flour**

2 large **eggs**, beaten

2 cups (475 mL) **bread crumbs**

2 tsp (10 mL) dried **oregano**

1 tsp (5 mL) **butter**

3 Tbsp (45 mL) pure **olive oil**, divided

1 cup (250 mL) canned **tomato sauce** (or homemade; see sauce in Collard Green Moose Rolls recipe, page 124)

¼ cup (60 mL) grated **Reggiano cheese**

¼ cup (60 mL) grated **mozzarella cheese**

HOW TO PREPARE BREAST MEAT FOR MAKING A SCALLOPINE OR ROULADE

Remove the skin, if any, from the breast; reserve skin if required in the recipe. Butterfly the breast, by laying it flat on a cutting board and holding it down with one hand. With your other hand, insert a boning knife into the side of the breast and slice through the meat, horizontally, as you would if you were filleting a fish. Stop cutting about ¾ inch (2 cm) from the edge, so that the top and bottom layers are the same thickness but still joined together.

Open up the breast meat like opening a book. Place the meat on a sheet of plastic food wrap and cover with a separate sheet of food wrap. Use a meat tenderizer to pound the breast down to an even thickness. If you don't have a meat tenderizer, use the edge of a heavy pot. A scallopine should be pounded to a thickness of ½ inch (1.5 cm), whereas a roulade (a stuffed roll) should be pounded to a thickness of 1 inch (2.5 cm).

Discard the food wrap and prepare the meat as instructed in the recipe.

01 Heat a pot of water to the boiling point. Add the pasta and table salt, and let simmer for 10 minutes while you prepare the duck as described above.

02 Mix the thyme with 1 teaspoon (5 mL) of the kosher salt and a pinch of the pepper, and season each butterflied breast with this mixture.

03 Create a "breading station" with three bowls: flour in one, the beaten eggs in another and bread crumbs mixed with the oregano in the third.

04 Dredge the seasoned meat, one piece at a time, in the flour, shaking off the excess flour. Place the meat in the bowl of beaten egg, turning the meat over to coat it evenly. Then lift each piece of meat out of the egg, letting excess egg drip off before placing the meat in the dish of bread crumbs. Cover the meat in bread crumbs, gently patting crumbs onto it and turning it to coat evenly.

05 Drain cooked pasta. Stir in butter and remaining kosher salt and pepper. Pour pasta into a greased ovenproof casserole dish or serving pan. Set aside.

06 Preheat oven to 375F (190C).

07 When all the meat has been prepared, pour half of the olive oil into a sauté pan and heat to medium-hot. Lightly brown one piece of meat, and then turn it over and brown the opposite side. Use the remaining oil to brown the other pieces.

08 Top pasta with the duck breasts. Heat tomato sauce and spread over the meat. Sprinkle the cheeses on top.

09 Bake for 8 to 10 minutes, until the internal temperature of the meat reaches 155F (70C) or reaches the temperature Health Canada recommends, 165F (75C).

Pine Nut Variation: Replace the bread crumbs with ground pine nuts.

Sexy Duck Legs with Balsamic Glaze

MAKES 4 SERVINGS

W hat? Never heard of sexy duck legs? Well, beauty is in the eye of the beholder, and I think these barbe-cued legs are sexy!

1 wooden **skewer**
4 **duck legs** (1⅓ lb/600 g in total)
2 Tbsp (30 mL) **Sexy Chicken Spice Mix**
   (see recipe, page 26)
2 Tbsp (30 mL) **vegetable oil**

TO SERVE (OPTIONAL):
2 tsp (10 mL) **orange zest**
1 cup (250 mL) mixed **salad greens**

01 Poke three or four holes in the skin of each duck leg using a skewer. Season the legs with the Sexy Chicken Spice Mix and let stand for 30 minutes in a nonreactive dish (glass, ceramic or stainless steel) at room temperature. Rub the oil on the legs, and let stand for five minutes.

02 Heat barbecue to medium heat (350F/175C).

03 When the barbecue reaches temperature, turn down the heat on one of the burners to 300F (150C). Brown legs for four to five minutes, skin side down, in the high temperature zone and with the lid down, without moving them so that their skin doesn't tear and also so that they develop good colour.

04 Move the legs to the lower heat zone of the bar-becue and cook, turning frequently and keeping the lid down. Cook duck legs until they reach an internal temperature of 165F (75C). Use a thermometer to test the temperature.

05 Remove legs from heat and let rest, loosely cov-ered with foil, while you prepare the glaze.

06 Serve duck with Balsamic Glaze and garnish with orange zest and greens if using.

Baked Variation: Season duck as described. Bake in the oven on a rack set over a parchment paper–lined baking sheet at 400F (205C) for 20 to 25 minutes or until the bird reaches 165F (75C). Drain legs on paper towel while they rest after cooking.

Balsamic Glaze

MAKES ½ CUP (120 ML)

This glaze goes well on a variety of proteins, like poultry, beef, pork, large game and small game.

1¼ cups (300 mL) **balsamic vinegar**
¼ cup (60 mL) **maple syrup**
1 tsp (5 mL) kosher **salt** (or sea salt)
¼ tsp (1 mL) ground **cloves**

01 Combine the vinegar, maple syrup, salt and ground cloves in a small saucepan. Bring the mixture to a low simmer over very low heat and allow the liq-uid to reduce by three-quarters, stirring occasionally. Do not allow this to burn!

02 Once the mixture reaches a thick consistency (after about five to eight minutes), remove from heat. Brush some glaze on the duck legs or pour glaze into a squeeze bottle and use to make decorative drops or patterns on the serving plates.

Chestnut and Prune Turkey Roulade with Saskatoon Berry Compote

MAKES 8 SERVINGS

Do you want stuffed turkey without the hassle of roasting a whole bird and having to deal with trussing it, stuffing it, carving it and then deboning it for leftovers? Then turkey roulade will do the job. For the roulade (so named because it's shaped like a roll), you start with a turkey breast that you slice open and pound flat for stuffing and then you roll it up and roast it. Once it's done, you serve it in slices. Each serving includes both turkey and stuffing. Brilliant.

Indigenous chestnut trees and wild plum bushes used to be plentiful across the United States but they aren't anymore; still you can buy the ingredients for this stuffing recipe using the newer varieties of chestnuts and prunes commonly found in stores today. Here turkey is teamed up with a berry compote.

If you want to break this recipe into two stages, prepare the stuffing and compote a day ahead. They can be refrigerated overnight.

STUFFING:

12 cups large-diced sandwich bread (2.8 L; approximately 15 slices)
¼ cup (60 mL) medium-diced dried prunes
¼ cup (60 mL) pure olive oil
½ lb (225 g) pork sausage (or diced breakfast sausage), casings removed
2 Tbsp (30 mL) butter
¾ cup (180 mL) small-diced celery
¾ cup (180 mL) small-diced onion
½ tsp (2.5 mL) kosher salt (or sea salt), plus more as needed
½ tsp (2.5 mL) ground black pepper, plus more as needed
2 cups (475 mL) White Stock (see recipe, page 39) or store-bought unsalted chicken stock
⅓ cup (80 mL) finely chopped roasted chestnuts

TURKEY:

1 whole boneless turkey breast (2½ lb/1 kg), with skin on
1 tsp (5 mL) dried marjoram

½ tsp (2.5 mL) kosher salt (or sea salt)
¼ tsp (1 mL) ground black pepper

01 To make the stuffing, spread the bread over a baking sheet and leave in the open air overnight so that they dry out thoroughly, or dry them in a 250F (120C) oven for 15 minutes. Set aside.

02 Place prunes in a cup or small bowl and cover with water. Heat in the microwave on high for one minute. Let the prunes soak in the warm water for five minutes; drain.

03 Heat oil in a large saucepan over medium heat. Cook sausage meat, uncovered, breaking it up with a spoon, until it loses its pink colour (about three to five minutes). Drain off excess oil and reserve.

04 Turn the heat to medium-low and add butter, celery, onion and salt to the meat. Cook for five minutes, stirring frequently. Add pepper and stir.

05 Heat stock in a small saucepan or in the microwave to the boiling point. Remove from heat. Add 1 cup (250 mL) of the stock, plus the bread, prunes and chestnuts, to the sausage mixture, and stir to combine well. Transfer mixture to a large mixing bowl.

06 Deglaze the pan by adding some of the remaining stock and scraping up the brown bits stuck to the pan. (Normally stuffing is made on the dry side because it will absorb fat from the roasting bird, but this mixture should be fairly dense, moist and heavy when it goes into the oven, as there is no fat to absorb from a turkey breast.)

07 Add the rest of the stock to the pan and stir. Pour over the stuffing and combine well. Adjust the taste of the stuffing with more salt and pepper as needed. Set stuffing aside to cool.

CONTINUED ...

08 Preheat oven to 400F (205C).

09 Remove the skin from the turkey breast and reserve. Butterfly the turkey breast as instructed in "How to Prepare Breast Meat for Making a Scallopine or Roulade" in the Duck Parmesan with Wild Rice Fusilli Pasta recipe (page 196).

10 Shape the butterflied breast meat into a rectangle. Season both sides with marjoram, salt and pepper.

11 Carefully spoon the stuffing in an even row along one of the longer edges of the meat, leaving about 2 inches (5 cm) of space along this edge.

12 Keep the stuffing together as much as possible as you roll the meat into a tight roll, starting from the side with the stuffing. Once the roll is completely formed, wrap it up in the reserved turkey skin.

13 Tie butcher twine around the roll, tying it every inch (2.5 cm) or so for the full length of the roll to keep it firmly together. Place the roulade on a parchment paper–lined baking pan. Brush roulade with the reserved oil using a pastry brush, and season the roulade with more salt and pepper on the outside.

14 Bake for 30 minutes, uncovered, and then turn down heat and bake at 350F (175C) for another 30 minutes, or until meat reaches an internal temperature of 165F (75C). Baste the roulade from time to time using the reserved oil.

15 Let the roulade rest, loosely covered by foil, on a cutting board for about 15 minutes before serving.

16 Remove string and slice. Serve with Saskatoon Berry Compote or with Brown Sauce if you prefer (see the Roasted Goose with Hazelnut Stuffing and Giblet Sauce recipe, page 206).

Saskatoon Berry Compote

MAKES 2½ CUPS (600 ML)

Did you know that the city of Saskatoon got its name from the saskatoon berry, which got its name from the Cree, who call it *mi-sask-wa-too-mina*? The saskatoon berry is also called Pacific serviceberry, western serviceberry, western June berry, chuckley pear, sugar pear, Indian pear, shadberry or just "saskatoon." Regardless of the name, this berry was a traditional staple for the Cree and Blackfoot on the prairies, since it was good, fresh or dried, in meat or in soups, and the bush's bark was carved into tools.

Blueberries are a decent substitute for saskatoon berries, but they are not the same. Saskatoon berries have a taste that is a little earthier, and they make a nutty-tasting compote that goes well with poultry or game birds of any kind. Maple sugar is dehydrated maple syrup; look for it in fine food shops or health food stores, or use brown sugar instead.

2 cups (475 mL) **saskatoon berries**, fresh or frozen
¼ cup (60 mL) **maple sugar** (or brown sugar)
¼ cup (60 mL) **water**
2 tsp (10 mL) **lemon juice**
Pinch ground **cloves**

01 Place all the ingredients in a small saucepan and bring to a simmer. Simmer for 10 minutes on medium-low heat, stirring frequently. If the mixture is not thick enough to coat the back of a spoon, simmer it for five to seven minutes more, stirring frequently.

02 Remove compote from the stove and pour into a server. Chill compote for 10 minutes before serving. Chilled, this compote will last for up to two weeks.

Apple Cider Brined and Roasted Turkey with Cranberry Sauce

MAKES 12 TO 14 SERVINGS

If you find turkey comes out dry when you roast it, then brining is for you. Brining in saltwater gives birds a juicier texture, not to mention all the flavour the seasonings add! Stuffed turkey sure has come a long way in the centuries since the first Thanksgiving dinner that Indigenous people shared with Pilgrims at Plymouth, Massachusetts!

This recipe poses a brining challenge, though: you will have to come up with a plan to figure out how to brine your turkey so that it is totally covered and chilled overnight. If you have a pot large enough to keep the turkey submerged (not floating) in the brine, that's excellent. Alternatively, use a flatter container like a roasting pan or a 5 gallon (19 L) bucket, and put the turkey inside a strong plastic bag large enough to hold the bird as well as all the brine. I recommend that you get a brining bag. A garbage bag is *not* strong enough or food-safe.

This recipe will make enough brine for a bird up to 18 pounds (8.2 kg) and is suitable for farm-raised and wild turkey.

You will need to start preparing the recipe a day ahead to get the brining done, and you could also make the Cranberry Sauce a couple of days in advance for better flavour.

BRINE:

8 cups (2 L) **White Stock** (see recipe, page 39) or store-bought unsalted chicken stock
4 cups (1 L) **apple cider**
4 cups (1 L) **water**
⅔ cup (160 mL) kosher **salt** (or sea salt)
⅔ cup (160 mL) **maple sugar** (or brown sugar)
16 cups (3.8 L) **ice water**

SPICE BAG:

5 fresh **sage** leaves (or ½ tsp/2.5 mL dried sage)
1 Tbsp (15 mL) whole black **peppercorns**
1 Tbsp (15 mL) dried **juniper berries**
4 tsp (20 mL) sliced **garlic**

6 whole **cloves**
5 dried **bay leaves**
2 sprigs fresh **thyme**
½ tsp (2.5 mL) ground **allspice**

TURKEY:

1 fresh **turkey** (12–14 lb/5.4–6.4 kg), not pre-brined
1 **carrot**, cut in half
1 **celery** stalk, cut in half
1 **onion**, cut in half
1 tsp (5 mL) ground **black pepper**
⅓ cup (80 mL) pure **olive oil**

01 To make the brine, combine the stock, apple cider, 4 cups (1 L) water, salt and sugar in a large stockpot.

02 To prepare the spice bag, grind the sage, peppercorns, juniper berries and garlic in a mortar and pestle. Combine with the cloves, bay leaves, thyme and allspice; toss spice bag into the pot. Bring mixture to a boil, stirring to dissolve the salt and sugar. Boil for a couple of minutes. Stir, and let brine cool.

03 Remove the neck and giblets from the cavity of the turkey. Chill them if you are planning to make Giblet Sauce (see recipe on page 209); otherwise, discard.

04 Place the turkey in the brining container along with the brine, spice bag and ice water. Alternatively, if you are using a food-safe brining bag instead, put the bag inside a large bucket, put the turkey and spice bag in the bag, and pour the brine and ice water into the bag. Tie up the bag tightly. Either way, the liquid should cover the bird completely. Chill the turkey in the brine for 16 to 24 hours, turning the bird over at the halfway point.

05 Preheat oven to 400F (205C).

06 Remove turkey from the brine and discard brine and spice bag. Soak the turkey in cold water in a large pot or sanitized sink for 20 minutes to remove the salt. Pat the bird dry with paper towels.

07 Insert the carrot, celery and onion pieces into the turkey, or make a stuffing for it (see the Roasted Goose with Hazelnut Stuffing and Giblet Sauce recipe, page 206). Truss the turkey as described in "How to Truss a Bird" (page 208) and rub pepper and oil on it to help brown the skin without burning.

08 Set the turkey on a rack inside a roasting pan. Roast the bird, uncovered, breast side up, on the lower rack of the oven for 30 minutes, without turning it.

09 Lower the heat to 325F (160C). Roast for two hours. Baste the bird with pan drippings every 30 minutes.

10 If the bird gets too brown before it's done, cover the dark parts with pieces of foil. Use a thermometer to check that the turkey reaches an internal temperature of 180F (82C). Insert the thermometer in the breast area where the wing bone, shoulder bone and backbone meet (this is where the coldest part of the bird would be, due to all of the bones being in one area).

11 Remove the turkey from the oven and let rest, with a sheet of foil set loosely over it, for 30 minutes before carving. Use a turkey baster to remove the liquid fat floating on top of the pan drippings and discard. If you make Brown Sauce, use the drippings from the pan and the reserved neck and giblets.

12 Serve with Cranberry Sauce.

Cranberry Sauce

MAKES 2½ CUPS (600 ML)

This classic sauce made with a classic North American berry really is the perfect complement to roast turkey—but it's just as good with poultry or game birds of any kind. Store excess sauce in the fridge for up to two weeks.

1 apple, peeled, cored and diced (preferably McIntosh, Red Ida or Honeycrisp)
1 orange, peeled and puréed
2 cups (475 mL) frozen cranberries, divided
1 cup (250 mL) chopped walnuts
1 cup (250 mL) maple sugar (or brown sugar)
½ tsp (2.5 mL) ground cinnamon
½ tsp (2.5 mL) ground nutmeg
Pinch salt

01 Place the apple, orange and half the cranberries in a medium-sized saucepan with the walnuts, sugar, cinnamon, nutmeg and salt.

02 Stir mixture and let cook over medium-low heat for three minutes. Blend with a hand blender off and on for 30 seconds to break down the fruit without puréeing it.

03 Add the remaining cranberries and stir; cook the mixture over very low heat for five more minutes.

04 Stir sauce and let cool partially. It will thicken enough within 15 minutes to serve hot, or let it cool to room temperature before serving.

Cedar Pheasant with Apricot and Plum Pan Drippings

MAKES 4 SERVINGS

My mom's homeland near Lillooet, BC, has scorching hot summers, harsh winters, sky-high mountains, raging rivers and desert-like terrain. For over 4,000 years, her people spent their summers fishing, hunting and gathering seasonal plants; they made shelter under covered cedar-pole frames with woven cedar mats inside, but in winter they lived in their pit houses to escape the brutal wind. To make these houses, a pit was dug in the ground and a framework of cedar poles erected within the pit; the framework was then covered with cedar bark and earth. Each pit house had only one opening and a cedar ladder to allow entering and exiting. It was extraordinary to see the remains of an ancient pit house community a few years ago, during my first trip to the area; the pit houses looked like mounds made by giant groundhogs. Art Adolph was kind enough to take Marlene and me on a tour.

Cedar is, without a doubt, one of the Creator's greatest gifts to my mother's people of the plateau region of BC. I am reminded of that when I cook with cedar, as in this recipe. Cedar is considered a sacred medicine in many Indigenous nations (along with tobacco, sage and sweetgrass), so it is customary to leave a handful of tobacco on the earth where the cedar is picked. And when the cedar is no longer needed, it is returned to the earth, with thanks. *Note:* Fresh cedar imparts a strong flavour, so a little goes a long way.

The brine is optional but recommended if your pheasant was wild; brining will tenderize and flavour the meat. Pheasant is a fairly lean bird, requiring flavour builders and moisture to roast without drying out. I partially stuff the bird in this recipe with stone fruits, garlic and onion but rely mostly on the savoury pan drippings for flavour. This recipe goes well with Caramelized Rainbow Pearl Onions (see recipe, page 226).

BASIC BRINE (OPTIONAL):

¼ cup (60 mL) kosher **salt** (or sea salt)
1 Tbsp (15 mL) **maple sugar** (or brown sugar)
8 cups (2 L) **water**

PHEASANT:

1 whole **pheasant** (2 lb/900 g)
¼ cup (60 mL) chopped **dried apricots**
½ tsp (2.5 mL) kosher **salt** (or sea salt)
¼ tsp (1 mL) ground **black pepper**
½ tsp (2.5 mL) chopped fresh **rosemary**
2 cups (475 mL) sliced fresh **plums**
1 cup (250 mL) sliced **onion**
1 Tbsp (15 mL) sliced **garlic**
2 Tbsp (30 mL) pure **olive oil**
2 sprigs fresh **cedar**, divided
1 cup (250 mL) **White Stock** (see recipe, page 39)
   or store-bought unsalted chicken stock

01 Combine brine ingredients together in a stockpot and bring to a boil. Let cool. Place bird in a tall container large enough to hold the bird and all of the cooled brine so that the bird is completely covered (not floating). Reserve the neck and giblets if you have them. Soak pheasant for two hours in the fridge. Rinse pheasant in fresh water very thoroughly before continuing with the recipe.

02 Preheat oven to 375F (190C).

03 Soak the apricots in warm water for 5 to 10 minutes.

04 Season the inside and outside of the bird with salt, pepper and rosemary (leave out salt if you brined the pheasant).

05 Drain the apricots and combine with the plums, onion and garlic in a mixing bowl. Stuff the bird with about half of the mixture.

06 Truss the bird as directed in "How to Truss a Bird" (page 208). Brush oil on the outside of the pheasant.

07 Place one cedar sprig underneath the bird in a roasting pan and place the remaining fruit and onion mixture, along with the neck and giblets (if using), around the bird.

08 Bake the pheasant, uncovered, for 20 minutes.

09 Heat the stock to the boiling point on the stovetop or in a microwave.

10 Pour the stock into the pan and place the second cedar sprig on top of the bird.

11 Every 10 minutes, baste the roasting bird with the pan drippings using a turkey baster, and stir the fruit and onions in the pan so that they don't burn. If you notice the bird is getting too dark in parts, cover the dark parts with pieces of foil.

12 Total cooking time should be from 50 minutes to one hour, but check that the internal temperature of the pheasant (and stuffing) reaches 180F (80C) before removing it from the oven.

13 Let the bird rest for five minutes, with aluminum foil loosely covering it.

14 Remove the cedar, neck and giblets from the pan, and strain off the drippings into a gravy bowl to serve. Discard the neck and giblets and return the cedar to the earth.

15 Spoon the fruit and onion mixture into a small bowl to serve. Serve the bird whole with stuffing intact for visual effect or in a separate bowl—your choice.

Roasted Goose with Hazelnut Stuffing and Giblet Sauce

MAKES 6 SERVINGS

If you have never attempted to roast a goose for a special dinner, try it. But first read "Cooking Birds" on page 192 for more background on cooking goose, and consider brining it if you are using a wild goose (do this a day ahead of serving). You could also make the stuffing a day ahead. You could start to make the Giblet Sauce after the goose is almost done so that the sauce and the goose are ready at almost the same time.

Tip

Save the goose grease that ends up in the bottom of the pan when cooking goose, and use the grease for making creamy mashed potatoes or for frying chicken. (Marge, my mother-in-law, says to rub goose grease on your chest when you have a bad cold.)

BASIC BRINE (OPTIONAL):

½ cup (120 mL) kosher **salt** (or sea salt)
2 Tbsp (30 mL) **maple sugar** (or brown sugar)
16 cups (3.8 L) **water**

STUFFING:

3 cups (710 mL) **water**, divided
½ cup (120 mL) **wild rice**, rinsed
2 tsp (10 mL) table **salt**, divided
Sprig fresh **rosemary**
3 cups (710 mL) large-diced **sandwich bread**
1 cup (250 mL) **dried cranberries**
⅓ cup (80 mL) **butter**
2 cups (475 mL) diced **onion**
2 Tbsp (30 mL) minced fresh **sage**
1 tsp (5 mL) fresh **thyme**, chopped
½ tsp (2.5 mL) ground **black pepper**, divided
1½ cups (350 mL) diced **celery**

1 cup (250 mL) diced peeled **apple**
½ cup (120 mL) chopped **hazelnuts**
1 cup (250 mL) **White Stock** (see recipe, page 39)
   or store-bought unsalted chicken stock

GOOSE:

1 fresh **goose** (9–10 lb/4–4.5 kg), with neck and giblets
3 Tbsp (45 mL) kosher **salt** (or sea salt), divided
2 Tbsp (30 mL) ground **black pepper**
3 Tbsp (45 mL) pure **olive oil**
½ cup (120 mL) melted **unsalted butter** (optional),
   for injecting

OPTIONAL GARNISH:

1 **orange**, sliced

01 Combine brine ingredients together in a stock-pot and bring to a boil. Let cool. Place bird in a tall container large enough to hold the bird and all of the cooled brine so that the bird is completely covered (not floating). Chill the neck and giblets. Soak goose for eight hours in the fridge. Rinse goose in fresh water very thoroughly before continuing with the recipe.

02 For the stuffing, begin by cooking the wild rice. In a medium-sized saucepan bring 2 cups (475 mL) of the water to a boil over high heat. Add the rice, ¼ teaspoon (1 mL) of the table salt and the rosemary. Cover and reduce heat to medium. Cook for 40 to 50 minutes, or until the rice is tender and the water is absorbed. Remove rosemary and discard. Drain off any excess liquid. Let cool in a large bowl.

03 Spread the bread cubes over a baking sheet and leave in the open air overnight so that they dry out thoroughly, or dry them in a 250F (120C) oven for 15 minutes. Set aside.

CONTINUED …

04 Pour the cranberries into a large glass and cover with water. Heat in a microwave for 60 seconds and let the cranberries soak.

05 In a large sauté pan, heat the butter. Add the onion, sage, thyme and a pinch of the black pepper. Cook over medium-low heat until the onion is translucent (about three minutes), stirring occasionally.

06 Add the celery, apple and hazelnuts, and cook for two minutes more, stirring frequently.

07 Drain the cranberries and add to the onion mixture, along with the wild rice and bread.

08 Heat the stock to the boiling point on the stovetop or in a microwave and add to the mixture. Mix well, remove from the heat and taste, adjusting seasoning with the remaining salt and pepper. Set stuffing aside to cool. Chill until you are ready to stuff and roast the bird.

09 To prepare the goose, pat dry with paper towel. Discard extra bits of fat from around the goose's neck.

10 Salt the inside of the goose with half the kosher salt (skip this step if you brined the bird). Stuff the bird. Reserve excess stuffing for baking separately (see variation below).

11 Truss the bird with a long piece of butcher twine (see sidebar "How to Truss a Bird"). This will help keep the legs and wings close to the body so that it looks nicer for serving. *Note:* Some people don't bother to truss goose before roasting it, but I do because it will stay together better this way and fit into most roasting pans more easily. If your pan is large, however, or if you are roasting a smaller bird, then you might not need to bother. An advantage to *not* trussing a goose is that it will roast more evenly and more quickly.

12 Preheat oven to 350F (175C).

13 Score the breast of the bird in a criss-cross pattern using a sharp knife, but do not cut so deep as to cut the flesh. Season the outside of the bird with the pepper and the remaining kosher salt (leave out the salt if you brined the bird), rubbing the seasonings into the skin. Brush the bird with oil.

HOW TO TRUSS A BIRD

Place the bird on your work surface, breast side up with the neck closest to you. Tuck the wings behind the back. Lift the legs at the back upwards towards you in order to slide butcher twine underneath the legs and the hip bones; pull the twine up and cross over the legs and pull tight. Pull the twine down under the ends of the legs and around the sides of the bird towards you and tie in a knot over the neck. Cut off excess twine.

14 Place goose on a rack set inside a roasting pan on the lower rack of your oven. Roast, uncovered, for three hours (or 2½ hours if your bird was brined). Do not attempt to turn the bird.

15 The rack will allow the solid fat on the bird to render, or melt, into liquid fat in the bottom of the pan; that is the savoury "goose grease" mentioned above. Every hour during the roasting process, use a turkey baster to suck up the rendered fat from the bottom of the pan into a grease separator (to collect if saving, or to discard) and baste the bird with the pan juices. Alternatively, just before you start to roast the goose, use a meat injector to inject the breast with the optional melted unsalted butter, injecting directly into and about halfway through the breast meat.

16 The bird may get brown on the breast before the legs are done, so cover the browned parts with pieces of foil, leaving the legs and lighter spots uncovered.

17 Check that the goose reaches an internal temperature of 180F (80C); check it with a thermometer in several places, including the thickest muscle of the inner thigh, away from the bone.

18 Once done, let the goose rest, loosely covered in foil, for 15 minutes while you prepare the Giblet Sauce.

19 Transfer the goose to a serving platter, and remove the twine. Garnish with orange slices if using.

Baking Stuffing Separately: Bake the stuffing on its own in an oiled loaf pan covered with foil for about 45 minutes to one hour at 350F (175C) or until the stuffing reaches an internal temperature of 165F (75C). If you have a family that loves stuffing like mine does, then you could double this stuffing recipe; roast half of it in the bird and the rest in a pan.

Giblet Sauce

MAKES 2 CUPS (475 ML)

The sauce made from the pan drippings will be light brown in colour and a great finishing touch for your meal.

Goose neck and giblets
4 cups (1 L) cold **water**
3 to 4 crushed black **peppercorns**
1 dried **bay leaf**
1 stalk **celery**, cut in half
½ **onion**
⅓ cup (80 mL) all-purpose **flour**
⅔ cup (160 mL) **water**
1 tsp (5 mL) kosher **salt** or sea salt (optional)

01 Cover neck and giblets in 4 cups (1 L) cold water and bring to a boil in a saucepan on the stovetop, along with the peppercorns, bay leaf, celery and onion. Lower heat and simmer for 40 to 50 minutes, uncovered. Strain stock, and discard the neck. Set stock and giblets aside.

02 Using a turkey baster, remove the rest of the goose grease from the pan you cooked the goose in, leaving the pan drippings. Place the pan on the stovetop and heat over two burners over medium-low heat. Using a wooden spoon, scrape the brown bits of pan drippings that are stuck to the pan. Pour in reserved stock and bring to a simmer.

03 Make a slurry by combining the flour with water in a small cup or bowl. Remove the lumps with your finger. Strain stock and add to pan. Bring back to a simmer.

04 Let the sauce gently simmer for five minutes. Stir and taste, adding salt if needed. Strain sauce through a sieve. Chop giblets and add to sauce. Serve hot in a gravy bowl.

CHAPTER 8
The Plants: Vegetable and Side Dishes

Question: What's another name for a Native vegetarian? *Answer:* A bad shot. I still think that's funny even if nobody else does, but the truth is, as much as Indigenous people are associated with a diet based on wild game, fish and birds, traditional diets were actually very rich in ferns, lichens, mosses, grasses, fungi, flowers, bulbs, tree barks, roots, nuts, leaves, needles, ashes, shoots, stalks, stems, berries and saps. And then there were the cultivated crops. Depending on where Indigenous people lived, the crops they grew included corn, potatoes, squash, tomatoes, peanuts, pineapples, avocados, beans, chili peppers, amaranth, quinoa and cacao. Survival meant capitalizing on the seasons and planning for future needs using everything that grew and provided nutrients. Even though lichens needed processing before they could be eaten, the Inuit, for instance, discovered nutritional value in eating the partially digested lichens they found in the stomach of caribou. Indigenous people also protected the food sources of the animals that they so heavily depended on for their own survival.

Agricultural societies like the Haudenosaunee continue to hold ceremonies to protect the crops, to mark planting times and to thank the Creator for the foods that enabled people to live for millennia. The connection between Indigenous people and plants has always been very strong, one of kinship, as is the connection with animals, despite attempts by federal governments in Canada, the United States, Mexico and numerous countries in South America to outlaw numerous cultural practices. Some nations in the US Southwest, like the Pueblos, Navaho, Hopi and Mojave, for example, have managed to carry on the rain dance tradition (during periods of extreme dry weather) even though it was outlawed for a time.

There are still some medicine people and traditional healers who know the habitats, medicinal properties and key preparations of plants indigenous to this continent. There are elders who devote their golden years to sharing this knowledge with the young. There are still hunters and fishermen (and women) living in Indigenous communities who know how to survive on the land yet don't need to compete on a reality show to prove it. I have so much respect for them all and have been very fortunate to have met several in my travels, especially given their small number. There is a lot to learn about what originally came from this continent, but acquiring this knowledge isn't easy. Traditional teachings on the subject are still carefully protected and not widely shared. A lot of plants that once grew here have become extinct. Others are threatened by environmental change.

My friend Ken Parker is the only First Nations person I happen to know who ever managed to establish a business selling seedlings, potted plants and trees, and seeds of plants that are indigenous to North America. Another friend of mine, Jonathan Forbes, went into the business of selling indigenous fungi, berries, tree saps, and so on, in raw, dried, ground and preserved forms (in jellies, syrups and vinaigrettes). I relied on both of these friends to supply me with my off-the-grid food supplies for my television show and was impressed by their ability to bring organic, hand-harvested, indigenous ingredients to market.

Let It Pour!

The thought of drought is frightening to those who live off the land. In Marlene's family, there is a well-told story about one visit her aunt Gladys Fisher had on her Saskatchewan farm from cousin Wilfred Bellegarde, who was chief of Little Black Bear First Nation. Gladys told him how worried she was about the condition of the crops due to an ongoing lack of rain. Cousin Wilfred went outside and chanted a song while beating on his chest and belly. Gladys saw a tiny black cloud in the distance, and when her cousin began to sing, it started to come closer. Within minutes, rain was pouring down, and it carried on for half an hour straight. She didn't know if he was just pretending or if he really knew what he was doing, but it didn't matter.

Tips for Cooking Vegetables

Regardless of where you get your produce from, you can preserve its nutritional value and appearance with a few standard cooking practices.

To prevent illness caused by food-borne contaminants, all vegetables should be washed under cold running water without soap (and that includes those that have been pre-washed *and* organic vegetables). Root vegetables should be scrubbed first with a brush.

Vegetables are best prepared when their colours, textures and nutrients are preserved as much as possible. These qualities are affected by factors such as the amount of water you use when boiling, water temperature, exposure to salt and acids, and whether or not you cover the vegetables while cooking. Here are some basic guidelines:

· Soak vegetables in cold, salted water for 30 minutes if they are organic or home grown, before cooking.
· Cook evenly cut fresh vegetables as briefly as possible.
· Put root vegetables in cold, salted water to begin cooking them.
· Put green vegetables and any others that grow above ground in boiling, salted water to begin cooking them.
· Canned vegetables are already cooked, so just heat and serve.
· Frozen vegetables are sold raw, partially cooked and fully cooked, so follow package instructions for cooking.
· When cooking a variety of vegetables, cook them separately and combine later, to preserve their colours and flavours.
· Serve fresh vegetables as hot as possible. (In the industry, we sometimes do it in two stages: the first stage is really just blanching in boiling water and then chilling them in ice water, and once the rest of the meal is just about ready, we cook them some more so that they are piping hot and still brightly coloured when served.)
· Use a fork, not a knife, to test vegetables for doneness.

Garlic Roasted Sunchokes

MAKES 8 SERVINGS

The sunchoke, which is a knobby tuber that resembles ginger root and has the texture of potato, has various other names, including Jerusalem artichoke, sunroot and earth apple. It's a species of sunflower that is indigenous to North America and has a long history of being prepared in soups by eastern woodlands First Nations. Sunchokes can be eaten raw in a salad, the way you might eat radish, or tossed into a stew, but I like to roast them in garlic as a side dish. When shopping, look for firm sunchokes with clean brown skin rather than soft ones or those with green spots or sprouts.

2½ lb (1 kg) **sunchokes**
1 Tbsp (15 mL) **lemon juice**
⅓ cup (80 mL) pure **olive oil**
4 tsp (20 mL) chopped **garlic**
1½ tsp (7.5 mL) dried **oregano**
1½ tsp (7.5 mL) kosher **salt** (or Salt Alternative, see page 32)
¼ tsp (1 mL) ground **black pepper**
1 tsp (5 mL) **lemon zest**
1 Tbsp (15 mL) chopped fresh **oregano** (optional)

01 Preheat oven to 400F (205C).

02 Wash and scrub sunchokes thoroughly. Peeling is unnecessary and I don't bother, but if you do, peel them using the edge of a spoon to scrape the skin off as you would from ginger root.

03 Slice sunchokes into ⅛ inch (0.5 cm) slices. Sprinkle with lemon juice to keep them from browning.

04 Combine oil, garlic, oregano, salt and pepper together in a large mixing bowl. Add the sunchokes and toss to coat. Spread mixture in a 9 by 9 inch (23 × 23 cm) baking pan.

05 Roast sunchokes for 45 minutes or until tender.

06 Toss with lemon zest and fresh oregano, if using, before serving.

Stuffed Acorn Squash

MAKES 4 SERVINGS

How many ways can you prepare squash? Probably as many ways as you can prepare potatoes. The Mohawk and Ojibway found many ways to cook squash: baking it whole over hot coals, boiling it with basswood leaves and mashing it, and flavouring it with deer suet and maple sugar. Isn't that something? The Onondaga preserved squash for later use by cutting it into long strips, stringing the pieces together, and drying it over fires before storing the dried squash in birchbark or wooden containers; the squash could be rehydrated later in water to make soup or bread. Some squash and gourds were used to make rattles for ceremonial purposes.

Acorn squash is considered a winter squash and has hard seeds and deep ridges going down the full length of its thick green skin. It sometimes has orange spots on the skin, which is okay. Look for heaviness when shopping for squash, and try to find squashes of about the same size if preparing this recipe for "company."

This recipe is an attractive and tasty side dish that would go well with Garlic Elk Short Ribs in Sour Cherry Sauce (page 140), Smoked Deer Sausage (page 142) or Broiled Ranch Deer Chops (page 145).

SQUASH:

2 whole acorn squashes (2 lb/900 g)

¼ cup (60 mL) pure olive oil, divided

½ tsp (2.5 mL) ground ginger

½ tsp (2.5 mL) Vanilla Salt (see recipe, page 22) or kosher salt

Pinch ground black pepper

STUFFING:

1½ cups (350 mL) White Stock (see recipe, page 39) or store-bought unsalted chicken stock

½ cup (120 mL) pearl barley, rinsed

Pinch table salt

¼ cup (60 mL) chopped pecans

¼ cup (60 mL) melted butter, divided

½ cup (120 mL) chopped mushrooms

½ cup (120 mL) small-diced onion

¼ cup (60 mL) small-diced celery

1 tsp (5 mL) chopped garlic

1 cup (250 mL) small-diced apple (preferably McIntosh, Cortland or Northern Spy), skin on

1 Tbsp (15 mL) chopped fresh sage

1 egg, beaten

OPTIONAL GARNISH:

1 Tbsp (15 mL) chopped parsley

01 Cut the tops and bottoms off the squashes and then cut them in half lengthwise. (Try to cut them so that each piece is level and about the same size.) Spoon out—and discard—the seeds and loose fibres from the centres.

02 Combine half the oil with the ginger in a small bowl. Brush the mixture on the inside and tops of the squash cups using a pastry brush.

03 Sprinkle Vanilla Salt and pepper on each piece of squash.

04 Heat 1 tablespoon (15 mL) of the remaining oil in a frying pan over medium heat. Add the squash and brown in batches (cut side down), adding the rest of the oil as needed to keep the squash from burning.

05 Preheat oven to 375F (190C).

06 Once all the squash cups have been browned, place them in an ovenproof baking pan or on a parchment paper–lined baking sheet large enough to hold all the pieces in a single layer, cut side up.

07 Bake the squash cups, uncovered, in the oven for 30 minutes while you prepare the stuffing. Before you remove the cups from the oven, test them with a fork to make sure the flesh is fork tender. If not, bake for a few minutes more. Remove squash from oven and tent with foil to keep warm. Leave the oven on.

08 Heat the stock in a microwave or on the stovetop almost to the boiling point. Pour it into a medium-sized saucepan, add the barley and salt, and bring to a boil over high heat. Turn heat down and cook barley for 25 minutes at a low simmer, covered. Remove from heat. Test to make sure barley is soft and chewy; if it is not, cook for a few minutes more. Set aside.

09 Toast pecans in a large saucepan over medium heat for two minutes. Remove them from the pan and set aside in a small bowl.

10 Add half of the melted butter to the pan you used to toast the nuts in, along with the mushrooms, onion, celery and garlic. Cook over medium-low heat for 5 minutes, stirring frequently. Add the apple and sage and cook for two minutes more, stirring frequently.

11 Return the toasted pecans to the pan, along with the rest of the melted butter. Stir in the egg to bind the mixture. Add the barley to this mixture and stir to combine well.

12 Scoop the stuffing into the squash halves. Bake for 10 minutes.

13 Serve squash garnished with parsley if using.

WILD RICE: TRADITIONAL VERSUS COMMERCIAL

Traditionally harvested wild rice comes in different colours and has grains up to 3 or 4 inches (7.5–10 cm) long. It cooks quicker than commercially grown wild rice and tastes a little smoky. It's hard, but not impossible, to find it if you search online.

Commercial wild rice is easier to find, is more economical and typically has shorter, black or dark brown grains from drying in the sun. This type of rice, which is technically a grass, takes longer to cook, so for timing purposes you need to know which kind you are using.

Both types of rice are cooked with four times the quantity of water, but the timings suggested in the recipes in this cookbook apply to commercial wild rice.

NOTE: Read "Wild Rice: Traditional versus Commercial" (page 215) before choosing the rice for this recipe.

Wild Rice Pepper Pilaf

MAKES 6 SERVINGS

Pilaf, a quick side dish, is really a simple rice dish using flavoured stock. It wouldn't be the same at all if you substituted water for the stock, because the water would not provide any flavour. Serve this dish as an accompaniment to a meat or fish dish. You can use vegetables other than peppers (e.g., mushrooms, zucchini).

2 Tbsp (30 mL) pure olive oil, divided

¼ cup (60 mL) diced green pepper

¼ cup (60 mL) diced red pepper

¼ cup (60 mL) diced yellow pepper

1 cup (250 mL) diced onion

1 cup (250 mL) wild rice, rinsed

4½ cups (1.1 L) Brown Stock (see recipe, page 40)
    or store-bought unsalted beef stock

2 dried bay leaves

½ tsp (2.5 mL) table salt

¼ tsp (1 mL) ground black pepper

1 Tbsp (15 mL) chopped parsley

OPTIONAL GARNISH:

2 Tbsp (30 mL) toasted pine nuts (or slivered almonds)

Tip

When cutting peppers into smaller pieces, place them on the work surface skin side down. This is safer than cutting them skin side up, because the skin is slippery.

01 Preheat oven to 350F (175C).

02 Heat a Dutch oven over low heat for five minutes. Add half the oil and raise the heat a little. Cook the peppers in the pot for five minutes. Remove peppers from the pot and set aside.

03 Heat the remaining olive oil in the Dutch oven and cook the onion for three minutes.

04 Add the rice to the pot, stir to coat it in oil and let it cook for three minutes.

05 Heat the stock in a microwave or on the stovetop almost to the boiling point. Add the stock, bay leaves, salt and black pepper to the pot all at once. Stir and let the mixture reach the boiling point.

06 Transfer the Dutch oven to the oven and bake the pilaf, covered, for 50 minutes.

07 Remove pilaf from the oven and place on the stovetop. Return the peppers to the pot at this point and stir them in.

08 Let the pilaf cook for 5 to 10 minutes more over medium heat, and add the chopped parsley.

09 For a little crunch, serve the pilaf with the optional toasted nuts sprinkled on top.

Scalloped Rutabaga

MAKES 8 SERVINGS

The prairie turnip is a root vegetable that prairie Lakota and Sioux harvested for cooking and for trading with nations to the south. It is also called prairie potato, tipsin, tipsinna and Indian breadroot, and is starchy enough to be dried and ground into a flour for making porridge or for thickening stew. Rutabagas are the next best thing to the prairie turnip and are much more readily available.

Try this recipe with Deer Osso Buco (see recipe, page 135). This dish is heavy and creamy and a little cheesy, but you can add more cheese if you want to, or leave it out altogether. To get the full benefit of the dish, you should not cut out the cream, however. When shopping for a rutabaga, choose one that is firm and heavy. It will probably have wax on the skin, which will be removed when you peel it.

3½ cups (830 mL) sliced **rutabaga** (⅛ inch/0.5 cm thick)
Pinch table **salt**
1 Tbsp (15 mL) **butter**
1 cup (250 mL) sliced **onion**

SAUCE:
3 Tbsp (45 mL) **butter**
3 Tbsp (45 mL) all-purpose **flour**
2 cups (475 mL) 10 percent **cream**
2 cups (475 mL) homogenized **milk**
¼ tsp (1 mL) ground **allspice**
1 tsp (5 mL) kosher **salt** (or sea salt)
¼ tsp (1 mL) ground **black pepper**

TO ASSEMBLE:
1 cup (250 mL) sliced **potato** (preferably Yukon Gold) (⅛ inch/0.5 cm thick)
1 cup (250 mL) shredded **Gouda** cheese (or Swiss)

01 Drop rutabaga into a pot of cold water with a pinch of salt and bring to a boil. Cook for 10 minutes. Drain.

02 Melt 1 tablespoon (15 mL) butter in a saucepan. Add onion and cook over low heat for five minutes. Remove onion from pan and set aside.

03 For the sauce, add 3 tablespoons (45 mL) butter to the saucepan and let melt over medium-low heat. Add the flour and stir with a wooden spoon to make a roux. Cook for three minutes.

04 Remove the pan from heat, gradually add the cream, and stir or whisk to remove lumps. Return the pan to the heat and let the sauce thicken for a minute, whisking a couple of times and making sure it doesn't reach the boiling point.

05 Add the milk to the sauce and whisk until it becomes smooth. Stir in the allspice, salt and pepper. Simmer for five minutes and then remove from heat.

06 Preheat oven to 350F (175F).

07 Ladle a third of the sauce onto the bottom of a greased 9 by 13 inch (23 × 33 cm) baking pan or casserole dish. Arrange about half of the rutabaga and half of the potatoes over the sauce, and top with a third of the cheese.

08 Pour half of the remaining sauce over the mixture. Add the rest of rutabaga and potatoes. Add half of the remaining cheese.

09 Pour the rest of the sauce into the pan, and top with the remaining cheese and cooked onion.

10 Bake at 350F (175F) for one hour.

11 Let the dish rest for five minutes before serving.

Simply Creamy Polenta

MAKES 4 SERVINGS

Polenta is a cornmeal dish that's generally associated with Italy, but it really originates from Indigenous people. Before corn from the Americas was introduced in Europe, people there used to grind farro, chestnuts and millet, spelt and chickpeas to make a porridge. The tradition of grinding corn and making it into a mushy dish began in Peru in 5000 BCE. Much later, the Seneca made *sagamité* with ground corn, water and wood ash. Haudenosaunee culture was founded upon corn; more than a staple food, corn was, and still is, sacred. Numerous agricultural Indigenous nations added maple syrup to mashed corn to make a sweet pudding, called Indian Pudding; these days the dish is typically made with lots of cream, brown sugar, vanilla and baking spices. See the Amaranth Birch Pudding recipe on page 265.

Polenta as we know it today is quick and easy to make and adaptable as a side dish for red meat, fish or poultry entrées. If you have never had it, think of Cream of Wheat cereal, or porridge, with salt and pepper instead of milk and brown sugar!

Before proceeding read "How to Choose Cornmeal" (page 221).

There are endless possibilities for how you can jazz up polenta, so you can make it often, in different ways. See the variations below for just a few ideas. If you don't know what to do with leftover polenta, cut it into squares and pan-fry it in a little oil or a little of the grease you saved after you roasted a goose at Christmas.

4 cups (1 L) **water**, plus more if needed
1½ tsp (7.5 mL) kosher **salt** (or sea salt), plus more if needed
¾ cup (180 mL) coarse yellow **cornmeal**
2 Tbsp (30 mL) **butter**

01 In a saucepan, bring the water to a boil. Season with salt.

02 Gradually add the cornmeal while stirring constantly with a rubber spatula or whisk. (Some chefs insist you use a wooden spoon for this procedure.) Lower the heat after all the cornmeal has been added and lumps have been removed.

03 Cook for 20 to 25 minutes over low heat, uncovered, frequently stirring to make sure the polenta does not stick to the pan.

04 Add the butter and taste. Adjust seasoning with more salt if necessary. Polenta should be creamy by this point, but if the cornmeal is still a little hard, add another ½ cup (120 mL) water and continue cooking for five more minutes.

Cheese Variation: Reduce the salt by half and add ½ cup (120 mL) grated Parmesan cheese at the end of the cooking process.

Herb Variation: Add 1 tablespoon (15 mL) minced fresh herbs such as sage or thyme to the polenta at the end of the cooking process.

Tomato Variation: Cook the cornmeal in Vegetable Stock (see recipe, page 38) instead of water, reduce the salt by half and add some sliced sundried tomatoes to the polenta about five minutes before the cooking process ends.

HOW TO CHOOSE CORNMEAL

Cornmeal is ground maize (field corn) and may be ground to different sized grains: fine, medium or coarse. Fine cornmeal is better suited to muffins or coatings for fried foods and is often confusingly labelled as corn flour. Medium cornmeal is used for making corn bread. Coarser cornmeal is better for making polenta and the coarsest is used for making grits. If cornmeal has been stone ground, then it's a whole grain, which means it's the most nutritious, but stone-ground cornmeal can become rancid, so you have to use it right away or keep it in the freezer.

When shopping for cornmeal you might come across "polenta," which is a cornmeal specifically suited to making polenta, and it comes in both slow-cooking and quick-cooking (par-cooked) types. Polenta is not the same as masa harina, which is cornmeal made from ground hominy that was cooked in limewater first; that is used for making tortilla shells.

Cornmeal also comes in various colours. Blue cornmeal is hard to find (and it's really a grey colour, not blue); it's more nutritious than yellow (the most common) or white cornmeal (the mildest).

Maple Baked Beans

MAKES 6 SERVINGS

Native Americans introduced New England settlers to pit-baked beans flavoured with maple sugar and bear fat, and this was the precursor to what is commonly known as Boston Baked Beans today, which typically is made with salt pork, molasses and brown sugar. Salt pork isn't the easiest ingredient to find in stores at times; if your butcher doesn't sell it, try a fish market that also carries traditional Maritime groceries, or try a Caribbean market, but you might need to use bacon instead for this recipe. Also, you can use navy beans or any other small white bean for this recipe if you have trouble finding great northern beans.

2 cups (475 mL) great northern **beans**

8 cups (2 L) **water**, plus more for soaking beans

½ lb (225 g) **salt pork**

1 cup (250 mL) large-diced **onion**

3 Tbsp (45 mL) **molasses** (preferably blackstrap)

3 Tbsp (45 mL) prepared **mustard**

¼ cup (60 mL) **tomato paste**

½ cup (120 mL) **maple syrup**

1 tsp (5 mL) kosher **salt** (or sea salt)

Pinch ground **cloves**

01 Soak beans, covered by a minimum of 2 inches (5 cm) of water, in the fridge overnight in a large container (the beans will expand).

02 Drain out the water and rinse the beans well.

03 Bring soaked beans and 8 cups (2 L) water to the boiling point in a covered saucepan. Lower temperature and simmer, covered, until beans are tender (about one hour). Drain off liquid and reserve. Set beans aside.

04 Heat a Dutch oven over very low heat for 10 minutes. Raise heat to medium. Remove any rind from the salt pork and cut the pork into large dice. Sear the pork—without moving it—in the pot for five minutes. Add onion, stir and cook over low heat for five minutes.

05 Add the rest of the ingredients to the Dutch oven, including the beans and half of the liquid they were cooked in. Bring to a simmer.

06 Bake for three hours at 300F (150C), covered, but check each hour to make sure beans don't dry out. As needed, add some of the reserved water in which the beans were cooked.

Andean Mountain Potato Cakes

MAKES 8 SERVINGS

Potatoes and corn are two of the world's four basic food crops (rice and wheat are the other two), so you could say that Indigenous farmers changed the world. (Funny I never learned that in school!) Estimates are that starting somewhere between 7000 and 5000 BCE, Indigenous peoples in the Andean mountains of either Peru or Ecuador started cultivating potatoes, which they developed into a staple food. Potatoes were just one crop that fuelled the Incan empire. To this day *llapingachos* (potato cakes) are prepared in Ecuador and Colombia (and served with cheese or peanut sauce as in the Tangy Bass Fillet with Peanut Sauce recipe, page 168). This recipe is a simplified one using ketchup instead.

I learned really quickly when I got married that there are two things we can never run out of at home or there will be consequences. One is tea and the other is potatoes. We go through a lot of tea and potatoes, and this is a good way of using up leftover mashed potatoes—assuming they are not overly creamy or overly seasoned (if they are, you won't need the added salt and pepper, but you might need to add more flour to thicken them up enough to fry).

3 cups (710 mL) mashed **potatoes** (preferably Russets or Yukon Golds)
½ cup (120 mL) all-purpose **flour**
½ tsp (2.5 mL) table **salt**
¼ tsp (1 mL) ground **black pepper**
1 tsp (5 mL) ground **cumin**
1 **egg**, beaten
¼ cup (60 mL) diced **green onion**
2 Tbsp (30 mL) chopped fresh **parsley**
⅔ cup (160 mL) shredded **mozzarella**
¼ cup (60 mL) **vegetable oil**, divided
½ tsp (2.5 mL) **achiote seed** seasoning (or ¼ tsp/1 mL sweet paprika and ¼ tsp/1 mL turmeric)
ketchup (optional)

01 Heat the mashed potatoes if cold. In a mixing bowl combine the potatoes with the flour, salt, pepper and cumin.

02 Add the egg, green onion, parsley and cheese to the potato mixture, and mix well using a potato masher.

03 Heat half of the oil in a frying pan over medium-low heat. Add the achiote seed seasoning and stir to combine.

04 Form the potato mixture into hamburger-sized patties about ¾ inch (2 cm) thick (about ½ cup/120 mL of mixture each), using your hands.

05 Cook the patties in small batches of three or four at a time over low heat for 15 to 20 minutes or until browned on each side, using the remaining oil as needed.

06 Serve hot with ketchup on the side if using.

Steamed Tarragon Spaghetti Squash

MAKES 4 SERVINGS

Cultivation of gourds dates back to 7000 BCE in Mexico, according to scientists' best guess. Squash and pumpkin are in the same plant family as gourds. The spaghetti squash resembles a yellow melon and the flesh has an unusual texture—resembling spaghetti—when cooked and fluffed with a fork. The spaghetti squash is considered a winter squash since it is harvested in the fall and early winter. Choose a firm one with a hard rind when shopping; you might find it labelled "squaghetti," "vegetable spaghetti," "noodle squash" or "vegetable marrow."

1 spaghetti squash (1½ lb/600 g)
2 Tbsp (30 mL) melted butter
1 Tbsp (15 mL) orange zest

1 Tbsp (15 mL) chopped fresh tarragon
½ tsp (2.5 mL) ground black pepper
½ tsp (2.5 mL) table salt
¼ tsp (1 mL) ground nutmeg

01 Cut squash in half lengthwise. Spoon out seeds and discard. Place cut sides facing down in a steamer. Steam (unseasoned) for 15 minutes, covered.

02 Scrape the spaghetti-like fibres from the cooked squash into a bowl using a fork. Mix squash with the butter, orange zest, tarragon, pepper, salt and nutmeg until well blended.

03 Serve hot.

NOTE: Try to buy sprouts of the same size so that they cook evenly.

Oven Roasted Brussels Sprouts with Bacon

MAKES 4 SERVINGS

We have Jacques Cartier to thank for cabbage; on his third voyage to New France in 1541, he brought it here for planting. By the eighteenth century, Indigenous people were growing it. Brussels sprouts are a result of cross breeding cabbage but are not to be confused with the inedible skunk cabbage, an indigenous wildflower used by First Nations mainly for their broad leaves in storing food.

This dish is pretty simple to make, and it's versatile—I like it with red meat, fish and poultry. We have it in the fall, when aromas fill the house and nobody can resist peeking into the kitchen to find out what's going on. Nuts from the walnut tree, which is indigenous to present-day Canada and the United States, add crunch to the dish.

1 Tbsp (15 mL) pure olive oil
½ lb (225 g) diced bacon
3 Tbsp (45 mL) chopped walnuts
1 cup (250 mL) thickly cut red onion
2 tsp (10 mL) sliced garlic
1 lb (500 g) Brussels sprouts
½ tsp (2.5 mL) table salt
½ tsp (2.5 mL) ground black pepper

01 Heat a cast iron frying pan over medium heat for five minutes. Add oil and cook bacon until crispy. Remove bacon from pan and reserve.

02 Cook the walnuts in the same oil and remove them, reserving them along with the bacon.

03 Cook onion and garlic in the pan for two minutes.

04 Preheat oven to 325F (160C).

05 Wash the sprouts. Cut off any discoloured outer leaves as well as the bottoms without cutting off too many outer leaves. Cut the sprouts in half lengthwise.

Add the Brussels sprouts, salt and pepper to the pan, and cook for three minutes. Transfer the pan to the oven and bake for 20 minutes, uncovered, stirring once or twice.

06 Remove the pan from the oven, sprinkle the bacon and walnuts on top, and return to the oven for five minutes. Mix well just before serving.

Caramelized Rainbow Pearl Onions

MAKES 4 SERVINGS

How's this for living off the land: Indigenous peoples of the west coast of Canada used to steam nodding onions with other roots and vegetables in cedar-lined pits covered with lichen and alder boughs. Then they were dried or pressed into cakes—gourmet cooking if you ask me! But these people weren't the only ones to cook onions, and they used plant-based location naming systems to remember where they found them. Chicago is said to have got its name by the Miami in reference to where they picked onions: *shikaakwa*.

Onions of any sort become caramelized when roasted, and pearl onions are no exception. The rainbow variety includes red, yellow and white onions, which add a little splash of colour that makes them perfect as a super simple side dish to poultry or game birds. But you could definitely use just the white or yellow variety. Look for onions that are hard and do not have any black fungus, mould or green shoots.

This recipe is especially good with any meat dish when you want a little scoop of something extra on the side.

3 cups (710 mL) **rainbow pearl onions**
1½ Tbsp (22 mL) pure **olive oil**
4 tsp (20 mL) sliced **garlic**
1 tsp (5 mL) chopped fresh **rosemary**
¼ tsp (1 mL) ground **nutmeg**
¼ tsp (1 mL) table **salt**
¼ tsp (1 mL) ground **black pepper**

01 Preheat oven to 350F (175C).

02 Blanch onions in a pot of boiling water for 30 seconds with their peels on. Drain and drop them into a bowl of ice water. Drain again.

03 Peel onions and cut in half lengthwise, but try to keep some of the root attached to each half so that the onions don't completely separate when cooking. Mix the remaining ingredients with the onions in a mixing bowl.

04 Heat a cast iron frying pan over medium heat for five minutes. Add the onion mixture, and cook for three minutes. Then transfer the pan to the oven and cook for 20 minutes, stirring occasionally.

05 Remove from oven and serve hot.

NOTE: Don't eat fiddleheads raw as they may make you very ill.

Fiddleheads and Carrots in Sesame Birch Sauce

MAKES 4 SERVINGS

I offer no substitutes for fiddleheads. Either you have them or you don't. I can't think of anything that tastes or looks even remotely the same. It's as simple as that. If you can't tell by the name, fiddleheads really do look like the head of a fiddle. They are the little green tops of ostrich ferns before they grow up and unfurl themselves . . . like ostrich feathers. One elder was nice enough to show me her favourite fiddlehead picking spot on Bear River First Nation, Nova Scotia, one spring, but now I tend to just wait until they magically appear in my supermarket every April. Treat yourself to heirloom carrots in this recipe.

12 oz (340 g) whole **carrots** (about 6 thin carrots)
Pinch table **salt**
3 cups (710 mL) **fiddleheads**
2 Tbsp (30 mL) **sesame oil**
2 cloves **garlic**, thickly sliced
1 Tbsp (15 mL) **soya sauce**
1 Tbsp (15 mL) **birch syrup**
1 Tbsp (15 mL) **molasses**

01 If the carrots are too large to cook whole, cut in half. Drop the carrots into a saucepan of water, add salt and bring to the boiling point. Reduce heat and let cook for 10 minutes. Strain.

02 Thoroughly rinse the fiddleheads. Remove the brown bits and trim off the cut ends.

03 Heat a pot of water to the boiling point. Add the fiddleheads and boil for 10 minutes. Rinse and strain.

04 Heat a cast iron frying pan on high. Add the oil. When it starts to smoke, sear the garlic in it for two minutes.

05 Lower the heat to medium, and add the fiddleheads and soya sauce. Stir and let cook for three minutes. Remove the garlic and fiddleheads from the pan.

06 Add the carrots, molasses and birch syrup to the pan. Toss the carrots to coat them. Let heat for two minutes.

07 Return the fiddleheads and garlic to the pan and toss. Serve hot.

CHAPTER 9

On the Side: Bannock and Other Breads

There's a reason why real estate agents advise clients trying to sell their homes to bake bread or pies right before holding an open house. It seems that when you walk into a home and smell fresh baked goods, you don't mind the clutter in the closets or the flaws in the walls so much. Instant distraction. Your brain is too busy sorting through memories of childhood and happy times to notice imperfections in the property. Marlene's sister Nancy Johnson didn't have time for pies when she was selling her house, so she just put a pot of water on the stove and heated up some cinnamon sticks and cloves instead. Sold!

Before the arrival of Europeans in the Americas, Indigenous peoples might not have had wheat, but they were able to turn cattails, wild oats, corn, tubers, hickory nuts, hazelnuts, walnuts and acorns into coarse flour to make flatbreads of sorts. It was called s*apli'l*, *pegna*, *nabainaa* or *arepa*, depending on where they lived. However, after wheat flour, sugar, leavening agents and dairy products were introduced, Indigenous peoples developed new bread-making practices and their diet changed.

Bannock, a quick bread that Scottish settlers made, was quickly adopted into the culture of many Indigenous nations. Whether baked as one large piece or several smaller ones, it became a staple. These days, the fried version of bannock is called fry bread, which is served smothered in butter or lard, or with jam on top, or with a huge ladleful of chili (garnished with grated cheese and a sprinkle of shredded lettuce), as the ever-popular "Indian taco." (I challenge anyone to find a powwow that doesn't have at least one food vendor selling Indian tacos.) The bannock recipes in this cookbook feature herbs, buttermilk and berries instead, and I kick up the fry bread with hot peppers. Hello!

The difference between quick breads (such as baked bannock) and regular bread is that quick breads rely on baking powder or baking soda and salt to rise, and the dough rises as it bakes, but regular bread has yeast that causes the dough to expand before it bakes. Typical quick breads are muffins, cookies, cakes, pancakes, corn bread and banana bread. The difference between the two types of bread doesn't interest the person who eats the final product as much as it concerns the person who makes it, but yeast has interesting idiosyncrasies that bakers need to understand in order to be successful.

Yeast dough recipes generally take some time to prepare, since the dough has to "work" before it goes into the oven. The yeast kicks into action when it comes into contact with sugar and warm water. How you mix the dough (by machine or by hand) isn't as important as the proofing action that takes place afterwards when

the dough expands—doubling in size if all goes well. It will *not* go so well if you are working in a drafty location. Yeast is sensitive (like me!). Even if you use a bread maker, the machine will proof the dough before baking it.

Some recipes require you to punch the dough down after it rises and let it rise again before it goes into the oven, because doing so improves the texture of the bread.

Typical breads are sandwich loaf breads, donuts, bagels and pizza crusts, and you can make them with cake (block) yeast, active dry yeast or instant yeast. I am most accustomed to using active dry yeast, which is what I use in this cookbook. The only drawback to using active dry yeast is that you have to allow time for the yeast to get started in some water—that adds about 10 to 15 minutes to the recipe on top of the time for proofing. You can use that time to catch up on emails you didn't have time to read when you were busy berry picking.

GLUTEN-FREE BAKING

Gluten is essentially the "glue," or protein, in wheat, rye, barley and other grains that binds and stabilizes baked goods. Here's the thing about gluten: it's what makes baked goods light, airy, stretchy and moist—so you can guess what happens when you bake without it.

When you bake bread without glutinous flour of some sort (wheat is the most common), you have to fight to prevent it from becoming overly dry, crumbly and dense. To compensate for the absence of gluten, other ingredients are needed such as xanthan gum or guar gum (powders that acts as thickeners and stabilizers), oil, other liquids or eggs to bind the ingredients. What's more, various types of flours generally need to be combined for gluten-free baking. The late comedian John Pinette, who was known for his love of food, developed quite the opinion on gluten-free foods after his doctor informed him he was allergic to gluten. Pinette would ask the audience, "Do you know what has gluten in it?" His answer: "*Everything!*"

Lemon and Dill Buttermilk Scones

MAKES 12 SERVINGS

In just about every episode of my cooking show, I've had guests make bannock while we chat about this or that—their latest work, their art, and so on. On one show, my guest John Kim Bell, the well-known Mohawk symphony conductor, was making scones and hamming it up for the camera. He caught me off guard by asking, "David, do you know what a baker's dozen is?" And I answered, "13." He said, "Well this here is a Newfie's dozen—11!" I was speechless as I stared at what should have been 12 scone shapes. All I could think of was my entertainment lawyer, Larry Pasemko, freaking out in the editing truck and telling my director, Sidney Cohen, to cut and redo the segment because of possible legal action from insulted viewers in Newfoundland. But instead I heard laughter in my earpiece, so I figured the joke must be okay. That's TV scone making for you.

This scone recipe features buttermilk and an egg. Now, I don't care for buttermilk straight out of the fridge, although some people like to drink it even though it's milk that's been deliberately soured by a bacterial culture (as is the case with yogurt and cheese). It doesn't sound so appetizing when you think of it that way, but that's what it is. Regardless, buttermilk makes everything light and fluffy, whether pancakes, biscuits, cakes or salad dressings, so it's a nice treat. Just use regular milk or non-dairy milk if you don't have any buttermilk; the recipe will work, but the product won't be quite as creamy tasting as one made with buttermilk. Of course, scones are normally plain, but here I added citrus and herbs. Eggs are not traditionally used in scones, but they make the scones a little more golden in colour and add body to the dough. By the way, where I live, the "Nish" way to pronounce the word is "scon," not "scown."

This recipe goes well with Buffalo Canoes (see recipe, page 60).

2½ cups (600 mL) all-purpose flour,
   plus 2 Tbsp (30 mL) for dusting
2 Tbsp (30 mL) sugar
4 tsp (20 mL) baking powder
½ tsp (1 mL) table salt
¼ cup (60 mL) cold butter, cubed
3 Tbsp (45 mL) chopped fresh dill
1½ Tbsp (22 mL) lemon zest
1 large egg, beaten
1 cup (250 mL) 1 per cent buttermilk
½ tsp (2.5 mL) vanilla

01 Preheat oven to 400F (205C).

02 Combine 2½ cups (600 mL) flour with the sugar, baking powder and salt in a large mixing bowl (I always make bannock by hand). Add the butter and mix in using a pastry blender (or your hands) until the lumps are the size of peas.

03 Add the dill and lemon zest, combine and set aside.

04 In a separate bowl, combine the egg, buttermilk and vanilla. Pour the wet mixture into the flour mixture, combining them only long enough for the dough to stick together. Use your hands for this.

05 Dust the work surface with the remaining flour and flatten the dough on it to a thickness of 1 inch (2.5 cm). Cut out scones using a 2½ inch (6 cm) cookie cutter—or do what a lot of home cooks do on the rez: use a small empty soup can to cut the dough.

06 Place scones on a parchment paper–lined baking sheet and bake for 20 minutes.

Salmon Half-Moons

MAKES 8 SERVINGS

It boggles the mind to think of the risks my relatives face to catch salmon in the Fraser River. On top of the dangers of climbing down the incredibly steep, rocky riverbanks with all their gear to get to their favourite fishing spots on the Xaxli'p First Nation, families work together, leaning over the raging, light green water to hoist up full nets by hand. Then if they are planning to wind dry the fish, they clean them on the spot and cut them up into fillets, making long slits across the flesh to help speed up the drying process. Some families salt the fish at this point to cure it. Then they spread the fish out on wooden racks to wind dry the traditional way for a week or more; the quicker the fish dries, the better it is. Once it's dry they store it in food-safe plastic bags and have fish available all year long. They cover the first batch of fish with cedar branches for a few hours as they work on the rest so that the pungent aroma of the cedar keeps flies off. According to my mom, they collect the fish organs, heads, tails and bones and place them on the ground in a few distant spots. This distracts bears from the cleaning site so that the families can work in peace. Wow.

In this recipe, I use fresh salmon and store-bought puff pastry. Puff pastry is a good fit for the tangy flavours of the ginger and tarragon and a perfect texture for the salmon. Try this recipe with Cream of Celery Soup with Red Pepper Purée (page 94).

If you want to speed up the process of making turnovers (if doubling the recipe, for example), use a plastic dough press, which is also known as a turnover maker.

¼ cup (60mL) all-purpose flour for dusting
1 pkg (14 oz/400 g) puff pastry, chilled

FILLING:
1 beaten egg
1 lb (500 g) small-diced fresh skinless salmon
  (or canned salmon, drained)
2 Tbsp (30 mL) Greek yogurt
1 Tbsp (15 mL) finely chopped green onion
1 tsp (5 mL) chopped fresh tarragon leaves
1 tsp (5 mL) minced garlic

½ tsp (2.5 mL) minced fresh ginger
½ tsp (2.5 mL) lemon zest
¼ tsp (1 mL) ground black pepper
¼ tsp (1 mL) table salt

EGG WASH:
1 egg yolk
1 Tbsp (15 mL) water

01 Dust the work surface with flour and then cut the puff pastry into two pieces; dust the top of each piece with flour before rolling out using a rolling pin; each piece should roll out into a 6 × 18 inch (15 × 46 cm) rectangle. Let rest.

02 To make the filling, combine the egg, salmon, yogurt, green onion, tarragon, garlic, ginger, lemon zest, pepper and salt, in a mixing bowl.

03 Preheat oven to 400F (205C).

04 Use a 5 inch (13 cm) round cutter or a large empty soup can to cut out circles from the puff pastry, avoiding wastage as much as you can. (If any pastry is left over, you can mix it up with some Parmesan cheese and bake to make cheese sticks.)

05 Combine the egg yolk and water and brush the egg wash on the edges of the pastry circles; the wash will help the dough stick together.

06 Spoon about 2 tablespoons (30 mL) of the salmon mixture into the centre of each circle and fold the circles over to make half-moons. Dust your fingertips with flour and press down along the edges of the pastry to make a good seal.

07 Invert each half-moon on a parchment paper–lined baking sheet. Push down on the edges once again and brush the top of each moon with egg wash, which will make the pastry golden brown when it bakes.

08 Bake in the oven for 25 to 28 minutes.

Cranberry Muffins

MAKES 10 MUFFINS

Cranberries are considered a superfruit and are indigenous to North America, growing in bogs in the Atlantic provinces and northeastern United States all the way to the Midwest along the 49th parallel. Cranberries are so versatile that many different Indigenous people relied on them as a staple food to eat fresh, ground, mashed with corn to make a bread or mashed with game and melted fat to make pemmican. The Leni-Lenape called the berry *ibimi*, meaning "bitter berry," and used it as a medicine to heal wounds long before the Pilgrims decided to commercialize the berries and rename them after their leaves, which resemble the head and neck of a crane.

Pure cranberry juice is something to stock up on (as sour as it is) because of its healing properties. We usually mix it with orange juice at home to make it more drinkable. I think cranberries are a super fruit because of their colour, tangy taste and versatility in cooking and baking. Frozen whole cranberries are super for making sauces, syrups and compotes, but I am never without dried cranberries to use in salads and baking, as in this recipe.

½ cup (120 mL) softened **butter**

1 cup (250 mL) **sugar**

2 large **eggs**

2 tsp (10 mL) **orange zest**

2 cups (475 mL) **flour**

1½ tsp (7.5 mL) **baking powder**

1 tsp (5 mL) table **salt**

½ cup (120 mL) **milk** (or water), divided

1 cup (250 mL) **dried cranberries**

01 Preheat oven to 375F (190C). Grease muffin pan.

02 Cream butter and sugar together in a mixing bowl for three minutes, using a hand or stand mixer. Add eggs one at a time, mixing well after each addition, and then mix in the orange zest.

03 Sift together flour, baking powder and salt in a bowl. Fold half the flour mixture into the butter mixture. Blend lightly. Add half the milk and blend.

04 Add the remaining flour mixture and the remaining milk. Blend only long enough for ingredients to combine.

05 Fold in cranberries.

06 Fill muffin pan and bake for 20 minutes, checking doneness with a wooden skewer or knife that, when inserted, comes out clean.

07 Let muffins rest five minutes before removing from the pan and serving warm.

Métis Bannock

MAKES 6 SERVINGS

Bannock is basically a baking-powder dough made with wheat flour and formed into individual portions for baking, in the tradition of the Scots. Indigenous people made bannock by stretching the dough, wrapping it around wooden sticks propped up over a fire; this is the way our niece Cecilia Chum learned to make bannock from her Swampy Cree grandmother in Moose Factory First Nation.

With the advances of metal and cooking technologies, the Métis made bannock on pans set over hot coals or in wood-stove ovens, often in one large disc shape, with little holes poked on top to let out steam. Next time we get hit by a polar vortex and have frost quakes and loss of power for days on end, like we did in Toronto in 2014, we are going to try making Métis bannock in the fireplace!

The trick to baking bannock is to get an even dough texture (slightly elastic but not sticky) without overworking it, and to bake it at just the right temperature. Lard was easier to come by than shortening long ago, so that is what the Métis used, but nowadays people use lard and shortening interchangeably and bake bannock in the oven.

2 cups (475 mL) all-purpose flour,
　　plus 2 Tbsp (30 mL) for dusting
4 tsp (20 mL) baking powder
2 tsp (10 mL) sugar
½ tsp (2.5 mL) table salt
½ cup (120 mL) cold lard, cubed
¾ cup (180 mL) milk (or water)

TO SERVE:
Butter

01 Preheat oven to 400F (205C).

02 In a mixing bowl, combine the 2 cups (475 mL) flour, baking powder, sugar and salt.

03 Add the lard and mix with your fingers or a pastry blender until the mixture is well blended and lumps are the size of peas.

04 Make a well in the centre of the dough, gradually add the milk and, using two fingers or a fork, combine the mixture until it sticks together.

05 Lightly dust the work surface with the remaining flour and knead the dough very briefly. Shape it into a disc about 1 inch (2.5 cm) thick. Place the dough on a parchment paper–lined baking sheet and poke a few holes in the top of the dough, using a knife or fork.

06 Bake for 20 minutes or until golden brown. Serve hot in wedges with butter.

Blueberry Variation: Follow the recipe above but reduce the lard to ¼ cup (60 mL), increase the sugar by ¼ cup (60 mL) and add ¾ cup (180 mL) fresh blueberries after adding the milk.

Pine Nut and Savory Variation: Follow the recipe above but increase water to 1 cup (250 mL), and add 3 tablespoons (15 mL) chopped fresh savory and ⅓ cup (80 mL) chopped toasted pine nuts.

Hot Pepper Fry Bread

MAKES 8 SERVINGS

At powwows both north and south of the 49th parallel, fry bread is typically sliced open and smothered in margarine to go with corn soup. I know, I know—it's not good for you! That's why I treat myself to fry bread only on rare occasions.

If you have a deep fryer that shows the temperature, this recipe is pretty simple. Otherwise you can improvise by using a medium-sized pot, as long as you are very careful and have a thermometer (and a lid nearby in case the oil gets overheated and flames up). Enjoy fry bread with Hominy Corn and Kidney Bean Soup (see recipe, page 96).

2 cups (475 mL) all-purpose flour,
   plus 2 Tbsp (30 mL) for dusting
1 Tbsp (15 mL) baking powder
1 Tbsp (15 mL) sugar
1 tsp (5 mL) table salt
1 Tbsp (15 mL) red pepper flakes
1 Tbsp (15 mL) finely minced jalapeno pepper
   (seeds included)
1 cup (250 mL) warm milk
½ cup (120 mL) water
2 cups (475 mL) vegetable oil

OPTIONAL:
3 Tbsp (45 mL) chili sauce

01 Mix 2 cups (475 mL) of the flour with the baking powder, sugar, salt, red pepper flakes and jalapeno pepper in a mixing bowl. Make a well in the centre of the mixture and gradually add the milk and water.

02 Use two fingers or a fork to mix the dough, not a stand mixer. The dough will be ready as soon as it holds together, so don't overmix.

03 Form the dough into a ball and let it sit, covered, for at least 15 minutes while you heat the oil to 350F (175C) for frying.

04 Dust the work surface with flour. Cut dough in half. Cut each piece in half again. Do this again to make eight pieces. Toss each piece in flour so you can handle it without having it stick to your fingers.

05 Stretch each piece from the outer edges to flatten it (without tearing) to a thickness of about ⅓ inch (1 cm), and poke each piece with a fork a couple of times before cooking.

Tip

If you don't have a thermometer to get an exact reading of the temperature of the oil, cook one test piece of dough and watch to make sure the oil bubbles and the food rises to the surface fairly quickly indicating that it is cooked.

06 Very carefully, slowly lower the first piece of dough into the fryer, away from you and without splashing the oil. If there's room, add another two pieces and let cook. Do not put too many pieces into the oil at once, since that will lower the temperature of the oil.

07 Check that the oil continues to bubble during the cooking process. If it doesn't, then it is not hot enough; raise the temperature to 375F (190C). The longer the dough cooks in the oil, the more oil it absorbs, so try to fry the dough quickly.

08 Remove the fry bread from the oil once it's golden brown on both sides (about one minute or less), and let dry on a paper towel to absorb excess oil. Continue cooking until you finish the batch.

09 Serve immediately with a little chili sauce, if using, for extra heat.

Shawnee Cake

MAKES 8 SERVINGS

Shawnee Cake is the classic American cornmeal bread of centuries past. There's disagreement about the exact origin of this cake, though. It goes by many names—including Journey Cake and Joniken, which might be a term coined by early African Americans for cake made from corn; some historians say European colonists labelled this bread made by the Shawnee "Johnny" Cake, even though the Cherokee and Powhatan also made corn bread. In Canada, you might hear it called Indian Cake. Read more on cornmeal on page 221.

Warning: I am not going to argue over whether the cake should be a pan cake or a more substantial cake, made with milk or without, and so on, so please don't even go there. But one way or another, the colonists worked out how to make it after learning from Indigenous people—possibly the Pawtuxet—how to grind and cook corn. Over the years, the cake's been refined with the addition of ingredients such as milk, butter and leavening agents.

Enjoy this with a soup or stew, such as the Mango and Raisin Curried Elk Stew (page 104).

2 large **eggs**

1 cup (250 mL) 1 per cent **buttermilk**

½ cup (120 mL) **maple syrup**

¼ cup (60 mL) **sour cream**

1¼ cups (300 mL) medium-ground yellow **cornmeal**

1 cup (250 mL) all-purpose **flour**

2 Tbsp (30 mL) **sugar**

2 tsp (10 mL) **baking powder**

½ tsp (2.5 mL) **baking soda**

½ tsp (2.5 mL) table **salt**

3 Tbsp (45 mL) **butter**

TO SERVE:

Butter

01 Preheat oven to 400F (205C). Heat up a cast iron pan in the oven.

02 In a small mixing bowl, lightly beat the eggs. Add the buttermilk, maple syrup and sour cream, and combine until blended. Set aside.

03 In a larger mixing bowl, whisk together cornmeal, flour, sugar, baking powder, baking soda and salt.

04 Add the wet mixture to the dry ingredients. Stir very lightly—just enough to combine ingredients.

05 Remove hot pan from oven. Place butter in the pan to melt and swish it around to coat the bottom and sides before pouring it into the batter. Stir very lightly.

06 Pour batter into the pan and bake for 25 to 28 minutes or until a toothpick inserted into the centre of the cake comes out clean. Let cool on a baker's rack for 10 minutes before removing from pan.

07 Serve in wedges, with butter.

Birch-Laced Zucchini Tomato Tarts

MAKES 12 TARTS (4 INCH/10 CM)

This recipe may seem at first glance like some kind of modern Italian dish, but its main ingredients are indigenous to the Americas. Tomatoes and zucchini are gifts from the New World to the Old World. Birch syrup comes from birch trees, as strange as that may seem, but it's not a common ingredient— you may have to shop online.

You will need metal tart pans (also known as mini quiche pans) to make this recipe for homemade tarts. Tart pans, which usually have a removable bottom, are not the same as muffin pans, and normally have sharp, fluted edges that allow the delicate pastry to bake more evenly and be served without getting damaged in the process. If you don't want to invest in authentic tart pans, get disposable foil tart pans instead.

DOUGH:

2 cups (475 mL) all-purpose flour, plus ½ cup
   (120 mL) for dusting
½ cup (120 mL) cold unsalted butter, cubed
½ tsp (2.5 mL) brown sugar
½ tsp (2.5 mL) table salt
2 eggs, beaten
1½ Tbsp (22 mL) ice water

FILLING:

1 cup (250 mL) finely shredded peeled zucchini
   (green or yellow)
½ tsp (2.5 mL) table salt, divided
1 cup (250 mL) sliced tomatoes (or sliced cherry tomatoes)
½ tsp (2.5 mL) ground black pepper
½ tsp (2.5 mL) dried basil
1 tsp (5 mL) minced jalapeno (with seeds)
2 Tbsp (30 mL) birch syrup (or Worcestershire sauce)
⅓ cup (80 mL) grated fresh Parmesan cheese

OPTIONAL:

Freshly ground black pepper
Chopped fresh basil

01 To make the pastry, in a bowl combine 2 cups (475 mL) flour with the butter, brown sugar and salt, using a pastry blender; work the mixture by hand (only until it develops a mealy texture). Add the eggs and water, and blend using your hands.

02 Form the dough into a ball, wrap it in plastic food wrap and let it chill for at least 20 minutes in the refrigerator.

Tip

Place parchment paper above and below dough before rolling it to help keep it from sticking to the rolling pin.

---

03 Remove dough from the fridge, dust the work surface with the remaining flour and, with a rolling pin, roll dough out to a thickness of about ¼ inch (1 cm).

04 Preheat oven to 425F (220C).

05 Using a 4 inch (10 cm) cookie cutter or a large empty soup can, cut the dough into 12 rounds just slightly larger than your tart pans. Place the rounds in the tart pans and gently press the dough into place, cutting off any excess but keeping in mind that the pastry will shrink somewhat so don't be too hasty. Place the tart pans on a baking sheet. Poke some holes in the tart bottoms using a fork.

06 Bake tart shells in the oven for 10 minutes. Remove from oven and allow to cool slightly, but leave the oven on.

07 In a colander or sieve set over a bowl or pot, combine the zucchini and a pinch of the salt. Mix well and allow zucchini to drain for 10 minutes.

Tip

To cut a lot of cherry tomatoes in half quickly, spread them out on a shallow plate, cover with another shallow plate. Press down gently on the top plate with one hand and, using a breadknife in your other hand, slice through the tomatoes halfway between the plates.

08 Place sliced tomatoes on a parchment paper–lined baking sheet (skin side down if using cherry tomatoes). Season tomatoes with a pinch of salt, pepper and basil.

09 Bake tomatoes in the oven for five minutes.

10 In a mixing bowl, combine the zucchini, jalapeno and birch syrup. Spoon 1 tablespoon (15 mL) of the mixture into the base of each tart shell. Top each tart with tomatoes in a single layer. Sprinkle with cheese and freshly ground pepper if using.

11 Bake tarts in the oven for 12 to 14 minutes.

12 Remove tarts from tart pans. Garnish with basil, if using, and serve warm.

NOTE: You can find potato starch, cornstarch and xanthan gum in health food stores or bulk stores.

Gluten-Free Potato and Corn Bread

MAKES 1 LOAF

This recipe is gluten free (see "Gluten-Free Baking," page 230). It sucks to have celiac disease, as Marlene does, or be wheat sensitive like her sister Nancy. They have no choice but to learn to be creative using gluten-free flours, and that takes a lot of experimenting. (Our nephew James Chum, on the other hand, makes a point of asking for extra gluten in anything we serve him!) We've tossed more than a few rock-hard buns out the back door to the raccoons after not-so-successful attempts at gluten-free baking. You know they're bad when even the raccoons won't touch them!

Some people regard potato flour as a really versatile ingredient for making bread, as well as sauces and soups. To make potato flour by hand in the traditional way, you would need to cook and mash potatoes before dehydrating them and pulverizing them into powder. Can you imagine the work that was involved in doing all of this after first having to dig up tubers or drag them up from swamplands in a canoe or down from the mountains as Indigenous people have done for thousands of years in Peru? Incredible! In this recipe, though, I cheat by using potato starch and cornstarch. Don't confuse flour with starch. Potato flour is made from whole potatoes (i.e., skins included), whereas potato starch is just the starch from the potatoes. You can't substitute one for the other or the bread will be too dense and probably won't rise.

This bread is better toasted and buttered than it is plain, but it can be used for sandwich making or crouton making too. *Warning:* Since this recipe uses only two very fine starches, be prepared for bread that has an entirely different texture and colour than you expect bread to have, and eat it up as soon as possible, since it will become dry more quickly than regular bread.

1½ cups (350 mL) **milk**
1 pkg (2¼ tsp/11 mL) active **dry yeast**
1 tsp (5 mL) **sugar**
1½ cups (350 mL) **cornstarch**, sifted
1½ cups (350 mL) **potato starch**, sifted
1 Tbsp (15 mL) **baking powder**
1 tsp (5 mL) **baking soda**
2 tsp (10 mL) **xanthan gum**
1 tsp (5 mL) table **salt**
2 Tbsp (30 mL) liquid **honey**
¼ cup (60 mL) **vegetable oil**
¼ cup (60 mL) **water**

01 Preheat oven to 375F (190C).

02 Warm the milk in a microwave very slightly, to 105F (40C). Add the yeast and sugar. Stir and set aside, leaving the mixture undisturbed for 10 to 15 minutes to allow it to begin working (foaming).

03 In a medium-sized mixing bowl, combine cornstarch, potato starch, baking powder, baking soda, xanthan gum and salt.

04 Slowly add the milk mixture and the honey to the dry ingredients. Mix slowly with a wooden spoon. Add the oil and water, and mix. The dough will be heavy and thick; don't overmix it.

05 Scoop dough into a greased loaf pan. Smooth out the top and cut a line down the middle using a knife. Bake for 25 minutes. Test doneness with a wooden skewer or sharp knife that, when inserted in the loaf, should come out clean.

06 Let bread cool, covered with a dish towel, for 10 minutes to steam before inverting it onto a cooling rack.

CHAPTER 10
Sweets Before You Go

Chocolate. Vanilla. Maple syrup. Berries. These are some of the gifts of the Americas that forever changed dessert making throughout the world. Over 2,000 years ago, the Olmec, Maya and Aztec peoples cultivated cacao in Mesoamerica for trade, currency and for beverage making for the elite. Cacao beans were roasted, ground and seasoned with vanilla seeds and chili peppers to make a frothy, hot drink—hot chocolate! The Aztecs in Mexico called it *xocoatl*, from which the word "chocolate" originated. The chocolate recipes that follow pay tribute to that history.

As much as we might think of sugar as the foundation of all sweet things, it isn't. North American Indigenous peoples of the woodlands harvested berries for mashing and drying in the sun to make a fruit leather of sorts that was suitable for storage and travel. Maple syrup, maple sugar and maple water were just a few of the sweeteners First Nations used for flavouring and for energy. Some First Nations in Ontario and Quebec still make maple candy in the winter by heating kettles of maple sap to produce hot maple syrup and then pouring it onto snow to harden. It's an outdoor event that families look forward to attending in March each year.

Berry pudding was one of the treats numerous West Coast nations made using deer fat, black tree lichen, berries, the licorice fern and the blue camas bulb. Métis in Alberta used wild plums to make all sorts of desserts, including *poutine au sac*, a steamed pudding with raisins, spices, flour and sugar (in addition to buffalo meat). Talk about being creative! My cousins and aunts like to whip soopalallie berries (soap berries) in the summertime to make Indian Ice Cream. See the Urban Indian Ice Cream recipe on page 261 that I came up with. Obviously, there were all kinds of sources of sweets among First Nations long before they were ever introduced to sugar.

Yes, these days there is sugar in pies, cakes, cookies, frostings, chocolate, candy and even condiments like ketchup, mustard and relish, but sugar derived from sugar cane is a relatively recent addition to the diet of Indigenous people—it happened when Columbus introduced sugar cane to the West Indies. Before that time, for centuries in fact, the Indigenous peoples of Paraguay used stevia, a small wild shrub in the daisy family, as a food and medicine. Of course, stevia has since caught on big time as a sugar substitute and doesn't cause the same "rush" of dopamine in the brain that you get when you eat sugar. Stevia is good news for diabetics but not the best thing to use for baking. Agave syrup is also a sweetener derived from an indigenous, cactus-like plant from southern Mexico and is pretty good for baking.

Fruit is an excellent sweetener and I use it a lot in my recipes, but there are some differences between using fresh fruit and frozen fruit. Fresh fruit naturally tastes better than frozen, but it also has less moisture—which can be good or bad, depending on what you are making. If you are making a berry sauce to go with meat, it won't make much difference, but if you are making a pastry, excess liquid can be a problem, since it can make crusts mushy and start oozing out where you don't want it to. For that reason, before you bake with frozen fruit, it's generally wise to drain the liquid from the fruit once it's thawed (see, for example, Marge's Strawberry and Rhubarb Pie, page 252). One way to counteract excess moisture in fruit when baking is to toss it in a small amount of flour before using it. This will also help to keep the dough from changing colour (in blueberry pancake batters, for instance).

Tip
Use liquid measuring cups to measure liquids and dry measuring cups to measure dry ingredients.

Liquid measuring cups generally have a little more room at the top so that when you fill them with water or milk, for example, you can still walk across the room without spilling it all over the place; they should also have a spout for pouring. Dry measuring cups, on the other hand, are filled to the brim; they are good for shoving into a bag of flour and pulling the flour out, and you can then use a knife for slicing off the extra flour so that you get a precise volume. (You'd be surprised at the difference a little extra flour or shortage of liquid can make when baking.)

For my sweets recipes that call for sugar but don't specify what kind, I am referring to standard white granulated sugar. In a few cases I offer other alternatives, but I wouldn't experiment if I were you, as the results can be unpredictable. As for flour, I use all-purpose white flour for just about everything unless specified otherwise.

How to Melt Chocolate

Melting chocolate is not difficult, but there are a few options and other things you need to know that may not be obvious:

01 If you are working with **block chocolate**, chop it up before melting it. You could use chocolate discs, squares or chips instead.

02 **Heat** the chocolate in either
» **a microwave**—heat for 50 seconds at 50 per cent power, check and stir, heat for 15 seconds at 20 per cent power, check and stir, and continue this process until the chocolate is melted or
» **a double boiler**—heat while stirring , without letting the water boil dry. You can improvise a double boiler by putting a metal bowl over a pot of simmering water, making sure to leave space between the bowl and the water.

03 Use a **rubber spatula** for stirring.

04 **Never heat** chocolate beyond 120F (50C).

05 **Don't let any water or steam** get into the chocolate. (If it happens and the chocolate hardens, try adding some butter to rectify the situation, but I make no promises that will work.) Follow specific recipe instructions for adding any liquid to chocolate.

Chocolate Hazelnut Bark

MAKES 8 SERVINGS

Which is better: to make sweets for someone you love, or to eat something sweet made by someone who loves you? Either way, who doesn't love sweets—especially when chocolate is involved? This little number is so simple and worth making once in a while to have with friends over coffee after supper.

I've made this recipe using 70 per cent dark chocolate, in block form, and milk chocolate, in chips, with equal success, but you could also use semi-sweet chocolate squares. The only thing that could go wrong is if you somehow manage to get any liquid into the mixture; if that happens, you will find that your chocolate will instantly turn into a glob of cement right before your eyes. Therefore, do not substitute liquid vanilla extract for vanilla beans; if you don't have vanilla beans, go without.

1 lb (474 g) **semi-sweet baker's chocolate**, chopped
Pinch kosher **salt** (or sea salt)
1 tsp (5 mL) **ancho chili powder**
½ **vanilla bean**
½ cup (120 mL) chopped raw **hazelnuts**, divided
¼ cup (60 mL) raw **pepitas** (shelled pumpkin seeds), divided
¼ cup (60 mL) chopped **dried cranberries**), divided

01 Melt the chocolate (see instructions in "How to Melt Chocolate," page 246). Stir in the salt and chili powder.

02 Make an incision down the middle of the vanilla bean using a paring knife. Open it up and scrape the tiny black seeds out using the tip of the knife. Remove a tablespoon (15 mL) of the melted chocolate and mix the vanilla seeds into it. Add this mixture to the larger chocolate mixture. Stir to combine.

Tip
Store used vanilla beans in sugar to flavour sugar for baking.

03 Add half the hazelnuts, pepitas and cranberries to the chocolate. Stir very gently.

04 Pour the mixture onto a parchment paper–lined 9 by 13 inch (23 × 33 cm) baking sheet, letting it spread out to a thickness of ¼ inch (1 cm). Sprinkle the remaining hazelnuts, pepitas and cranberries on top.

05 Chill chocolate for two hours. Break chocolate bark apart to serve in rough pieces. Chill or freeze if desired.

Chocolate Dipped Aztec Berries

MAKES 4 SERVINGS

Chocolate dipped berries for dessert, anyone? These ones are a little unusual, however, and have a unique taste that's almost a cross between a tomato and a cranberry. The Aztec berry is also called the Inca berry, cape gooseberry, husk tomato, physalis, ground cherry, golden berry, husk cherry and Peruvian cherry. They come from South America originally, although their popularity spread wildly—settlers at the Cape of Good Hope in what is now South Africa grew them. They are a small orange fruit with paper-thin husks and are related to tomatoes. You might have come across them served in restaurants as a garnish for bacon and eggs. They are good just plain but even better covered in premium-quality chocolate.

1 pint (2 cups/475 mL) **Aztec berries** (with husks)
4 squares (4 oz/115 g) **dark chocolate melting wafers**
4 squares (4 oz/115 g) **white chocolate melting wafers**
2 tsp (10 mL) **coconut oil**

01 Melt the dark and white chocolate separately, either in bowls in the microwave or over simmering water on the stovetop (see instructions in "How to Melt Chocolate," page 246).

02 Warm the coconut oil if necessary to liquefy. Add half of the coconut oil to each container of melted chocolate and mix well.

03 Carefully pull back the husk on each berry and slightly twist it without removing it, so that you can use it to hold the berries as you dip them in chocolate.

04 Partially dip half of the berries in the dark chocolate and place on their sides on one side of a parchment paper–lined baking sheet. Partially dip the remaining berries in the white chocolate and place on their sides on the other side of the baking sheet. Chill the berries on the baking sheet in the refrigerator for five minutes.

05 Return the bowls of chocolate to the stove to keep warm if following the stovetop method, or reheat chocolate in a microwave.

06 Use a fork to flick some white chocolate onto each of the dark chocolate berries and place back on the baking sheet. Similarly, flick some dark chocolate onto the white chocolate berries.

07 Chill berries for one hour before serving them on a chilled plate.

Maple Pumpkin Cake with Cream Cheese Icing

MAKES 12 SERVINGS

Native Americans enjoyed pumpkins long before the Pilgrims arrived on the scene. Unfortunately, cooking pumpkins are hard to come by now. I've found it very difficult to get access to fresh pumpkins at any time other than October, and even then, stores usually carry just the decorative ones. So I keep canned pumpkin (pumpkin purée) in stock instead, and that is what's used in this recipe. There is another pumpkin option: growing your own!

I modified this recipe from our good neighbour Lauren Powers in Muskoka. Lauren and Marlene are both July babies so they used to share birthday celebrations. We really miss our times together with Lauren and Jamie Hassard, hanging out on the deck and jamming in their recording studio. It's where I learned to play the drums! But I digress. Lauren used gluten-free flour when she made this originally but I switched to regular all-purpose flour here and it works just fine. I added the icing because who doesn't like cream cheese icing?

CAKE:

1 cup (250 mL) **vegetable oil**, plus 1 tsp (5 mL) for greasing pan

3 cups (710 mL) all-purpose **flour**, plus 1 Tbsp (15 mL) for dusting the pan

4 **eggs**

1 cup (250 mL) **sugar**

½ cup (120 mL) **maple syrup**

2 cups (475 mL) canned **pumpkin purée**

½ cup (120 mL) **applesauce**

½ cup (120 mL) chopped **raw pepitas** (shelled pumpkin seeds) or raisins

1 tsp (5 mL) **vanilla**

3 tsp (15 mL) **cinnamon**

2 tsp (10 mL) **baking soda**

1 tsp (5 mL) **baking powder**

1 tsp (5 mL) table **salt**

½ tsp (2.5 mL) ground **ginger**

¼ tsp (1 mL) ground **cloves**

ICING:

¼ cup (60 mL) softened **butter**

¼ cup (60 mL) softened **cream cheese**

1 cup (250 mL) sifted **icing sugar**

1½ Tbsp (22 mL) 5 percent **cream**, divided

OPTIONAL GARNISH:

¼ cup (60 mL) toasted **walnuts** or edible flowers

01 Preheat oven to 350F (175C). Grease and flour a 10 to 15 cup Bundt pan.

02 Beat eggs and sugar together in a large mixing bowl. Add maple syrup and combine. Add the pumpkin, 1 cup (250 mL) oil, applesauce, pepitas and vanilla, and combine.

03 In a separate bowl, combine 3 cups (710 mL) flour with the cinnamon, baking soda, baking powder, salt, ginger and cloves. Add dry mixture bit by bit to the wet ingredients. Mix with a spoon until well combined.

04 Pour batter into the prepared pan and bake for 60 to 70 minutes. Test for doneness at 60 minutes. Let cool for 10 minutes with a clean dish towel on top before inverting onto a cooling rack.

05 Allow the cake to cool *completely* before icing.

06 To make the icing, beat the butter and cream cheese together with a hand mixer or stand mixer until the mixture becomes light and fluffy (up to five minutes).

07 Gradually beat in the icing sugar, mixing well to combine.

08 Add 1 tablespoon (15 mL) of the cream. Mix until combined, scraping down the sides of the bowl. Repeat this process until all the cream has been added and the icing is perfectly smooth. This will be a creamy icing.

09 Slowly pour it onto the inverted cake, very gradually, allowing icing to slip over the edges and down the centre.

10 Garnish cake with toasted walnuts if using. Chill before serving. Freeze extra slices in an airtight container.

Marge's Strawberry and Rhubarb Pie

MAKES 2 PIES

When they came to the Americas, the colonists were quick to put local berries and fruits to good use in pies. Up to that time, in Europe pies were primarily made with meat or fish, or unsweetened fruit, and the crust was inedible—designed purely as a means to keep the contents from going bad. The transition from savoury to sweet fruit and berry pies wasn't a long one. The discovery of fruits and berries in North America and the domestication of the plants settlers brought with them led to diverse pie ingredients, including rhubarb. Sometime over the years, desserts were adopted into Indigenous culture—especially anything made with rhubarb. Marlene's mom gets busy cutting up the rhubarb that grows in the backyard in early summer, freezing it along with seasonal fruit, like strawberries, so she can make pies all year long. Not bad for someone in her early nineties! When it comes to dessert, our family treasures her homemade fruit pies above anything else.

Pie dough is versatile. With this recipe, you can make fruit pies and tarts as well as savoury pies—anything from blueberry or pumpkin pie to tourtière (as in the Métis Deer Tourtière recipe, page 146). The best part is you can make the dough ahead of time and freeze it until you need it.

The secret to a flaky dough is to use cold fat. Pork lard is really the best for flakiness, and that's what Marge uses, but if you are not into that, then shortening and butter are your next best options. You can use one or the other or a combination of the two as long as they are really cold. A dough made with shortening will be flakier than one made with butter, and shortening is easier to work with than butter, but butter does taste a little better than shortening. So, it's up to you.

DOUGH:

4 cups (900 g) all-purpose flour,
  plus 2 Tbsp (30 mL) for dusting
2 tsp (10 mL) table salt
1½ cups (350 mL) cold lard (or shortening or butter), cubed
1 egg
½ cup (120 mL) ice water, plus up to 2 Tbsp (30 mL)
  if needed
1 Tbsp (15 mL) brown sugar
1 Tbsp (15 mL) vinegar

01 Combine flour and salt in a large mixing bowl.

02 Cut in the lard with your hands (or a pastry blender) if making the dough manually as Marge and I do. Break apart the lard until the lumps are the size of peas. Alternatively, if using a mixer, pulse the mixture just once or twice to make sure you don't overdo it. Set aside.

03 In a small bowl, whisk together the egg, ½ cup (120 mL) ice water, brown sugar and vinegar, taking care to remove lumps.

04 Make a well in the flour mixture. Pour some of the liquid mixture in the well, combining gently using a fork. Pour the rest of the liquid mixture around the outer edge of the flour mixture and combine. The dough will be ready when it is still quite crumbly. Test it by squeezing it in your hand to see if it sticks together. If it does, then form it into a ball; if it doesn't, add a little more ice water about 1 tablespoon (15 mL) at a time. Again, be very careful not to overmix the dough. If you do, your pie will not be very flaky.

05 Cut the dough in half and each piece in half again. Flatten each piece of dough into a round disc

CONTINUED ...

about 1 inch (2.5 cm) thick. Wrap the pieces separately in wax paper or parchment paper, place them in a sealed plastic bag and refrigerate for a minimum of one hour.

06 The dough should keep for three to four months in the freezer if you are baking later on.

07 Roll out each piece of chilled dough on a lightly floured surface to a thickness of ⅛ inch (0.5 cm), and transfer two of them to the pie plates. Cut off excess dough that hangs over the edge of the pans, but leave about ½ inch (1.5 cm) all around, as the dough will shrink.

PIE FILLING:
4 cups (2 L) frozen strawberries
4 cups (2 L) diced frozen rhubarb
1½ cups (350 mL) sugar
3 Tbsp (45 mL) instant tapioca (or all-purpose flour)
1 tsp (5 mL) ground cinnamon
1 tsp (5 mL) lemon juice
2 tsp (10 mL) butter

EGG WASH (OPTIONAL):
1 egg yolk
2 Tbsp (30 mL) water

SUGAR GLAZE:
1 tsp (5 mL) sugar
1 tsp (5 mL) cream

TO SERVE (OPTIONAL):
Vanilla ice cream

01 Preheat oven to 400F (205C).

02 Thaw the fruit, and strain off any juice and discard it.

03 In a large mixing bowl, combine the strained fruit, sugar, tapioca, cinnamon and lemon juice.

04 Divide the fruit filling between the pies. Dot the pies with butter.

05 I would egg wash the edges of the pie shells before covering them with the rest of the pie dough (mix the egg and water and use a pastry brush to apply) so that the fruit juices don't seep out. Marge never bothers to do this, so this step is optional.

06 Cover the pies with the two remaining circles of dough, cutting off the excess dough and crimping the edges.

07 Poke some holes into the pies. Lower the oven temperature to 350F (175C) and bake for 55 minutes.

08 Check the pies to see if they are slightly brown. Combine the sugar and cream in a small bowl. Brush this glaze on top of the pies, and put them back in the oven for an additional 10 minutes or so until perfectly browned.

09 Serve with vanilla ice cream if desired (and tea, of course!).

Wild Fruit Galette

MAKES 12 SERVINGS (TWO 10 INCH/25 CM GALETTES)

This recipe calls for fresh fruit, and in the best-case scenario, that would include the kind of wild black plums that are indigenous to this continent. If you find some, consider yourself fortunate. Indigenous varieties of plums are now difficult to find. The strawberries sold in stores today are also unlikely to be the varieties indigenous to Canada, despite the fact that berries used to be a prime method of sweetening food in Indigenous culture. Try this recipe with other fresh fruits, as suggested below, and double the recipe if you are really ambitious.

A galette is essentially a thin, open-faced pie with the edges folded up and inwards towards the centre, revealing luscious, hot, bubbling, seasoned fruit, but the Métis came to use the term to mean fry bread (see Hot Pepper Fry Bread recipe, page 236). My galette, though, is of the rustic French tradition, with fruit and dough.

In this dough recipe, I use butter—even though the pastry is not as flaky as when lard or shortening is used—only because it tastes a little better. Butter makes the dough harder to work with, however, so you have to be very careful not to overmix the dough or work it too much when rolling it out. You'll know if you have done that, because the dough will simply fall apart before you can add the filling! If that happens, put it back in the fridge for an hour to chill it and try rolling it out again. (If the idea of having to do this makes you a little nervous, use shortening instead of butter.)

DOUGH:

2½ cups (600 mL) all-purpose flour,
   plus 2 Tbsp (30 mL) for dusting
1 Tbsp (15 mL) sugar
1 tsp (5 mL) table salt
1 cup (250 mL) cold butter, cubed
⅓ cup (80 mL) ice water, plus up to 2 Tbsp (30 mL) more
   if needed

FILLING:

2 cups (475 mL) thinly sliced fresh plums (or peaches,
   pears, nectarines or apricots), skin on
1 cup (250 mL) sliced fresh strawberries
¾ cup (180 mL) sugar
3 Tbsp (45 mL) cornstarch
1 Tbsp (15 mL) orange zest
¼ tsp (1 mL) cinnamon
¼ tsp (1 mL) nutmeg
¼ tsp (1 mL) table salt

EGG WASH:

1 beaten egg
1 Tbsp (15 mL) sugar

01 To make the dough, place the flour, sugar and salt in a large bowl, and mix well.

02 Add the cubed butter and mix with a pastry blender, or by hand, rubbing the mixture between your fingers until a coarse meal forms.

03 Add ⅓ cup (80 mL) ice water and blend only long enough to make a rough dough. Add up to 2 tablespoons (30 mL) water if needed. Divide dough in half and form each half into a ball. Flatten each into a disc about 1 inch (2.5 cm) thick.

CONTINUED ...

04 If you are planning to use the dough the same day, wrap each piece individually in wax paper or parchment paper and refrigerate for a minimum of one hour. Otherwise, freeze rounds of dough wrapped in parchment paper or wax paper inside a freezer bag until ready to use. (Note that the dough should keep for three to four months in the freezer.)

05 Roll out the chilled dough on a lightly floured work surface to a thickness of $\frac{1}{8}$ inch (0.5 cm). Cut out two circles about 12 to 14 inches (30–35.5 cm) across. Slide the dough onto two parchment paper–lined baking sheets. Chill pastry.

06 Before making the filling, preheat oven to 400F (205C).

07 In a bowl, toss the fruit with the sugar, cornstarch, orange zest, cinnamon, nutmeg and salt. Let fruit sit in a sieve for a few minutes to strain.

08 To assemble the galettes, starting from the centre of each circle of pastry, arrange the fruit slices in a spiral, with minimal overlapping, leaving up to 2 inches (5 cm) bare at the edge of each circle. Gently fold the bare pastry over the fruit, overlapping the pastry as needed to round the edges and leaving most of the fruit exposed.

09 Brush the beaten egg on the exposed pastry and sprinkle with sugar.

10 Bake for 30 to 35 minutes or until pastry is golden brown and filling is bubbling.

11 Let rest before cutting for serving.

Wild Fruit Variations: Use any of the following in place of the wild plums: huckleberries, blueberries, pitted cherries, sliced apples or strawberries.

Mexican Chocolate Spice Cake

MAKES 8 SERVINGS

This is a moist cake made in the Mexican tradition of combining vanilla and cocoa with cayenne pepper and other spices. There's just a hint of spice, so you can ramp it up if you want more kick. The batter can also be used to make cupcakes, but I use a round cake pan. Just a little dusting of icing sugar and fruit, and you're done!

2 cups (475 mL) all-purpose flour

1 tsp (5 mL) baking soda

1 tsp (5 mL) ground cinnamon

1½ tsp (7.5 mL) cayenne pepper

1 cup (250 mL) butter, plus 1 tsp (5mL)
   for greasing baking pan

½ cup (120 mL) sifted cocoa powder,
   plus 1 Tbsp (15 mL) for dusting

¾ cup (180 mL) brewed black coffee at room temperature

2 eggs, beaten

2 cups (475 mL) sugar

½ cup (120 mL) buttermilk

1 Tbsp (15 mL) vanilla

¼ cup (60 mL) icing sugar

TO SERVE (OPTIONAL):

Handful fresh raspberries

Whipped cream

01 Preheat oven to 375F (190C).

02 Sift flour, baking soda, cinnamon and cayenne into a mixing bowl. Sift again. Set aside.

03 Melt 1 cup (250 mL) butter in a large saucepan over low heat. Add ½ cup (120 mL) cocoa powder and whisk until smooth. Whisk in the coffee and heat to lukewarm. Remove from heat.

04 Add the eggs, sugar, buttermilk and vanilla to the cocoa mixture and stir to combine. Whisk in the dry ingredients very lightly. Small lumps are okay.

05 Butter a 9 by 9 inch (23 × 23 cm) cake pan and dust with cocoa powder. Pour in the batter.

06 Bake for 30 minutes. Let cake cool for 20 minutes, covered with a clean tea towel before loosening edges and inverting onto a serving plate.

07 Sift icing sugar onto the top of the cake. Serve with fresh berries or whipped cream if desired.

Wild Blueberry and Rhubarb Jam Cookies

MAKES 2 DOZEN

Wild blueberries have been on the menu for the Innu, Mi'kmaq and Maliseet longer than recorded history. They carved berry rakes from wood to harvest the indigenous fruit in large volumes for use in all sorts of sweet and savoury dishes, for medicine and for making dye for baskets and clothing. Rhubarb, though, is not indigenous to North America, and I understand it took a long time to make its way to Turtle Island from Asia via Turkey and the Hudson's Bay Company, but by the late 1800s rhubarb had become a staple of First Nations. It's one of my favourite plants, and I know a lot of First Nations people just love it. I remember that when I was little, Mom used to make thumbprint cookies using strawberry jam out of a jar. I use homemade Wild Blueberry and Rhubarb Jam in this shortbread-like cookie recipe instead.

Pine nuts come from—where else?—pine trees! These days the pine nuts you get in grocery stores generally come from pine trees growing in the Mediterranean; however, various northern Indigenous nations used to gather pine cones in the fall, shaking them to loosen the nuts and then toasting them over a fire and saving them for winter snacks. That isn't easy, but if you wait for the nuts to fall to the ground, then you'll have to fend off squirrels.

If you want to eat pine nuts as a snack, just toast them on a tray in the oven at 250F (120C) for a few minutes first, which helps to release the oils and gives them a little more crunch. For this recipe, I use raw pine nuts, since they will bake in the oven. You could use any other raw, unsalted nuts.

2 cups (475 mL) all-purpose flour
½ tsp (2.5 mL) baking powder
½ tsp (2.5 mL) table salt
½ tsp (2.5 mL) vanilla
1 cup (250 mL) butter, softened
½ cup (120 mL) sugar
2 eggs
½ cup (120 mL) chopped pine nuts
⅓ cup (80 mL) Wild Blueberry and Rhubarb Jam (or other jam)

01 Preheat oven to 350F (175C).

02 In a medium-sized mixing bowl, whisk together flour, baking powder and Vanilla Salt (or regular salt if using). Set aside.

03 Cream butter and sugar in a larger mixing bowl. Separate egg yolks from egg whites. Add egg yolks (and vanilla if using) to butter mixture and blend well. Reserve egg whites.

04 Gradually add flour mixture to butter mixture and blend well. Using your fingers, work the dough until it sticks together and forms into a ball. Form 1 inch (2.5 cm) balls of dough.

05 Gently beat the egg whites. Dip cookies in the egg whites to coat them evenly and gently roll them in the nuts.

06 Place cookies on a parchment paper–lined baking sheet. Flatten them by making a ½ inch (1.5 cm) depression in the centre of each ball with your thumb.

07 Bake for 15 to 18 minutes or until lightly browned. Let cool.

08 Fill the thumbprint on each cookie with 1 teaspoon (5 mL) of jam.

Wild Blueberry and Rhubarb Jam

MAKES 8 SMALL JARS

This jam will look like, but won't be as sweet as, pure blueberry jam. The tartness of the rhubarb makes the difference. I made this from rhubarb that grows in our yard. Marlene and her mom picked it, rinsed it, cut it up and froze it in freezer bags in June so that we could enjoy it in jams and pies in the fall and winter. This recipe calls for frozen fruit, which you should thaw and strain (save the juice) while you prepare the jam jars.

The hardest part of making jam is getting the equipment ready. It bears repeating that you must use proper canning jars, not just any glass jars that are lying around the house and once contained pickles, peanut butter or tomatoes, for example. These days, it's easiest to use single-use metal lids that have a built-in rubber seal, and reusable metal rings for keeping the lids on tight to prevent food poisoning. In this recipe, a water bath method is used to process the jam.

For more details on preparations and canning timing for high-altitude locations, read the instructions that come with purchased fruit pectin.

3½ cups (830 mL) chopped rhubarb, frozen
2½ cups (600 mL) wild blueberries, frozen
1 pkg (2 oz/60 g) powdered fruit pectin
1 Tbsp (15 mL) lemon juice
½ tsp (2.5 mL) butter
5½ cups (1.3 L) white sugar

01 Thaw frozen fruit separately in two large colanders or sieves and let drain while you prepare the equipment.

02 Using the "sanitize" cycle of your dishwasher, sterilize your equipment: jars, bands, lids, tongs, jar lifter, canning funnel, headspace remover (also called a bubble remover), and a metal or rubber ladle. Alternatively, wash your equipment in hot soapy water and then submerge in water in a large stockpot or canner with a metal rack inside; rapidly boil for 10 minutes. Keep sterilized equipment hot until ready to use.

03 In a large stockpot, heat strained rhubarb and ½ cup (120 mL) of rhubarb juice to the boiling point. Reduce heat and simmer for five minutes, uncovered, stirring from time to time.

04 Add the blueberries, along with the pectin and lemon juice. Mix well to combine, using a potato masher to mash the fruit a little. Increase heat so that the mixture comes to a boil again. Stir in the butter.

05 Cook fruit over high heat for five minutes, stirring to make sure the jam does not stick to the pot. Now the fun begins.

06 Add the sugar and let the jam return to the boiling point. Boil the jam on high heat for 1 minute, stirring constantly. This is the part where you have to be careful: hot blue jam will spew out volcano style onto the walls and onto your face and clothes if you don't watch out, but never mind, it will be worth it in the end, so just keep cooking and stirring and don't burn yourself (wear an old shirt with long sleeves). The jam should thicken up significantly. Remove the pot from heat and let cool for five minutes.

07 Use the tongs and jar lifter to place the hot jars and other equipment on a baking sheet lined with a clean dish cloth. Using the funnel and ladle, pour jam into the hot jars, leaving ¼ inch (1 cm) headspace at the top for expansion. (Some people use a sanitized ruler, holding it next to the rim of the jar, but I just eyeball the space.) Slide the plastic bubble remover around the inside of each jar a few times to release trapped air bubbles. Wipe the rims of the jars clean with a very clean dish towel. Place a sterilized lid on each jar, and screw on a ring just until you feel resistance (meaning you should be able to open the jars without much effort).

08 Return canner with canner rack to the stove and fill about two-thirds full. Bring water to a boil. Lower filled jam jars into the pot. There should be at least 2 inches (5 cm) water covering them. Let process in a rolling boil, covered, for 10 minutes. Do this part in batches if you need to, instead of cramming in too many jars at once. The jars shouldn't touch. Remove canner from heat and let cool for five minutes.

09 Leave the rack in the canner but remove the jars from the water and let cool for 24 hours at room temperature without moving them. (If your counter is natural stone or a cold surface, prevent the jars from cracking by placing them on some dish towels.) You should hear the jar lids make popping noises as they cool. After 24 hours, test the seals by pressing down on the lids; if they pop back up, then you don't have a tight seal, so eat the jam within a few days. You can store jam that has been properly sealed for up to a year. Write the date the jam was made on the jar.

NOTE: Frozen berries are better than fresh berries for making a purée due to their extra liquid.

Urban Indian Ice Cream

MAKES 4 SERVINGS

When Mom was little, she used to help her sisters pick soapberries when they ripened in the heat of August so that they could make Indian Ice Cream, which they called *sxuxum* ("hoo-shum"). This was a special treat and not something I ever got to try when I was growing up, since we could never get any soapberries in Toronto. If you live inland in BC, you might come across them by other names: foam berry, buffalo berry and sopallalie.

Although soapberries were dried, made into drinks and used as a medicine in much earlier times, my mom and her relatives generally harvested the berries to whip into a creamy pink dessert using cedar branches. Some Indigenous nations in the region sweetened the mixture with salal berries, but others used fireweed. Nowadays they use sugar.

My aunt, Marge Kelly, still likes to have a little soapberry juice in water for energy every now and then. This is very popular with our elders, some of whom enjoy the juice with a lemon wedge. Cousin Gracie Kelly bakes with these berries on occasion and was nice enough to ship me some soapberries that she canned last summer so that I could make my own Indian Ice Cream. I included my aunt's recipe in the Soapberry Variation below, but for those of us who can't get our hands on the berries, I experimented with whipping cream, raspberry purée and egg whites. We liked the outcome, so here's my Urban Indian version of the recipe.

1²⁄₃ cup (400 mL) frozen **raspberries**, defrosted
½ cup (120 mL) pasteurized **egg whites**
   (or 4 fresh egg whites)
1 cup (250 mL) 35% **cream**
2 Tbsp (30 mL) **sugar**
½ tsp (2.5 mL) **lemon juice**

01 Drain raspberries in a sieve over a bowl, saving the juice. Use a spoon to force all the raspberries through a sieve, leaving only seeds. Discard seeds.

02 Whisk the egg whites in a small chilled bowl on medium-high speed using a hand mixer. Slowly add the sugar and continue mixing until peaks form. Chill egg white mixture.

03 In a large chilled bowl, whip the cream on medium-high speed until soft peaks form. Gently fold the whipped egg whites into the cream.

04 Slowly pour the raspberry puree into the egg-and-cream mixture. Add the lemon juice and gently stir until combined.

05 Pour the ice cream into serving bowls and chill for 1 hour before serving.

Soapberry Variation: Blend 3 Tbsp (45 mL) fresh crushed soapberries (or 2 Tbsp/30 mL canned crushed soapberries) with ½ cup (120 mL) ice water in a chilled bowl using a hand mixer over high speed until hard peaks form. Test the mixture by turning the bowl upside down; if it stays in position, it is thick enough (otherwise keep blending). Mix in ¼ cup (60 mL) sugar. Serve immediately.

Wolf Paws with Blueberry Dip

MAKES 8 TO 10 SERVINGS

Relax! These are not actual wolf paws. They are a deep-fried dough made to resemble wolf paws and are served with a sweet fruit sauce for dessert. Kids love them, and I'm a big kid.

1 cup (250 mL) warm **water** (105F/40C)

2¼ tsp (11 mL) active **dry yeast**

2 tsp (10 mL) **sugar**

3 cups (710 mL) all-purpose **flour**,
plus 2 Tbsp (30 mL) for dusting

1 tsp (5 mL) table **salt**

2 tsp (10 mL) plus 8 cups (2 L) **vegetable oil** for deep-frying

2 Tbsp (30 mL) **icing sugar**

01 In a small bowl, combine warm water, yeast and sugar, whisking slowly. Set aside for 5 to 10 minutes or until bubbles form.

Tip

If no bubbles form after combining the yeast with water and sugar, then either your water might have been too hot or your yeast might have been too old, so start again with a new package of yeast.

---

02 In a mixing bowl, whisk together 3 cups (710mL) flour and salt. Add 2 teaspoons (10 mL) oil to the flour mixture and mix well. Alternatively, make the dough with a stand mixer.

03 Add the yeast mixture to the flour mixture and knead dough by hand for about 8 minutes or blend with mixer on low speed for five minutes. Cover dough with a damp cloth and keep in a warm place for 25 minutes. The dough should double in size. This is a good time to make the Blueberry Drizzle.

04 Punch down the dough and knead again for five minutes, cover again and keep in a warm place for 15 minutes. The dough should double in size again.

05 Flatten dough out to a thickness of ½ inch (1.5 cm). Form the wolf paws by cutting the dough into evenly sized triangles about 5 inches (13 cm) long and 3 inches (8 cm) wide on one end, into which make three cuts. When it cooks, the dough will expand to form four "toes." Dust the paws very lightly with flour and keep covered until ready to fry.

06 Heat 8 cups (2 L) oil to 350F (175C). Carefully fry the dough for one to two minutes per side, and place cooked paws on paper towel or a metal screen to drain.

07 Serve with sifted icing sugar and Blueberry Dip.

Baked Variation: If you prefer to reduce calories, you can bake the paws instead of deep-frying them. Just brush them with oil and bake on a baking sheet in a 375F (190C) oven for 12 minutes.

Chocolate Variation: Drizzle melted semi-sweet chocolate over the paws and dust with sifted icing sugar.

CONTINUED ...

Blueberry Dip

MAKES 2½ CUPS (600 ML)

This is a very simple sauce you can make with any type of berry, sweetened by agave syrup, and you can use this as a dip or over cake or ice cream. The agave cactus was used for millennia by Indigenous peoples of Central America and the northern parts of South America for twine, clothing, shoes, medicine and food. Native Americans of the Southwest roasted the crown of the plant underground and ate the leaves like artichokes. Some credit the Aztecs with inventing tequila using agave, but in this recipe I use it as a sweetener.

2 cups (475 mL) frozen **blueberries**
⅔ cup (160 mL) **agave syrup** (or maple syrup)
½ tsp (2.5 mL) **lemon juice**
½ tsp (2.5 mL) **vanilla**
1 Tbsp (15 mL) **cornstarch**
2 Tbsp (30 mL) **water**

01 Bring berries, agave syrup, lemon juice and vanilla to a boil in a medium-sized saucepan.

02 Cook over high heat for five minutes, stirring occasionally.

03 Combine cornstarch and water in a small bowl and remove lumps. Pour into the berry mixture and continue cooking for two to three more minutes while stirring to thicken.

04 This dip will keep in the fridge for two weeks.

Amaranth Birch Pudding

MAKES 6 SERVINGS

Multiple Indigenous nations traditionally used corn to make what we call "Indian Pudding," and that is what inspired me to make this recipe using another ancient grain. Amaranth resembles quinoa, is sold whole and in ground form for baking, and goes by other names including "kiwicha," "velvet flower" and "love lies bleeding" (because of its drooping red flowers). This plant is indigenous to present-day Peru but spread to the point where pre-Columbian nations across the northern region of South America, Central America and Mexico found multiple ways to use it. Aztecs made a gruel out of the seeds (sweetened with agave syrup). Amaranth became the secret weapon of the Incan Empire due to its high protein content, which is why the Spanish tried drastic measures to destroy it altogether. Luckily for us, they failed.

Marlene usually cooks amaranth in water and flavours it with a little maple syrup and butter to eat as a gluten-free breakfast but, in this recipe, I kick it up a notch to make it into a creamy dessert flavoured with agave, maple sugar and earthy birch syrup. Maple sugar is dehydrated maple syrup but you can use brown sugar instead, and molasses is the best substitute I can think of for birch syrup in this recipe. Enjoy this dessert with coffee after supper.

1 cup (250 mL) whole **amaranth**

4 cups (950 mL) **water**, plus 3 cups (710 mL)
   more for water bath

1 **cinnamon** stick

½ tsp (2.5 mL) table **salt**

2 **egg yolks**

½ cup (120 mL) 35 percent **cream**

1¾ cup (415 mL) **coconut milk**

½ cup (120 mL) **maple sugar** (or brown sugar)

2 Tbsp (30 mL) **butter**

¼ cup (60 mL) **raisins**

1 tsp (5 mL) **vanilla**

3 Tbsp (45 mL) **birch syrup** (or molasses)

GARNISH (OPTIONAL):
Blackberries

01 Preheat oven to 350F (175C).

02 In a large saucepan combine amaranth, 4 cups (950 mL) water, cinnamon and salt. Bring to a boil.

03 Lower heat to a slow simmer and cook, covered, for 60 minutes, stirring frequently. Discard cinnamon stick. Remove amaranth from heat, uncovered, and set aside.

04 Place egg yolks in a large bowl and beat lightly. Set aside.

05 In a small saucepan, heat cream, coconut milk and sugar almost to the boiling point and whisk to remove lumps. Once it starts to bubble, remove from heat. Very slowly pour half of the cream mixture into the egg yolks, whisking constantly to combine.

06 Pour the rest of the cream mixture into the bowl. Add butter and whisk to combine. Pour the mixture into the amaranth and whisk to combine well. Add raisins and vanilla and mix.

07 Divide mixture between 6 individual-sized oven-proof ramekins and place in a 9 × 13 inch (23 × 33 cm) baking pan. To prepare a water bath, heat 3 cups (710 mL) water to a boil and pour into the baking pan, around the ramekins. Transfer baking pan to the oven and bake for 1 hour. Puddings should be light brown in colour and thickened.

08 Remove from oven and drizzle 1½ tsp (7.5 mL) birch syrup around the outer edge of each ramekin. Chill ramekins overnight before serving, then add a blackberry or two for garnish.

Acknowledgments

Chi Meegwetch (big thank you) to Jim Lastman, who took me under his wing and showed me the ropes on dealing with the public when I was just a young boy selling newspapers at Yonge and Queen; to Frank Burger, who taught me as a youth to see the world with open eyes; to George Chen, who went out of his way to help me attend chef apprenticeship training; to the late Brian Cooper, who made it possible for me to become a professor of culinary arts way back when; to Jo-ann Archibald, my cousin, who made me aware of the importance of listening to elders; to all my relatives out in Lillooet, BC, who live for the salmon to this day; to all the elders and community cooks I've met over the years who spent time with me sharing their knowledge and stories; to APTN for giving me the stage; to George Brown College for giving me a classroom; and to all my culinary students, who make teaching such a joy.

Thanks to my neighbour, John Smee, who made a most willing recipe taste tester and photography coach; to Cheryl Cohen, our thoughtful and reassuring substantive editor, who confirmed for us that it is normal to change your mind and what you wrote over, and over, and over again; to our copy editor, Sarah Weber, who fine-tuned and fact-checked; to Nicola Goshulak, assistant editor, who worked with us to tell the stories through photos; to Anna Comfort O'Keeffe, our very patient and calm managing editor, who walked us through this whole process; to all our friends and family members whose birthdays, barbecues, dinners and parties we've missed over the last two years as a result of working on this book; and, of course, to my lovely wife, Marlene. If it wasn't for her, this cookbook would not have been possible.

Index

About the Authors

Chef David Wolfman, member of the Xaxli'p First Nation, is an internationally recognized expert in wild game and traditional Indigenous cuisine. He has been a culinary arts professor at George Brown College in Toronto since 1994 and was also executive producer and host of a popular APTN program, *Cooking with the Wolfman,* which aired in Canada for 18 years and is now airing in the US.

Marlene Finn, Métis, is an education consultant, former director of the National Aboriginal Achievement Awards and former vice president of the Canadian Council for Aboriginal Business.

Together, Marlene and David deliver cooking demonstrations and workshops on Indigenous food and family nutrition. They do restaurant makeovers, provide hospitality and tourism training to First Nations, and sell culinary knives. David and Marlene live in Toronto.